CHANGELING

The Autobiography of
Mike Oldfield

Mike Oldfield

This paperback edition first published in
Great Britain in 2008 by
Virgin Books Ltd
Thames Wharf Studios
Rainville Road
London
W6 9HA

First published in hardback in 2007

ISBN 978 0 7535 1307 1

Typeset by TW Typesetting, Plymouth, Devon

14

Penguin Random House is committed to a sustainable future for
our business, our readers and our planet. This book is made from
Forest Stewardship Council® certified paper.

Printed and bound in Great Britain by Clays Ltd, Elcograf S.p.A.

CONTENTS

PROLOGUE – EXEGESIS – SUMMER 1978

The seminar is being held at a big, modern hotel on the Cromwell Road in London. Thursday evening is a get-in, sign-up, pay-your-money affair. When we arrive, at about seven o'clock, about fifty people are already there. They are mainly assistants, just helping out; everybody is quite friendly. I've been lucky, I haven't been photographed much so nobody recognises me. They only know my first name, which I've told them is Mick.

Other 'trainees' start to arrive and we all shuffle around; nobody really knows what they are getting into. The assistants explain to us what is going to happen. We are told the rules: after the session starts, we will not be allowed any alcohol, there is no smoking and we will not even be permitted to use the loo, we'll have to wait for the break. We're told to be back at the hotel at 8.30 a.m., prompt. Rosie and I have arranged with Richard Branson to stay on his houseboat that night, so off we go.

When we arrive on the Friday morning, all the assistants' attitudes have changed. They appear cold, unfeeling, almost robotic. They are not reacting or responding, approving or disapproving; they are just being neutral. I presume that is part of the strategy. In normal life, we are so used to interacting with others to get approval or praise, or, if we don't like them, to make them feel insecure. The assistants are being completely blank, which is very disarming.

There are about eighty of us. We file into a room and sit down, feeling uneasy. Suddenly the leader, Robert D'Aubigny, strides in. He is very smartly dressed, with immaculately coiffured dark hair. Robert is a very charismatic character; some people just have that gift. He stands at the lectern, with a blackboard behind him, and starts to talk.

Robert begins his lecture by describing some very basic things about the human mind, about relationships and how they work. We are encouraged to take notes: he is drawing diagrams, for example a fly in a bottle, bashing its body against the sides, never thinking to fly up to the top. He makes it funny, sometimes hilarious: we are all laughing.

A microphone is passed around and, one by one, we explain what we want to get out of the seminar. People have all kinds of insecurities, different reasons why they have come. When it comes to my turn, it is panic attacks. I want to not panic; I want to be comfortable in my body and my life; I don't want to keep thinking that I don't belong here, that I have ended up on the wrong planet, completely alienated.

One of the concepts Robert explains is 'running a racket', like a Chicago speakeasy, or a drugs racket: it's a dishonest way of running your life, where you're not facing the truth, lying to yourself. We all go up to the front and speak to the whole group, under the guidance of Robert. It soon becomes obvious that every person in the room, male or female, has some kind of 'racket' going on in their lives. Sometimes, Robert actually has to force it out of people. He can tell when someone is avoiding the issue by their body language, or through techniques like laughing, saying it's ridiculous, flirting and so on. Robert drums that out of them, he's saying, 'I am not interested in the façade you put up, to block what you really feel. Demand of yourself, what it is in your life that is blocking your progress.'

One by one, we all reveal our rackets. This isn't some weepy, hippy, New Age thing with poor, self-doubting, miserable types, these are all professional people who have paid to be here. Rosie, my sister's boyfriend, a kind of 'Hell's Angel' character with a massive rose tattoo on his chest, is right next to me, smiling. He finds the whole thing quite amusing. I know he can be aggressive, even dangerous, but he takes things as he finds them, on the surface. He thinks it is funny how different everyone is, all living their personas so differently. It gives me confidence, having Rosie there. I don't know why, he is just a reassuring presence beside me.

We look at how we behave as human beings, often very stupidly: we can follow a self-destructive course to make our lives a failure. We can make it someone else's fault: act the victim when things go wrong. Robert explains how, in nearly every case, this can link back to a childhood experience. Often we are just punishing ourselves, but it can be difficult to see that. Sometimes we need to be shown it and accept it.

After a while, a couple of people start saying, 'It's all right listening to you, but I want a break now, I need to go to the loo.' Funnily enough, that's another way of not confronting things. You can distract yourself, go to the loo, have a cigarette, have something to eat, go for a walk. Robert won't hear of it. He says, 'Well, if you're not going to take this seriously, you can leave now and we will give you your money back.' Several people do leave, but the rest of us stay where we are. We've already agreed we wouldn't do that, so we have to obey. It is almost like a boot camp.

We are told a first step is to come to terms with our parents, and with our own childhood. Robert tells us how a great many people can ruin their whole lives by burying some kind of resentment. When we do have a break, some people go out and call their parents to say, 'I forgive you for whatever you did to me.'

Robert shows us a technique of taking control, by standing aside from the kneejerk reaction to things. He tells us a good way to do that is to make a choice, however you are feeling. If you're feeling insecure, you can say to yourself, 'I'm very insecure and I can't do that.' It can be tough, but the mere act of choosing the feeling that you don't like somehow dissipates the energy of it, takes away its power. Robert explains it's like a black bubble that you can stick a pin into.

We finish fairly early on the Friday. I am feeling a little uneasy: I know I'm going down a road I have been avoiding all my life, and I'm not sure I really want to find out what is down there. That night I sleep badly on the boat: there is a sense of dread that I can't shake off.

Going back on the Saturday, I feel that, somehow, I'm going to be in for it: I am actually going to have to *do* something. I don't have a clue what it is, however. During the day, one by one, every single person goes up and explains in more detail why they have come. When it comes to my turn, I explain about my mother, my panic attacks, how I feel completely paranoid, alienated, scared all the time, about my drinking and being a virtual alcoholic. I am anonymous, so I can't explain about being successful and all that goes with it. Maybe this is when I am singled out by the organisers, as one of the people who will need some kind of additional treatment.

We go out for a break in the early evening. When we come back, each of us takes it in turns on the stage. We have to show we can confront somebody. The assistants come up to us, and we have to stand in front of them without laughing, or saying, 'Hi, how are you?' or any of the normal business people use to get approval, to impress or to dominate. We simply have to look them straight in the eyes, to act as a human being without all the elaborate rigmarole that normally goes with civilised society, with human relationships.

Gradually they go around the room, in the order people are sitting. When I have to go up, I feel terrified. As I stand in front of this person, I find myself confronting the stark nature of my humanity. Something sinks in, that all the effort we make in our lives to be liked, loved, respected or feared, it is all unnecessary. I realise I can just exist, and let other people exist, rather than trying to bend them to be what I want. I can simply be there and not do anything.

I feel slightly elated after that, but then it is the end of the evening and there remains a terrible dread inside me. That confrontation was tough enough, and I don't have a clue what to expect on the Sunday. That night, I don't sleep at all.

On Sunday morning, we troop back into the room and start again. This time we are role-playing. We have to do some outrageous things: first some macho 'trainee' has to come up and behave like a woman, to sing a song like, 'Itsy Bitsy Teenie Weenie Yellow Polka Dot Bikini'. Then a female will get a correspondingly macho task, like being a bomber pilot. I presume this is to teach that there is no fundamental difference between male and female. These roles are ingrained in our upbringing, they're something we learn at school.

Later that afternoon we begin the final process. I know my time is drawing near. They single out a young man and we all watch as he goes through an excruciating, terrifying experience. At the end I can see he has this glow, his eyes are dewy. Then, I know it is my turn and I am petrified. Finally, the time has arrived for me to go into the lion's den.

I walk into the centre of the room, feeling like a man condemned. I stand before Robert, putting myself totally under his control. I am in a cold sweat and trembling. 'Start breathing,' he says, as he signals me to lie on the floor. As I lie there, I feel the panic starting to swell up inside. 'Now then, breathe deeper,' he says, so I do that for a couple of minutes. 'Go on, breathe deeper, start to make a noise with every breath, whatever noise you feel like,' says Robert.

My breathing becomes deeper and deeper. I am diving into a pit where some unknown demon lives, this thing that has been torturing me for years and years. Then the sound comes, at first a groan, which builds slowly into a scream. After two or three minutes, the scream is as full blown as any human being could possibly articulate. Later, I will be told that I screamed so loud the hotel residents started complaining: they thought someone was being murdered in the room.

I am lying in the centre of the room, screaming and breathing so deeply that I am hyperventilating between the screams. I can't go any further. My skin is raw and wet, it feels like it is the first time it has made contact with the outside air. I find myself in this enormous space outside my consciousness, the one I've suffered nightmares about before. I am stuck in this place, literally *inside* my own panic, experiencing it, living it.

Suddenly I feel my legs lifting up. I am being supported by I don't know what, I'm dangling by my legs. Soft cushions are pressing up against me and pushing really hard, pushing all the fear and the terror away.

I realise I am a baby, an infant being born. I have gone back in time and I am reliving the memory of my own birth. When you read about rebirthing it's a very gentle, New Age thing. But this is not gentle at all; this is the real McCoy, like a real birth. It feels more like Armageddon.

Gradually I am laid down and put in the recovery position. My breathing subsides, and my consciousness starts to return. The feeling is indescribable. I have confronted my terror, my panic, and it isn't the devil at all: it is the tiny, newborn infant inside me. As I lie there, I can feel the glow I had seen with the man who went before me. I can barely believe it. I have confronted my worst fear, what I thought was the devil himself, and I have found out that it was a harmless, little child.

I start to chuckle, with absolute relief and euphoria. It is over.

1. BEGINNINGS – 1953

G iven everything that would happen in my life, the beginnings were all quite mundane. I was born in Battle Hospital in Reading on 15 May 1953. I don't think it was a particularly difficult or traumatic birth, not for my mother anyway. My parents were in their thirties then: my father was about 33 and my mother was four years older, at 37. I did ask my mother about it all later, and my father, but I understand it was all fairly run-of-the-mill.

We first lived in a semidetached place on Monks Way, quite near to the centre of Reading. I have some very, very early memories of the place, stored in some kind of infant memory bank; I think it's quite rare to have memories of that early time. I remember the way the sunlight used to stream through the windows; I also have very early, warm memories of my mother. I remember breast-feeding, and an incident when I saw a person – somehow I knew it was my sister – opening the door of the room and saying, 'Oh, excuse me,' and shutting it again. I have no idea how old I was when that happened. I remember that the material of the old cloth nappies was a bit itchy; I remember the feel of dirty nappies, how awful it felt when you were all dirty, and how nice it was when you were clean. I can remember wearing a bib and hating it, and preferring to be covered in food. I remember I always loved having buttons to push. Perhaps every baby loves buttons – push something and something happens, like magic.

When I was still very young, about three or four, we moved to a small, detached house in Western Elms Avenue, just a short distance from Monks Way. It used to be a well-to-do district of Reading: my father was a local GP so I suppose my parents might have been considered quite well off. My mother had an Irish helper called Kathleen, I think. It's all very hazy: I can remember having a brother and sister, but because they were older and closer in age to one another (Sally is six years older than me and my brother Terry is four years older), they were a pair and were quite distant from me. They were playmates, and I don't think they wanted much to do with their little baby brother. They weren't particularly nasty to me, but they didn't seem to like me very much either, at the time. Occasionally Sally was asked to baby-sit me for the afternoon: she used to take me to the cinema and I remember being dragged along the road and dumped in a seat at the pictures. Meanwhile, Terry occasionally deigned to allow me to join in his games of cricket.

My mother was a vibrant, very strange character. She was Irish Catholic, but I remember she used to answer the telephone in a very upper-class voice, like the Queen. 'Doctor Oldfield's residence,' she would say, but I knew it wasn't really her natural way of speaking. From time to time she would recite poems that went on for hours, these epic, Celtic stories, and when she was happy she could also do proper Irish dancing. She would do it completely naturally. It was extraordinary: she was a pure Irish woman, totally Celt.

As I got older, my mother started becoming more distant. Before starting school at five, I spent long periods playing on my own, waiting for my father to come back. I presume my mother was busy getting on with other things, so she left me to be on my own. Of everyone in the family, I got on best with my father. I remember when he was out at work, sometimes my mother would lock me in a playpen, which felt like a cage. Maybe I cried a lot or irritated her in some other way, because she would say things like, 'Wait till your father gets home, he's going to smack you!' I think all I had done wrong was whining or crying, and he never did smack me. I adored my dad. We got on really well and I would always look forward to him coming home.

In those days, patients could ring up any time they wanted their doctor: they had my father's personal number. I can hardly remember a time that he wasn't phoned up in the middle of the night at least twice, sometimes three or four times. He'd have to get up and go and see them. I would hear his car coming back, he'd come up the stairs to bed and then, 'ring, ring', the phone would go again.

To this day, I have a terror of telephones because of that.

I have so many happy memories. We used to go on holiday to the Isle of Wight, which I loved for various reasons. It took quite a long time to get there in those days: there weren't any motorways, so it was a fair journey. Mum and Dad would sit in the front of our Morris car, and us three children would sit in the back. To pass the time, my mother would recite her long, epic poems, which were fantastic. She could also pronounce the longest village name in Wales – Llanfairpwllgwyngyllgogerychwyrndrobwllllantysiliogogo goch. We were all terribly impressed by that, and I remember we would keep asking her to repeat it.

From Southampton we would cross on the ferry to the Isle of Wight, and go to this little cottage. Most exciting of all, it had two channels on the TV; back home we only had BBC, but the cottage had ITV as well. I remember seeing my first TV advert, which was brilliant: it was for Colgate toothpaste, I think, with some kind of fountain twiddling down. I remember fossil hunting on the beach, and on one holiday I started learning to swim with my father; unfortunately a wave knocked me over and everything went blue. I was scared of the water for quite a few years after that.

Travelling anywhere always took a long time. We've got some old film from an 8mm camera of the family visiting Beaconsfield model village – from Reading, that was probably a couple of hours' drive. Once or twice a year we would go to stay with my grandparents in Margate. That was a heck of a journey as well, taking six or seven hours. Margate was a lovely seaside town – I don't know if everybody thought that, but it was lovely to my little eyes. It had funfairs and rides on the pier, and the sea was amazing: I've always loved the sea air and, though I wasn't much of a swimmer, I just liked to be by it.

My grandfather used to run a duty-free shop on one of the ferries, a really old paddle steamer with two wheels, one on either side. It was called the 'Queen of the Channel' or something like that. I can remember going with my grandfather on a wonderful trip to Calais from Ramsgate. He was a charming man, indeed both my father's parents were gentle, lovely people: visits were always peaceful and happy. I remember my grandmother playing at her upright piano; I was told she used to play in the pub, years before. I used to love sitting at the piano, with all those keys laid out in front of me, the feel of them and the sound they made.

When was it that I knew I was different? From when I was very young, I was always watching, observing, taking it all in; but it was more than that, I knew there was more to life than I could grasp. I couldn't have explained what it was to anyone at the time, or how it felt to me, but even when I was small I had what you could call 'atmosphere antennae'. I would pick up signals, like a radio, it was all very strange. Still today I have this ability to feel atmospheres of places.

It was, and is, like tapping into another world. I've always had the feeling that there's some 'big thing', somewhere out there but not quite reachable, like a fairy castle, up in the clouds or on top of a mountain. I remember once, on the Isle of Wight, I was sitting on a little beach on a beautiful, sunny day. From a distance, I watched as a massive ship was pulled out across the Solent, I imagine from Portsmouth. Later I learned it was the last voyage of HMS *Vanguard*, the last battleship in the British fleet. I know it was a terrible machine of warfare being towed away to its demise, but it just looked dignified and proud, very beautiful in a way. That ship always reminded me of the feeling that there was something else, somewhere in the distance, unreachable.

Sometimes I would pick up closer feelings: they were more like presences around me, not on our physical plane but on a spiritual plane. It felt almost as though if I could only lift this invisible veil I would actually be able to see them. Sometimes the presences would feel good, sometimes not so good. Even now I often feel there is some entity, call it my muse, my inspiration or my guardian, somewhere around me, protecting and helping me. I also think there are a few of the opposite around, being extremely unhelpful. I don't know what to call them, my little demons, perhaps, or gremlins: they are always trying to make things go wrong.

I didn't know if it was just me that had these feelings, or whether everyone felt like that. I did know I wanted to find out what they were. I always wanted to try to get closer to that place, to lean out towards wherever it was. With my 'antennae' I could sense so much that was unknown, if only I could find the door I felt I might be able to reach it. It's very hard to explain, but I think all these feelings inspired me, much later. I wanted to use music to explain how I felt, but also to reach out, to get closer to the unknown. If I were a talented poet I would probably try to write a poem about it.

When I was a bit older, I used to go with my father on his rounds. He would take me to some interesting places: once, we went to a couple of appointments on Battle Farm in Reading, where they have the Reading Festival these days; back then, it was just a little farmhouse. Sometimes I would actually go in with him and see the patient; other times I would sit in his old Morris car. I would notice how people were so pleased to see him. 'Oh, Doctor, thank you, I'm so glad you've come,' they would say.

We didn't talk much, my father and I. I'm still not a conversationalist, but there were so many interesting things happening, I enjoyed just observing, soaking them up. His interaction with his patients, the way he kept his appointment book. I can still remember him listing out the names and addresses, and crossing them out when we'd visited them all. I remember driving to the different locations, visiting him in his surgery and seeing all of his sterilisation equipment – he used to do minor surgery, removing warts and so on (I think he even did vasectomies).

Once or twice when I was with my dad on his rounds, I experienced this strange feeling. He wouldn't let me go in with him, and I knew something must have happened. It was like that extra-sensory feeling you get in the middle of the night, when you think you have heard something downstairs and your consciousness spreads out and becomes super-sensitive. When it happened, time seemed to slow down and everything around me seemed to be aware of it: the trees, the grass, the air, the sky, the sunlight, the wind. I would be sitting in the car listening to the birds, when suddenly they would be singing really loudly, much louder than usual. When my dad came out he would be carrying his death-certificate book, a big, long thing, flapping like a sheet in the wind. Only then would he say to me that somebody had died but, somehow, I already knew.

At that time I didn't know what death was, but there was this definite feeling of finality. I think older people know it, anyone who's been to a funeral, there's the sensation of something having come to an end. It was only much later on that I really 'got' what death was, but I had the earliest glimpses. I had a cat called Sooty around that time. When

Sooty died, it was such a tragic, devastating event that it became ingrained in my character. I felt that if I really liked something living, it was going to disappear before long.

Of course, I didn't connect any of this with God, or religion or anything like that. My mother sent me to Sunday School – catechism we used to call it – and I would sit in this very cold little chapel with various other children, learning about something incomprehensible which had no relevance to anything I knew or understood. I remember once the priest, Father Scantleberry, asked this little girl, 'What is sin?' She said, 'If you are naughty, God puts a big spot on your tummy.' I think he had been explaining it was a stain on your soul, and she interpreted that as a spot on your tummy. The priest and his helpers would talk about death then, the fact that you had to be good in your life, because if you sinned too much you could go to hell, or to purgatory. When I asked about the awareness I felt of a spiritual presence, it was explained to me as Jesus or God, with all the complicated theology that was associated with it, the Holy Trinity and all that. I tried to grasp what they were talking about, and learned the basic Christian moral code, which I still try to practise.

My mother wanted me to have a social life, which was probably quite logical, but for me it was hell on earth. Unfortunately, I just wasn't that good at getting on with kids of my age. I wasn't that interested, and even when I tried to interact with other children, it always seemed that my gremlins would mess things up. I did have a younger friend for a while but I didn't like him very much. I remember we were experimenting with my father's golf clubs in the garden: Dad had been trying to teach me how to swing the club back and turn your head as it swept behind you. Then, as you thwacked the club back down, onto the ball, you were supposed to follow through with your head. Of course, as I swung the golf club backwards and looked up to the top of the club, skywards, I didn't realise my little friend had put his head where the golf ball was. Completely innocently, I swung it back down and I smacked him right in the eye with the club. To my surprise, his mother went completely bananas at me. 'How could you do this to my poor little boy,' she screamed, as she shook me. I told her it was an accident. I didn't think I had done anything wrong but that was the last I saw of that kid.

I remember how my mother would send me to parties or organise a party for me, for my birthday. I would be dressed up in a pair of shorts and an itchy shirt, then all these strange children, boys and girls, would walk through the door. They were complete strangers to me, I didn't know who on earth they were. They would give me a present – I quite liked that part – but then I had to play with the strangers. I didn't know what to do with them. It ended up that they played on their own, while I sat twiddling my thumbs and shuffling my feet. We would sit down to a children's tea of trifle, jelly and all that, then they would all troop off and say to my mum and me, 'Thank you for having me.' Once they'd all gone, at that point I dived into my presents, thinking at least I'd got something out of it.

I was quite happy in my own company, anyway. From when I was very young, I was a very 'laddish' kind of boy, doing macho, daredevil things. Once, when I was only about five or six, I fashioned a home-made parachute out of bed sheets so I could jump off the roof of the house, much to the dismay of the old lady over the road, who instantly came over and told my dad that his son was trying to commit suicide. To me it felt quite logical to strap on the sheet and jump off the roof. I didn't know what fear was in those days, I felt invincible! That didn't mean I was particularly brave; I just didn't realise that I could hurt myself, I didn't have a concept of fear. I have probably been lucky that I haven't had too many bad accidents – at the time I thought I could get away with anything. My God, did that change later, but in those early days I was completely fearless.

I'd been very impressed by the way the lifeboats had slid down the ramp on holiday, so in the garden I made a cardboard-box lifeboat station, with a little pulley winch made out of a stick and string, tied on to a little boat. I made the whole garden into a playground to resemble the ocean. It was all real to me, all in miniature. I did the typical thing of building plastic kits as well – I loved Spitfires and Hurricanes – and I was determined to become an RAF pilot when I grew up. I did it all quite happily on my own, just for my own enjoyment. Looking back, it was a great gift that I was not doing things for the approval of others; I think I got that from my father. He would sometimes have a day off and then we would spend time making stuff together. He was into making model aeroplanes, real ones that he could fly. He had a film he used to show us of him flying his models from the runway at his base in Egypt, when he did national service just after the war.

Off the back of my parents' bedroom we had a little attic, which was our workshop. We'd have a test bench where we would start model aeroplane engines. We even had a tiny diesel engine, which worked on compression. I remember flicking the propeller hundreds of times until it eventually got going. From a very early age I'd had a curiosity of how things worked. Dad took the time to show me how things could be put together, how the pieces would fit, and then he would encourage me to build the model aeroplanes with him. It would take months to make one. We'd build them properly with balsa spars and cover them with paper, then paint them beautifully. Ever since, I've always loved building things. I still love model planes.

My dad was part of the Reading Model Club, so we would go out to different places to fly them. The way they worked was magnificently ingenious: each aeroplane had a huge elastic band through the middle, not to work the propeller but to give power to the mechanism that turned the rudder. You could only turn the rudder left and then sequentially right, so if you wanted to go right twice in a row, you would have to go right then left–right; if you wanted to go left, you would have to go left then right–left. You always had to remember what you did last time, as the transmitter box only had one button on it.

Unfortunately, Dad wasn't very good at controlling the aeroplanes. As soon as he launched a plane after months of work, it would crash and he'd take it back in the car in hundreds of pieces. Or, 'What was my last command to this thing . . .' he would ask, as it rapidly disappeared from view. He was far better at building the planes than flying them.

He was also a great handyman. I helped on lots of projects – when he laid a new concrete path, I drew the lines in the concrete. The slabs were unbelievably heavy for me. I tried to lift one up but couldn't; of course my dad was able to lift it, but he didn't suggest we lift it together. Because of that incident, perhaps, I've had a whole lifetime of DIY phobia. I can put a model helicopter together, or insert a piece of circuitry into a Macintosh computer, with the tiniest screws and pieces; however, if it's anything to do with building work, I'm useless at it. If I try to drill a hole, either the drill breaks or it goes scooting off somewhere and ends up scratching the whole thing. Perhaps it's because of a feeling of not being as capable as my father. It's one little mistake I've tried not to make with my own children. If I was to see one of my kids trying to do something that was too difficult for them, I would suggest, 'You won't be able to do that yet on your own, let me help you,' rather than have them fail to do it by themselves.

I was very determined, however; I think I got that from my father as well. I remember once he built me a kind of box-cart. It wasn't like any old go-kart, it actually had the gears from a car in it. We went to the local junkyard and found a gearbox from an old car. My dad installed that in my box-cart, then he put in a gear stick so I could actually change gears. Unfortunately, due to the gear ratio, even at full pedal the car would only go at 0.01 mph. With the models and the box-cart he taught me that if something doesn't exist you can create it – even if you have to go and find something, cut a piece off an old car and stick it on. Still today I have a terrible reaction if someone says something can't be done. I get outraged, and I bloody well find a way it can work. I'll never give up.

It was the same with the feelings I had about the unknown presences, this sense of yearning. I wondered whether I could work out what they were, if I thought about them hard enough. I don't know if later I sensed I could bridge the gap with my music.

All in all, though, my early experiences were those of living within a normal family. We would have family meals together, my mother used to cook for us every evening, things like shepherd's pie and steak and kidney pudding. On Sundays we always went to church, and then we had Sunday dinner together as a family. My mother didn't seem to have any problems, but I later learned from my father that she did, we were just not aware of them. My father says she was moody and would switch off from time to time, but to us she seemed to be a reasonable, strong woman, very proud of her status as a doctor's wife. I think I was fairly secure and fairly normal, apart from the fact that, when you're a child, you think your parents are the same as everyone else's: everybody's dad gets up four times a night and has people ringing all the time!

Then, suddenly, it was all turned on its head.

My first school was a Catholic convent school called St Joseph's on Upper Redlands Road, on the other side of town: my sister Sally was already going there. I vividly remember my first day: my God, what a shock that was. That morning, my parents dressed me up in my school uniform, which felt horribly itchy. I had to put on this thing called a tie, which I had never worn before. My mother and father took me by car and went with me into the school. All around me, everyone looked completely alien, like nothing

I had ever seen. All the teachers were nuns, dressed in black and white habits. There were a lot of other children around, with strange-looking toys. All I could do was stare around me, taking it all in. I felt lost, like a fish out of water.

I was just five years old. When my parents left I was completely lost. I felt abandoned.

It was from that moment, I started to realise I wasn't the same as everybody else. I could see other children were all joining in, quite happily playing games in little groups. The other children didn't approach me and ask me to play; I didn't want to approach them either, so I just skulked around, watching. One part of me was wondering why they didn't invite me to join in, while another part of me was thinking, well, I wouldn't want to, anyway. It wasn't that I felt particularly different; more that everybody else seemed to fit in with each other, but not with me.

I knew I was being left out, but had no idea why. In one way I longed to be able to play, to run around with the other children, but I didn't know how to change the way things were. I just had this feeling there was something wrong with me. The other boys and girls used to chase each other but no one would be interested in chasing me; I saw some children who were very popular, who everybody wanted to know and be with, but nobody wanted to try and be with me. I don't know what put them off. I was on my own, I didn't really understand anything about it, and I hated it.

Things didn't improve as time went on, and I started to be singled out by the others. On one occasion, I was standing in line waiting for something and this older child, a girl I had never seen before, came up and smacked me, for no reason whatsoever. I chased after her and smacked her back. Unfortunately the nuns only saw me smacking her, so I was dragged off by the scruff of the neck and shaken. I was told I had sinned and was going to be punished. I was absolutely terrified: I thought my nice, calm little life had gone completely crazy. I said to myself, 'What am I doing here?' All I longed for was when I would be taken out. At the end of every day my dad would be there to pick me up and I couldn't wait to get in the car, back to safety with my father.

I was only about six months at St Joseph's, before I was sent to a junior school called Highlands. I don't know why I was moved. It was a pretty little school, up in Tilehurst in Reading. The school was run by this old lady called Mrs Peach. Highlands was a little better than the terrifying world of the nuns at St Joseph's. It was almost in the country, a collection of buildings set in a kind of garden or park. When it was good weather we had our lessons outside, under the trees. I remember smelling leaves in the sun, that sun-drenched, nature smell.

At Highlands, I think the boys left at eight and the girls stayed on until they were twelve. It wasn't a bad school, and I probably got the most useful education I ever had there. I can remember learning to read, having trouble with the word 'all'. I couldn't work out how you could have two 'l's, and you didn't say, 'al–l'.

Mrs Peach would always read to us from the Bible after assembly; she would encourage us to ask questions about God and the Bible. We would put our hands up and ask, 'What does it mean when it says God is the Trinity?' but she would explain in religious dogma, and we would end up none the wiser. I had no experience of religion, or God, or spirituality apart from what came out of those times, and my experiences at catechism classes: it was only when I reached my thirties that I really started to appreciate what a beautiful world we live in, and connected the spiritual side of being human with anything remotely religious.

To me, church was just something you did. We often went to a church in Pangbourne: I remember sitting through the ceremony with everybody talking in Latin, swirling incense around the place. On the way home, my mum and dad would stop at the pub. They went in and had a beer, and they'd leave me in the car with a packet of crisps and an orange juice. That was my favourite part of going to church! I did like the organ music as well – later, I had a friend who I used to call 'the reverend' because he was quite religious. He used to be able to play Bach's *Toccata and Fugue in D Minor* on the organ; he can't have been more than about twelve years old. I remember how he used to hammer between one note and lots of other notes, seesawing between different notes to build up that lovely, repetitive riff. Perhaps that was my first inspiration for *Tubular Bells*, all those years ago.

Some time around my sixth birthday I was deemed ready to take my first confession, and to take the sacrament. I went into the cubicle with Father Scantleberry and he asked me to tell him my sins, but it just so happened that particular week I couldn't remember having done anything wrong so I said, 'I haven't sinned.' Father Scantleberry seemed to be very upset about that, particularly as I couldn't go through the ceremony unless I actually confessed to some sins. He said, 'Yes, you have, tell me,' so just to shut him up I told him that I lied to my mother, I hit my brother, I stole this and that, and so on. He sent me off to say ten Hail Mary's, and I thought, 'What on earth is going on?' I really, honestly, couldn't think of anything I had done wrong, but I was being punished for it anyway.

After I had said my Hail Mary's and I'd had my first sacrament on a little plate, my mother must have thought she had done enough for me. They let me off after that and I didn't have to keep going to church any more.

I must have been quite a worry to my mother, thinking back on it. Presumably for good reasons she had wanted to teach me how to have a social life, but it wasn't the kind of life I wanted. There were some kids I got on with, but that was more on my terms. They were older kids, about eight or nine, and I suppose they didn't fit in, like me. Our garden backed on to a railway cutting and, as children do, we climbed over the fence and went down and put pennies on

the line, pranks like that. These were the last days of the
steam trains: I remember the different kinds of engines, they
were fantastic when they came rolling through. For some
reason they used to stop right at the end of our garden and
make this kind of 'choo-choo-choo' sound, where the
wheels would spin on the tracks and the steam would go
'shhoooop!' pushing out huge globules of smoke. I was
fascinated by it all.

We would creep down the side of the railway through the
trees, me and my older friends. We'd go a long way
following the line: further on there was a bridge, from
where you could get down to the ground by holding on to
a big branch. It was quite long, about twenty or thirty feet,
so it would bend at just the right speed to act as a lift: we
would hang on to it and lower ourselves down. We made a
camp in the trees, down beside the railway, out of bits of
boxes and plastic sheeting; we used to keep stuff like
chocolate bars or bottles of Coca-Cola in there. Seeing the
trains going past from our camp was just fantastic. Then
one day a big gang came in and mucked it all up, and that
was the end of our camp.

For some reason things weren't so bad with the older
kids. They accepted me, perhaps because I was happy to
join in with what they wanted to do, and they seemed happy
enough to join in with me. I remember happily playing in
our street in Reading with my friends with our box-carts
and footballs up and down the road. At night we used to
look at the stars. I had a star map, and me and another boy
would regularly stay up late and, with the map, try to
identify all the different stars, the planets and the constella-
tions, trying to grasp the distances involved. We would
spend an entire night, until the sun came up in the morning,
just looking at the stars. I just loved it, and I still do.

I was always an inquisitive child. I remember a book at
home called *Medical Jurisprudence and Toxicology*, which
I later found out was about medical pathology and the law.
There were photographs in there that had me reeling in

horror, people with their throats cut or impaled on railings, or being savaged by dogs, all things a doctor might have to know to practise. It was horrific but it was real – of course, your average six-year-old would be fascinated by that. That's why I have always had so much respect for doctors, or people like paramedics and firemen. My God, what these people have to deal with.

Apart from my older friends, all I wanted to do at home was be with my dad and his models. Eventually I started to build some of the aeroplanes myself, at the model club. Dad sent me down there with our kit, and I sat there with these people, sticking screws in and working the soldering iron. I still love soldering irons.

The last big family holiday we had, we managed to get all the way to the Costa Brava in our little Morris. It was a mammoth drive, through France and across Spain. We had to fly across the Channel in an enormous car transporter, from Bournemouth or Southampton airport. They were quite popular for a while: I believe they could take four cars, the passengers would sit in this small compartment with about twenty seats, and this big twin-engined machine would take off, somehow. It was my first ever plane journey, and when we landed in Cherbourg it was my first time in a foreign country. I was very excited.

It took us a week to drive all the way down through France. Eventually, in some mountainous region, probably the beginning of the Pyrenees, the engine on the Morris clapped out. We took the car to a local garage, where the very helpful French mechanic worked out what was the problem – something to do with the pin in the float chamber of the carburettor. It looked as if we'd have to order a part so we'd be stuck there for days, but this mechanic found a pin from somewhere and managed to solder it in. It was a Heath Robinson kind of repair, but lo and behold, the engine started up again! Off we went, across the Pyrenees and down towards the north of Spain.

Back then, the Costa Brava was still being built. The entire place was a building site, I don't remember seeing one hotel that was finished. We stayed in a little bay called Rosas – they had just about finished a few rooms of our hotel. We drove round the coast and found a tiny, old fishing village, not a touristy place at all. Next to the sea were some rocks: I still couldn't swim then, but I remember jumping off the rocks and into the water. It was so glorious, I suddenly started swimming for the first time.

That was a wonderful holiday. I remember going on to a beach and never being so hot in my life; I remember drinking *Cacaolat* for the first time, this Spanish chocolate milk, which was delicious. I drank bottle after bottle of it. One morning, the hotel waiter appeared and one side of his face was puffed up like a balloon, he was in desperate agony. He'd seen the internationally recognised 'physician' sign on my father's car, the snake and the sword, so had come to ask my dad if he could help. Dad gave him some antibiotics, and thereafter he was the big hero of that little hotel.

If the holiday had been a delight, the journey home was a total and utter nightmare, spent with my mother being sick by the side of the road, or being up most of the night. We didn't know what was wrong at the time, but my mother had contracted salmonella food poisoning, perhaps from some shellfish she'd eaten. She was not just a little bit sick, but desperately sick. My dad tried to get the journey over with quickly: he must have driven overnight because instead of taking a leisurely week, we did it in about three days. I think Dad wanted to get Mum back to England as quickly as possible, to get her into hospital. When we got back to England, my mother was put straight into quarantine, in the isolation ward, it was that serious. She had to stay in hospital for a week or two.

It was soon after that, that she became pregnant.

2. LOST IN MUSIC – 1960

Christmases at home were glorious, traditional family affairs. My mother would decorate the house, dress the tree and make the dinner with all the trimmings; she was a really good cook. I remember being taken to church to midnight mass, sitting through this ritual and not really understanding anything that was going on, but that was all part of it. The best part of all, of course, was the presents.

The best Christmas ever was in 1960, when I was seven years old. That particular year, my dad had made me a beautiful model of the *Ark Royal* aircraft carrier. It was complete with little tiny planes, each one individually painted. I remember that Christmas like it's locked in my brain, because of that model. The fact that my father made it and hand-painted it himself really impressed itself on me. When I was later to write music, maybe that was part of why I wanted to pay great attention to detail, to make sure it was something really special. To be worthwhile I knew it had to be really big, epic and important, not something to be thrown away. Perhaps those feelings all go back to that wonderful Christmas present.

On the wall at home hung an old guitar: every Christmas my father would take it down off the wall and play it. He knew three chords – C, F and G – and he would sing in a very nasal voice, 'Jimmy Crack Corn', 'Danny Boy' and something about a blue tail fly. I would just look at this guitar, up there on the wall, but I don't think he actually let me pick it up and play it until one day I asked about those three chords, and he showed me where to stick my fingers. I remember the stretching and how uncomfortable it was to put my fingers on the frets to play the C. All the notes sounded just awful, the F was a terribly difficult chord to play. G was easier because I only needed one finger to make the chord, if I only played the top four strings.

In those days, the main source of music in the house was my sister's room. Sally was the only one who had a record player: it was a Dansette, a very simple player with a wooden lid and built-in speakers at the front. By the time I was eight, she was playing all this modern music up in her room, a lot of Elvis and bands like the Shadows. Often she'd be up there with her boyfriend: my dad used to call it 'horizontal disco snoggery'. I don't know how she got the player – it was probably a present from my parents. If so, I'm sure it's one my dad regretted ever after. There was one track she used to play, it built up to the chorus, 'and the heavens cried'. Dad would be saying, 'Not the bloody heavens crying again!' Typically a record would have a scratch on the disc, so would repeat and jump. 'Are you lonesome tonight, tonight, tonight . . .' – I remember that a lot.

I became more aware of my sister when she had been having piano lessons and could actually read and play music. That was impressive. There was a small, white grand piano in the living room: I used to tinkle around with it from time to time, sit there and fiddle, and make up pieces of music. Once I composed something and I announced to my sister that it was called 'The Dying Swan'. She thought the title was hilarious and fell about laughing, because it was such a simple piece. Sally was a very good ballet dancer at the time and went up to London every week, to the Royal Academy of Dancing. They still had variety back then, at local theatres: there would be a comedian, juggler, a magic act, and one time Sally was the dancing piece.

Downstairs we had a radio, a big, old contraption. There were only one or two radio stations but it was on quite often. I remember listening to *Children's Hour, Listen with Mother* and that kind of thing. Once I wrote in to the BBC with a request, something like 'The Runaway Train Came Down The Track'. I listened for about one year solid but they never played it.

We had a TV as well (black-and-white, obviously), the one with only one channel. Sometime around then I discovered the screwdriver – what a wonderful instrument that was. When everyone was out and the house was empty, I would take the TV completely to pieces: I'd take the back off, unscrew the whole thing and take all the valves out. I think I probably took the radio to pieces as well. You could take the back off with it still working, with all the glowing of the valves and the smell of ozone. It was like it was alive, a magical world of glowing, smelling parts. This was in the days when electronics was vaguely understandable: if it was explained, you could fathom out how things worked. All the same, I did get quite a few electric shocks fiddling around inside.

I remember once there was some band playing on the TV, and somebody in the band had an electric guitar. I just loved the sound of that, I remember thinking how great it was. One of my sister's boyfriends was pretty good with the acoustic guitar, he could play in the really intricate, finger-picked guitar style that was popular at the time. I was very impressed and it started me off wanting to play like that as well. So I reached down the old guitar that was hanging on the wall and began tinkering around with it. I started with my C, F and G chords, and then I learned a couple more like A minor and D.

That was all long before I even thought of being a musician, however. Apart from looking at the distant stars, I didn't really think beyond my house, my school and my street: my little life, my little bubble that I lived in.

In the spring of 1961, our parents told us that Mum was expecting a baby. I would hold her tummy and feel movement in there; in the drawer, I saw the new baby clothes and all that kind of thing. I just thought 'yuk' and wondered why anyone would wear those funny garments. Life went on as normal, as if nothing were happening, until one day both my mother and father disappeared. I think we were looked after by friends of my parents. Dad popped back for the odd night to sleep for a bit, but was gone for days at a time. My mother was gone completely.

Eventually, my father came home. He said that Mother had given birth to a baby boy; I think they called him David. Dad told us the baby had a heart defect and had died due to this hole in the heart. It was many years later that I learned this wasn't true at all; the baby had been what would have been called a mongoloid child, with Down's syndrome. He lived for about a year and my mother was given the opportunity to look after him, to take him home. However, she didn't want to keep the baby so he had been looked after in some kind of health-care centre. I have never found out why they told us that he died – perhaps they thought it was better to shield us from the truth.

The next thing I remember at the time was when Dad said, 'We're going to see Mummy now.' We all went in the car, down to a convalescent home in a seaside place, somewhere like Worthing or Eastbourne. There she was: she sort of looked like Mum but there was something different about her. She looked paler, perhaps; I couldn't say exactly what it was but she just didn't look the same.

Eventually Mother came home, and it was then that she went to pieces. There were many other things happening around that time, such as changing school to St Edward's, at the top of Western Elms Avenue. St Edward's happened to be run by Mrs Peach's husband; while I quickly discovered this new school was a nightmare, the main thing I remember at that time was events at home.

It didn't happen straight away; it took a few months before I even knew anything was wrong. Nobody talked about it, I just became aware of the sound of crying after I had gone to bed. I remember waking up at night and hearing this wailing noise, a howling sound like a wounded animal, which went on and on. Eventually I would hear the doorbell ring, which would be my mother's doctor coming. She was being prescribed pills to help her sleep: in those days, sleeping pills were barbiturates, which are highly addictive. I don't think they are even legal any more but they really would knock you out. Trouble was, once you'd had a few of them, you couldn't get to sleep without them. During the day Mother would be very groggy, but she started getting panicky and so she had to have other drugs for the day, things like Largactil, which made her dry-mouthed, and even more woozy and out of it.

From that point on the nights were always the same: I got used to having disturbed sleep. My father wasn't allowed to be her doctor, she had to have another doctor, so there would be the ringing of the doorbell and her doctor would come up the steps. I remember once hearing the wailing of sirens and seeing a blue light outside in the middle of the night. When I came out of my room there were these two ambulancemen carrying my mother downstairs on a stretcher. She was sitting upright in her nightie, with a blanket around her.

I was just about turning nine years old when my mother was sectioned under the Mental Health Act for 28 days. She was put into Fairmile Hospital near Reading – we got a hell of a shock the first time we visited her there. The place was full of sick, unhappy, weird-looking people. There were people in the corridors in desperate mental situations, they'd be sitting babbling or walking around like zombies, probably all drugged up to their eyeballs. My mother would be up in her room, sitting on her bed. She wasn't like the other people we had seen but she was as white as a sheet, and looked really scared. Seeing my mother in there was quite a shock, which I found very confusing. I didn't understand what I was doing there, or why my mum was there in the first place.

I remember when my dad went to bring her home. They arrived back at the house with an album for me by Bob Dylan, his first one: I hadn't heard anything by Bob Dylan before. They also brought me a flowery shirt and a kipper tie, the sort everyone was wearing at the time. I thought everything would be back to normal, but it was just the beginning of a cycle that was to last for years. She was great for two or three days, just like old times, and then things would go downhill. Eventually, after a few weeks, she would go back into hospital and stay there a while, before coming out and starting the cycle all over again. Mother was at all kinds of different hospitals; she went to Fairmile quite a lot.

Over time my mother became addicted to the pills: barbiturates to help her sleep, various tranquillizers for daytime, and antidepressants which she took to fend off what I now believe were the same panic attacks I was later to suffer from. These were very strong drugs, not like the beta-blockers of today. They subdued and numbed her consciousness, and made her fuzzy-headed, slurring her speech and her movements; she wasn't the vibrant person she had been before the whole thing had started.

Meanwhile, my whole life started to unravel. I'd always looked up so much to my parents, assuming they'd always protect me. Up until then I had felt secure; I hadn't thought anything bad could ever happen to me.

Somehow it all made me withdraw even more into myself at school. St Edward's was a preparatory school, all very prim and proper; my brother was in the top class and I was in the bottom class, four years below. It was not a nice place: perhaps Roger Waters went to a similar school because in Pink Floyd's *The Wall* concerts, the big teacher with the cane looked exactly like St Edward's headmaster, Mr Peach. He was a walking caricature – tall, skinny and bald with wisps of hair; he would carry a huge cane, which he used very often. If you did three things wrong in a week you were taken up to the attic and Mr Peach would make you bend over and whack you with his cane, several times.

Unfortunately I don't think I was really very academic. I didn't enjoy studying, I couldn't really understand the relevance of school at all. I'm grateful in hindsight that somebody taught me how to read and write, because I can now do both; I also have a love of history that was all to do with the history teacher at St Edward's – he taught like he was telling a story. I was fascinated by ancient history. In the library there was a book called *Believe It or Not*, which was full of wonderful, strange tales. I found it really interesting that there were things in the world I didn't know about, but I didn't like to be taught anything; I liked to learn it for myself.

I wanted to rebel in my own way, so instead of being good at studying, I became an expert cheat. With a pencil sharpened to a needle point, I would write the entire results of a French or English test in a space the fraction of a postage stamp. I would spend an entire weekend just writing it out, in absolute miniature. It took ages but I loved doing it. When I was cheating at tests, I felt at least I had some control and that was all down to working in fine detail. I had very good eyes at that time; the answers would be invisible to me now, with my eyesight.

I remember once, I was accused of cheating in a French lesson when in fact I hadn't been cheating at all: I'd been stretching my back. The feeling of being accused of something I was not guilty of affected me deeply: it took me back to my first school, when the older girl had hit me and I'd hit her back, and I'd been punished for it. I was quite happy to be punished if I'd done something wrong, but not if I was innocent.

Perhaps I would have coped better if my home life hadn't been falling apart. At lunchtime I used to come back from school to get myself some food; I'd heat up a tin of beans or a steak and kidney pie. My mother would be at home but she'd be completely out of it, slumped in her armchair with a cigarette in a holder. I didn't particularly notice if there were bottles of alcohol around, but I do remember a smell of alcohol, so she'd probably had a few drinks.

My mum used to have a silver case for her Piccadilly cigarettes. I remember taking a couple when I was around nine or ten years old, and smoking them down in the garden. My brother and sister both smoked by this time, but I wasn't trying to rebel – I just wanted to see what smoking was like. Unfortunately I liked it, and I loved the feeling of dizziness. After a while it became habitual to come home, have lunch, smoke a few fags and listen to an album or two.

It was about the same time that I discovered alcohol for myself. I used to take back all my parents' Worthington beer bottles to the shop to get the deposit money. One day, I thought I might as well try it, and with the change I said, 'Can I have a couple of bottles of beer for my mum and dad?' So I brought them back and drank them. Until then I didn't understand what alcohol was; when I tried it I was overjoyed, I had never felt so wonderful in my life. I thought, 'Ah, this is what I have been looking for!' That became a regular cycle, about once a week. I had to wait for the bottles to build up, and when the crate got full I said, 'I'll take them back,' and I managed to get a couple of bottles each time. They'd have forgotten by the time I got home so they never asked for the money. When there wasn't enough, I used to steal a few shillings from my mother's purse. I still have a complex about that. Every time I open my tobacco pouch, it reminds me of her purse and I feel a wave of guilt.

Over time, my mother's condition was getting steadily worse. I don't know if she thought the baby had been some kind of punishment for marrying a Protestant, or maybe her depression was something genetic from her father. Whatever it was, the cycle continued of going downhill, going to hospital, returning home then going downhill again. It took about three months each time; my parents must have been absolutely desperate, as nothing ever seemed to make a difference. At one point my mother started saying she was hearing voices, so my parents decided to call in Father Scantleberry from the church up the road. I only heard about this later, but I was told he came to the house and conducted a practised and established exorcism ritual. Apparently he found something, or he felt there was something. Whatever it was, they got it out of the house and into the car, then they drove down to the outskirts of Reading and let it out there. Afterwards my mother got one of these pictures of Jesus with a sparkly, little candle lamp underneath it, which she put in the hall.

The exorcism didn't seem to make any difference however. Either it wasn't a spirit causing the problem or it came back again, but the cycle continued regardless.

After a year or so of these cycles, we were all suffering; I don't think my brother and sister were having a particularly good time of it. I didn't see them much, by then we were all living quite independently of each other. Sally seemed to spend most of her time out with her boyfriend or up in her room. Meanwhile, when Terry left St Edward's at the end of the year, he was sent off to a boarding school called Douai Abbey, a very strict place run by Benedictine monks. It wasn't very far from Reading but he was a boarder anyway, so I didn't see much of him either. I used to be taken to visit him there; it was cold and horrible and there were strange men wandering around in white tunics. Luckily I avoided it; he hated it and used to run away. I remember it became quite the thing to run away from boarding school: there was a vicar's son called Jonathan Birch down the road, who ran away from his school. It was very exciting, the police were involved and everybody was searching for him. My sister discovered him hiding in the woods down at the bottom of the avenue. She would take him bits of food like bread and chocolate, keeping him alive while he was holed up. He was found and sent back to school eventually, but I think he just ran away again.

Meanwhile my parents were trying to hold it all together at home. They still tried to have a social life – a couple of times they tried having garden parties. I think it was more my mother's idea: rather than wanting to invite all these people to have a nice time, it seemed to be more to maintain her status. My dad painstakingly put in these coloured bulbs everywhere and my mother fussed around getting the food ready. I remember the doorbell ringing and ringing; as guests arrived, there would be the sound of laughter. I think as the alcohol flowed and evening came, the whole thing went downhill. I would go to bed and I remember how they would look miserable the next day. I don't know what went wrong exactly.

We still used to go on holiday to Margate to see my paternal grandparents. It was always very peaceful when we were there, so it was a great relief to go down.

One of the few things I enjoyed at St Edward's was the singing lessons. We would sing traditional old English songs like 'Barbara Allen', with the music teacher playing the upright piano. I was in the choir at school, and I had a reasonable soprano voice. We went every Christmas to sing at the Carmelite nunnery just around the corner from the school. The nuns would be sitting hidden behind a screen but I could feel them there and we would sing carols to them without any accompaniment. I remember how we used to sing 'Good King Wenceslas': Mr Peach would be the king, one of the boys would be the page and then the rest of the choir would be the chorus. A couple of times I was the page, which I really enjoyed.

Mostly, however, I was feeling like I needed something to get into. I was lost at school, I was lost at home, my mother had gone sick and I was looking for something to do. I was still strumming on my father's guitar and listening to albums by folk players like Bert Jansch, which I would get from the record library. I loved the way they played by picking the guitar with their fingers, so I started to have a go at that as well. I persuaded my dad to buy me an acoustic guitar, called an Eko, a six-string, and before long, in every single spare moment I was playing that guitar. I would listen to the records I had borrowed, and I'd spend hours trying to work out how to play a particular instrumental, or even just ten seconds of it. I'd put the album on with the needle up, then I'd move the needle backwards and forwards and play along with it, over and over again.

It was like a switch went on in my head: I'd finally found something that I really liked, and I really wanted to do. I did nothing else for at least a year: I would stay up until two, three o'clock in the morning, just practising. I'd come home from school, go up to my room and practise until I fell asleep, and then wake up in the morning and play again before I went to school. I practised the entire weekend from Friday when I came home, all the way through Saturday and Sunday. I put everything, every single resource in my brain, to understanding that guitar and achieving what I could with it. I must have looked completely obsessive, but for me it was a way of escape.

I believe we have an instinct for things like music, a kind of sixth sense, which defies all rational explanation. A poet can describe it in words, but a musician can only try to explain it in musical terms: I've tried hard to describe this instinct in my own music. For me at the time, however, music felt more like a place, a sanctuary. When I was playing I could cut myself off from everything else that was going on, at home and at school; somehow I could lose myself in the rhythms and the notes. When I was practising, it felt like I was working towards something; music gave me direction. Perhaps that's why I was so obsessive about it – I certainly don't know what else I would have done if music had not come along.

Gradually I started to be able to improvise on my own using all the techniques I had learned. I could listen to a piece of music and work out a bass line, a melody line and the finger-picking, all at once. That's still my technique: when I play the electric guitar I finger-pick, and not many people play like that any more (funnily enough, I believe Mark Knopfler came from the same background – that's why he plays with his fingers, because he started in folk clubs). By the time I had got to nine or ten I had really progressed: I could finger-pick very well, and was making up my own tunes. A great, very happy, by-product of playing guitar was that suddenly I became popular. From being a lonely child who nobody wanted to talk to, as soon as I got out my guitar and started playing it, people were, 'Wow, hello', and interested in me. This obviously wasn't the only reason I played but from that point on, it meant I could get attention. I never went anywhere without my guitar: I was Michael Oldfield with the guitar, and we were inseparable.

Someone introduced me to a banjo player called Eddie Moss, who lived in a prefabricated house in Tilehurst; a lot of people lived in such places at that time. Eddie was a colourful character – nowadays you'd say he was a bit of a 'Del boy' – even though he was only about twelve or thirteen; he organised our first gig in some village hall, at a fête. When it came to the day I was terrified. I couldn't believe I was going on stage, even if it was only to play two very simple songs. It seemed to go down well: to have even one person clap was a completely new experience for me. From that moment on there was no doubt in my mind. It sowed seeds in me that I really wanted to do this, to be a musician.

I started going to a few social clubs on a Saturday afternoon, just to see who was playing. There were bands playing 'normal' music: before the 60s explosion of really interesting music that (I suppose) was drug-related and LSD-inspired, there was a period of pleasant, harmless music – Cliff Richard and the Shadows, Gerry and the Pacemakers, Jet Harris, the Searchers, that kind of thing. It was pop music, which wasn't that interesting to me. Far more interesting were the folk clubs, where I could go and see what I thought were 'proper' musicians. Sometimes I'd go with my sister and one of her best friends from school, a girl called Marianne Faithfull.

The standard of guitar playing in the folk clubs was really astonishing. It wasn't a question of strumming a few chords, it was really intricate stuff. I don't know where it came from, perhaps from the States. People were playing this fantastic music, finger-picking almost to the level of classical guitar, but in folk styles. This was long before anyone thought of using a guitar as a kind of sex symbol – you would *play* your instrument rather than posing behind it. I suppose later there were good rock guitarists like Jimi Hendrix as well, but in the folk world it was playing real instruments, properly, that mattered.

At the clubs in those days, you could just join in with whatever was going on. Once I'd started to make my own instrumentals, or the beginnings of them, from playing in various village halls with Eddie, I started playing the folk clubs. The other musicians were much older than me, they would be playing an Irish song and I would be weaving my intricate embroidery around it. I would sing a bit of the harmony line as well: everybody sang in the folk clubs. I didn't talk much: people would be in groups chatting away, and I would be playing my guitar. We shared the experience and I didn't have to socialise much. I was accepted because of my playing, and that was enough for me. My guitar was my voice, my way of communicating.

If it hadn't been for school, I wouldn't have been so desperate to have an alternative life. School was so restrictive and claustrophobic, and the punishment system was so especially awful, with the canings. It seemed to me there were a lot of people working at the school who didn't like children; they seemed to want to torture them. I became quite indignant about it. At that time you could leave school at fifteen and already I was counting the days to my fifteenth birthday, when I wouldn't have to go there any more.

It didn't help that I never wanted to do things the normal way; I always wanted to do things not just my way, but in a different way. Call it my Irish side: I can be extremely stupid about the simplest thing and not see something that is totally obvious to others, but at other times when there is a problem I can find a most ingenious way of solving it, which will not be obvious to anyone but me. Sometimes I just want to do things in a different way to how they would normally be done. This might explain how, when I started to write and compose music, I wanted to do it in a way it hadn't been done before.

By that time I was sure that, whatever happened, it would have to be me that made it happen. With my mother and father being drawn ever more deeply into their own drama, I was becoming more independent than ever.

3. THE CLUBS – 1963

Despite everything that was going on at home, I was still able to spend a lot of time with my father. When I was about ten, he joined a glider club at Lasham aerodrome and started learning to fly real gliders; he talked about taking me up in a glider one day. One cloudy, rainy day he picked me up early from school and we went to the gliding club. Everybody used to have to go and help get the glider, a Slingsby trainer it was called, with an open canopy, two seats side by side. I remember holding on to the wing and helping to push it to the winch. Then it was my go. This thing went up almost vertically, then the pilot disconnected the winch rope. I just couldn't believe it, it felt like a visit to another world. I saw houses looking like toys down below, and I listened to the whistle of the wind through the canopy. It was a marvellous feeling.

That was before I got scared of everything, of course. I still used to spend time with the kids in my street, down at the railway line and in the trees, getting up to things I probably shouldn't have done. When I was about ten years old I discovered *Exchange and Mart* magazine. In there I found an advert for a Matchless 350 scrambler bike. It was selling for six pounds, including delivery. I don't know where I got the money; I must have got a bit here and a bit there, scraped together from savings and what my parents gave me. Maybe I stole a bit from my mother's purse, I don't know, but I organised it all without telling anybody. One day a lorry arrived at our house, and this Matchless 350 scrambler rolled out the back.

I don't think my dad was very pleased. Once he saw it there, though, he seemed to realise, 'OK, he's got it, we may as well find somewhere he can ride it.' He was so well respected that he managed to get permission for me to use a gravel pit, somewhere up near Tilehurst. One of his patients lived close by and I was allowed to keep my bike in their garage, on condition that I wheeled it along the road to the gravel pit and only rode it once I got there.

I was in total heaven at the pit with my Matchless 350. Before long I had become bloody good at riding it: I could do these big leaps and land upright. I remember there was a dip that went down nearly vertically, then it went up over this hummock. I could jump off there and land, and I never fell off. When my father used to come off his rounds, he'd turn up and watch me leaping around on my bike. Sometimes he even brought me a bottle of Coca-Cola and a bar of chocolate. I think in some ways he was quite proud to see me doing something out in the fresh air and enjoying it, rather than sitting around watching TV.

One day these three, cool-looking guys came along with their bikes and saw me riding around the gravel pit and going over the jumps. I was a bit scared of them. They looked much older, probably about fourteen: I thought they were going to gang up on me and beat me up. One of them tried to do the jump that I had just done. I remember him flying through the air but then he went completely vertical, with his whole legs skywards, holding on to the handlebars. As the bike came crashing down I thought he was going to be killed. They looked at me with a bit more respect after that happened.

I have always had this thing about motorbikes, and I still do.

All through my time at St Edward's I can't think of a single friend I had at school, though I did have my older friends. I wasn't against making friends, I was very happy to meet new people: on one occasion Eddie Moss, who had organised my very first gig at that little village hall, suggested I should come along to a St John's Ambulance meeting. As well as studying the basics of medicine, which I thought was appropriate because my dad was a doctor, it was a social, youth club kind of place as well. So I went along, just for something to do.

When I arrived I found there were lots of people there, boys and girls who actually wanted to be there, unlike school. They were friendly enough but, as usual, I felt like a fish out of water. I suppose it was quite interesting learning about first aid: I remember someone would volunteer to be a victim of an accident, then people would spend an hour making up their leg to look like it was terribly wounded. They'd stick a piece of a dog bone on with tape and cover it all with slime, fake gore and blood, then you were supposed to know what to do with it all. I did find it all a bit dull, though the people were all right (if a bit dull as well).

One evening I looked out of the window and saw this rocker hanging around outside, looking really menacing. He was wearing a leather jacket and had a proper motorbike, a Triumph Tiger Cub. To my surprise he popped his head through the window and we started chatting. He was called George Offerdahl, he was Norwegian and eighteen years old. He said something like, 'Coming for a ride on my Triumph?' – which sounded a lot more interesting than first aid. So George and I started going off together, on his bike: I would go on the back because I was too young to ride on the roads. We must have gone hundreds of miles together, all the way from Reading to places like Hayling Island and High Wycombe.

Inevitably I became a rocker like George, with a leather jacket and jeans; we would regularly stay out until one or two in the morning, on his motorbike, or in cafés, or walking the streets. I don't know what we were doing, just hanging around. In the centre of Reading there were always mods and rockers, constantly out stalking each other and occasionally fighting. I was always scared of the mods but we had to swagger around, chewing gum and looking tough just like everybody else. I do remember George being thumped by a mod one evening.

We became great friends. It was my first experience of that kind of person, the wheeler-dealer type that is typical of car salesmen (or, for me now, motorbike salesmen); he was exactly the same breed. With my parents acting as they were, George the rocker with the motorbike became a kind of mentor to me. I'm not sure my parents were aware of what I was doing; they were probably just relieved I came back every night, or at least, most nights. Even if I was very late, I was obviously around and surviving: as long as I didn't come back hurt, drunk or damaged they let me get on with it. We didn't really eat together any more as a family, I just went to the chip shop and lived on fish and chips.

I was still riding around the gravel pits on my Matchless 350, but then I made a few mistakes. One was because I liked to take things to bits. George had shown me how to remove the clutch and replace the clutch plates, so I decided to change the plates in the garage where my bike was kept – at the house of my father's patient. Unfortunately, he was very religious and I didn't realise that you're not supposed to do things like that on a Sunday, it being the Sabbath. This man got terribly cross with me. Then I forgot to put clutch fluid in, so as soon as I rode it, after a couple of minutes, the plates melted inside the engine. I had to do it all again: the second time I think George helped me to do it properly. Shortly afterwards, I was also caught riding the bike on the pavement rather than pushing it, so that was that, I was elbowed out of there.

I had a complete life by then, with my older friends, like George and the other kids in my street. I was only eleven or twelve but I looked much older, I looked more like seventeen or eighteen. For some reason I was drawn to older children, and they were drawn to me. Normally the last thing older children want is a friend that is three or four years younger, but it wasn't like that at all. I was tall for my age: with my family life disintegrating I shot up in height and physical maturity, so perhaps my body instinctively thought, 'You've got to grow up quickly!' I've still got stretch marks on my back, because I grew so fast.

As we got older we got to do some rather unpleasant things down by the railway, like creeping along the track all the way to the railway sidings, and going inside the trains at night-time when there was nobody around. It was not exactly vandalism, but it wasn't really allowed: I was led astray by an older, rather reckless, boy at the time. It was bloody exciting, though. I didn't have any parental control of any sort, as everything at home was falling apart. I did give up smoking for six months when I reached twelve, but my life was too stressful so I took it up again.

This all went on for a couple of years until suddenly, one night, I was sauntering back home when my dad drove up and screeched to a halt in his car. He said, 'Your mother's been so worried about you, you've got to come home quickly.' I got back home and there was my mother in her nightie, trembling with worry. It was like she'd suddenly remembered she had a son, and that had thrown her into a panic about where I was and what I was doing. I was told never to stay out late again.

Of course, by the next night they had completely forgotten, and I did stay out late again. That was the last time I remember anybody worrying about what I did.

It was around this time my father started to go to catechism classes. He went for around six months and then converted to Catholicism. He probably did it in the hope of curing my mother, to help make her more relaxed. Perhaps for the same reason, at about the same time I changed schools again. St Edward's was a Protestant school, but my parents took me out of there and put me into a Catholic school called Presentation College. It was just around the corner, near where we used to live in Monks Way. Indeed it was run by monks, Catholic brothers from the Presentation order.

Presentation College was an awful school, in terms of both discipline and teaching ability. The monks were cruel and vicious. At St Edward's the beatings were a kind of ritual, they were civilised and organised: you would bend down and get your four or six strokes, stiff upper lip, as you were expected to do. I was never actually beaten there, but apparently, in Presentation College the headmaster would literally beat you around the room. I constantly lived in fear of the 'brothers', as we called them.

Ironically, it was at Presentation College that I first learned about other religions. Our physics teacher was a little chap, whose name was Islam Nabi Jaffrey. I don't know which country he was from, but he was an Islamic person, a Muslim. He was the most useless physics teacher you could possibly imagine, but he became a very important character in my life. One day, instead of asking about physics, somebody asked him about his own religion. Suddenly the whole class went completely silent. We had all been indoctrinated as good Catholics, and we were all fascinated to know about another man's religion. Every physics lesson from then on became a lesson in Islam instead of physics. We wanted to know all about Allah, about our teacher's praying and rituals; I've forgotten most of it but at the time I found it all very interesting indeed. I believe that was one of the first steps that led me to challenge the status quo and the indoctrination I had been put through. Here was a completely different way of looking at the world, rather than the narrow-minded view I had been taught. I'd been led to believe it was the truth and the only truth, and yet here was another perspective. I was absolutely fascinated.

It was a very international school: in my class there were people from different parts of the world. Some of them were a bit strange, but they were people I could actually get on with. One chap was from Rhodesia (now Zimbabwe). He had been shot in the leg when he was a child, and would show us his bullet wound. Another was from Tenerife in the Canary Islands, he was kind of half-caste, a bit dark-skinned, not a typical Anglo-Saxon. I found it fascinating that he lived in such an exotic place. I actually asked him to help me learn Spanish, so he taught me a few words. He lived in Los Palmas, and told me they quite often found tarantulas on the doorbells, so they had to be careful when they were ringing a doorbell in case they squashed one.

These people were very strange to me: they were from a different place, nothing like the people from my area. They were special somehow, different; they just stood out as not being ordinary, and I wasn't interested in ordinary people. They also looked older, like I did. It wasn't a question of heart-to-heart friendships; I would hang out with them in the playground and not say much.

All the while, I was trying to decide what to do with my life. I had been thinking about joining the RAF – that was what I had thought I was going to do for my whole life up to this point. I loved aeroplanes and books about aeroplanes, and I loved the idea of flying: I could hardly walk down the street and not think about flying an aeroplane. Music was starting to take over, however. It was something I found very natural to do and, on the upside, I almost had a career as a musician already. Since the age of eleven, I had been able to go to a proper, professional folk club and play so well that, rather than just clap, the crowd really would *clap*, they would think it was great. It's almost like I knew there was something different planned for me, I wasn't destined to do what I had always thought I was going to with my life.

When I was about twelve years old, I was offered a residency at Reading Folk Club together with a chap called John Burgess, which meant we were playing there every week. It was in the basement of the Rising Sun pub near St Mary's Butts in the centre of town. I even remember the boss's name, Sydney Luckington. We were a proper resident duo: we used to get about four pounds for the gig, which was enough to keep me in Number Six (the cigarettes we used to smoke in the clubs) and get me a few beers. We did mainly traditional songs, like Irish rebel songs, and some songs that I'd written myself. My sister was playing a little bit in the clubs as well, sometimes along with her best friend Marianne. Sally began to notice me a little bit around that time, and I started to play a little with her.

I was still going on trips with George the Norwegian until one day he didn't turn up. Eventually, he rang me from hospital. He'd had a motorbike accident and had completely shattered his leg. He had to spend nearly a year in hospital, having bone grafts from his other bones to stick in his leg. I went to visit him a few times but that was the end of our friendship.

From that point on, my life was folk clubs and playing music. I wasn't really socialising, I didn't really talk that much: the people I was with were older and more advanced, and by this time I was using my guitar as a means of communication anyway. I was so immersed in my music, it really was becoming an escape from the horrors of daily life, like school and family, my mother's sickness and everything else that was going on at home.

I just loved the guitar. It wasn't that I just discovered that I was good at it one day – I was practising very hard, right at the edges of obsession. I remember on one occasion, John Renbourn came to our folk club. I was so knocked out by his playing that I instantly begged, borrowed or stole his album and set myself the task of learning his instrumentals note for note. I couldn't play them at first but I wouldn't rest until I could, this poor little needle going backwards and forwards on the vinyl, probably hundreds and thousands of times before I got the hang of it. It was bloody difficult finger-picking, playing one melody with the bass and one over the top. It's difficult telling one finger to do one thing when another is doing something completely different; the fingering was sometimes agonisingly painful. I'd keep playing over each bit, until I could copy it note for note. It was such a wonderful achievement when I could actually do it.

I wanted to be like John Renbourn, not as a singer-songwriter but as an instrumentalist. I used to love the classical guitar of John Williams and Julian Bream, and I loved flamenco guitar, people like Paco Peña. Flamenco guitar is beautiful; I still love the energy of it. I can play a little bit but not like the real thing. I was always playing, and I still am always playing, even in my head. When I am asleep my fingers are playing something on my guitar, they are never still.

I also started to play electric guitar. In the Exchange and Mart shop I saw a Futurama 2 electric guitar, which cost eight pounds: after I had pestered him for weeks, my dad caved in and bought it for me without telling me. One day I came home and saw it in my parents' bedroom, leaning against the window. My heart stopped! Some time later my sister's boyfriend brought an amplifier to our house, a Watkins Tremolo, which fitted in the back of his car. It was an old Austin Healey or something like that: a bit like a Ferrari at the time, if you could afford it. To keep me quiet, they used to let me borrow the amplifier while they went out.

Amplifiers were great. I discovered you could get a pick-up, called a Lawrence pick-up, which would fit on an acoustic guitar. I bought one of those, so I could plug my Eko acoustic into the amplifier. When I wanted to get an amplifier of my own I couldn't afford a Watkins Tremolo, so my dad found a little shop that sold an amplifier in chassis form. It didn't have a housing; it came in a cardboard box with all the chassis and the components inside, a little old radio speaker and a couple of wires coming out. That was my very first amplifier. I plugged my acoustic guitar with this Lawrence pick-up into my chassis in its cardboard box, and it sounded fabulous. I loved the feeling of playing and it being so loud.

I remember coming home from school one day and hearing a different kind of music floating down the stairs. Sally had put Beethoven's fifth symphony on her record player, which made a change from the usual things she would play, Elvis Presley and the like. I don't know why she'd put it on, perhaps it was part of her schoolwork, but I just couldn't believe this music I was hearing. I was totally enthralled. I didn't have enough money to buy albums, so the next day I went straight down to the record library and rented all kinds of classical music. I loved the way a piece of music would start up with one idea that would develop into something different; it would be reprised in a different form and various instrumentals would echo its themes. Instead of the ding-a-ding of the songs I'd been used to, it was an enormously rich and complex musical world. It was like walking into St Peter's in Rome, if you have only been in a little village chapel. I was filled with awe.

I was too confused at the time to know whether I had any special talent for music, but I did know that I understood music like other people didn't. I felt it and saw it very deeply, with crystal clarity. When I listened to a piece of classical music I could see all its components, its parts and how they fitted together. I didn't just sit back and think, 'Oh, that's nice.' If someone said something like that I would be furious with them, 'What do you mean, can't you see what's going on? It's brilliant!' Music to me was something different, a vast kaleidoscope of magic and wonder. To this day my mind boggles at how superficially some people listen to music.

I got this idea that I would love to be a classical composer, so I started reading about composers and looking into their lives. After a while that whole idea went out the window, but I still couldn't get enough of the music. I taught myself the basics of writing music from a teach-yourself book. I wasn't that great at it but I knew the difference between a crotchet and a quaver; I knew 'every good boy deserves fudge' and all those kinds of things.

By that time I had a solo slot at the Red Lion in Reading, and I was playing in folk clubs around Reading with a musician called Chris Braclik, who was Polish. Chris and I would do a lot of Irish songs and we were pretty good. I had various musician friends – real, proper friends – all about eighteen years old, and by this time we all had residencies in the clubs. I was learning all the time, different ways of playing, of improvising. It must have been something to do with my age that it all went in so deeply, so it's part of my brain's programming now. I'm always amazed when I pick up a guitar, and think, 'I can still do this.' I suppose it's like riding a bike or swimming, it's a knack.

It's a great thing to be able to really specialise on your subject. That's how we advance as a civilisation, when somebody really, completely understands it. Music wasn't something I was taught, it just came out of the blue. It didn't replace anything at the time because there wasn't anything there to replace. I had finally found something that interested me and the by-product was that I became socially acceptable. Suddenly, I was impressive.

Most of all, music to me was a whole new way of coping with life: it was a sanctuary, a refuge, I felt safe there. Music was a different reality: in fact, it was more real to me than normal reality. When I shut my eyes and entered the world of music I was amongst friends, the instruments were like soul mates to me. Every instrument had a character: the tiniest of whistles would be a little, floating creature while a bass would be a deep, warm thing; electric guitars could be angry, acoustic guitars could be soft and loving. It was a complete world and I was very happy there.

* * *

Family life, meanwhile, was not good.

When Mum was in hospital, my dad had to cope with everything. As well as doing his job, going to his surgery in the day and getting up for his calls in the middle of the night, he was also looking after us and sometimes cooking for us. At work, he was having trouble with his practice: his partner was a much older, distinguished doctor who was an alcoholic and had problems of his own. It must also have been very difficult for my father that he wasn't able to treat my mother, it just wasn't allowed.

Unsurprisingly, after a few years of this, the stress really started to tell on my father. It showed itself in various ways, like him becoming angry and edgy. Looking back on it, it was a major burden for him to carry on his job with an alcoholic partner, and cope with a sick wife plus three children. I can totally understand, but at the time it was terrible for me. My dad had always been the rock that we all depended on. He was a doctor: he was supposed to make everybody better. From my childhood perspective, I believed he was endowed with godlike powers of healing; nothing could go wrong as long as Dad was around. To see him crumble was a tremendous loss for me. I had been so close to him and trusted him to hold things together, so to see him suffering was like, 'My God, even *he's* falling apart.'

One day, my dad took a whole load of pills as well, a handful of tranquillizers. He was completely out of it, lying in bed, and it was quite shocking to see him in that state. Funnily enough that brought out the mothering instinct and nursing ability of my mother, who suddenly came back to life and started looking after him. Of course, when he recovered from that things went back to how they were: Mum with her cycles, the ambulance in the middle of the night and the hospital again. I remember thinking, 'Well, now who's left to look after me?' Terry was off at school and was out most of the time when he was home; my sister helped out for a time, but then she went to university in Bristol, which seemed a long way away. The other doctors were pretty useless to my eyes, they didn't really seem to care. I suppose nowadays we would have someone like a social worker, but back then there wasn't anybody like that.

Around the end of our time in Reading my father had really lost it. I remember hearing sounds of violence from my parents' room in the middle of the night. I was frightened and angry with my father, angry with myself for being angry with my mother, I was angry with everything. On one occasion my father attacked me over some stupid thing, going to bed or something like that. I can't remember exactly what but we had what was nearly a full-blown fist fight. I was left feeling quite insecure: perhaps it was to do with this fight that I wanted to be able to protect myself.

Since George was no longer around, I was also very uncomfortable walking the streets of Reading late at night, what with the gangs of mods and rockers. I never actually got into a proper fight but I wanted to feel stronger. Somebody introduced me to weightlifting at the Reading YMCA; there was an ex-Mr Universe there, this great, big, muscular black man. I decided I wanted to have big muscles like him, so I started working on my physique, in the gym at school.

I also started having judo lessons, which I loved. I managed to get one step up from the bottom, which is a yellow belt, but then we moved from Reading and I never carried it on.

ON FAMILY – 2007

Sometimes my mother would disappear for a week or two, in between her sickness and going into hospital. We never knew where she went, but many years later, I finally met one of her sisters, my aunt, and she told me my mother used to go and see her. For some reason this auntie didn't want to become part of our lives; we never even knew she existed at the time. It's almost like my mother had been ostracised, not only by her parents but by her whole family; they didn't want anything to do with her, or her husband and children. It was all very strange.

My mother's maiden name was Liston. I wanted to find out why she was the way she was: we knew she was from Charleville, a little place in Cork in Ireland, but that's all she would tell us. Many years later I hired private detectives to investigate my mother's past. It took the agency about three years, but eventually I found where she had lived.

My mother was born to a very poor, very Catholic family of ten or eleven children. I know they didn't have much money: I've seen a photograph of their very small house. I have a picture of where my grandparents are buried, and they don't have a gravestone, it's just bare ground. My grandfather was well known and liked in the area. Apparently he spent some time in jail for poaching, but whether it was a real jail, or just the local police station nick, I don't know. He had a love of fishing, something my brother Terry has inherited: he now spends a lot of his time travelling the world, salmon fishing in Norwegian fjords and places like that.

With the help of the detective agency I managed to track down a number of cousins. Later I was contacted by one of them, who told me my mother's sister was still alive, so I arranged to go and meet her. She was a very old lady when I met her, living in this little place in Leatherhead, in sheltered accommodation. What she told me was extraordinary. She said that in about 1915 my grandfather, her father, had gone down to the pub and simply disappeared from their lives. Back home, they didn't know what had happened to him.

Just a few years ago I managed to track down some of his military record. He was in the Royal Munster Fusiliers and he'd fought in France during the First World War. In about 1917 he was discharged and put in the labour corps, building roads and generally clearing up the mess. I don't know if he had even wanted to join up. He could have been down the pub getting a bit drunk (I am sure he liked to drink), and maybe he was press-ganged or otherwise persuaded. You would have thought he would have gone home and told someone, but we don't know what it was like in those days.

I went to Ypres, to prove to myself that he was really there and just to feel the atmosphere. At the Menin Gate there is a memorial, where I found an inscription of the Royal Munster Fusiliers. Some had died and were listed there, round the back of the monument. I wondered if my grandfather knew some of those people. I remember walking through some of the war graves and seeing all the different flags. There were several Canadian regiments and, of course, the insignia of the Royal Munster Fusiliers. Near the town some of the old trenches survive and you can still see the holes in the trees. We're not talking about one bullet hole, but entire trees riddled with hundreds of holes.

The whole area around Ypres was a big focus of energy, and I just wanted to be quiet there. Even though the countryside has healed since those days, the scars of that conflict, the aura of those terrible times, is still there. Instead of blocking it off, saying, 'Don't be stupid, it was a long time ago,' I felt it was very important that I should immerse myself in it, get the feel for it and come to terms with it, like grieving. I feel it has all helped in my life. Now it doesn't upset me, only in the general sense that any normal person would feel, thinking about the carnage of that war.

Having to go from the fields and forests of County Cork and face that: what a massive, indescribable nightmare it must have been. About two or three years later my grandfather came home: my aunt said he was a changed man. It was just before the Irish Revolution, so he may not have been very popular. I believe that the people who fought in the British Army were thought to be traitors to the Southern Irish, so life could have been made hell for him by some of his fellow countrymen. It probably was the same for all the Irish people at that time, who came back from the war.

My aunt didn't want to go into great detail, but she said that of the ten or eleven children, all those born after he came back had some kind of psychological problems, not just my mother. I don't know if any of them survive now, but apparently the children born before he went off to war were reasonably well balanced.

When my mother moved over from Ireland, she went into service. I think she wanted to have status in life; perhaps she was ashamed of her poor background, the life she left behind. Maybe people at that time looked at Great Britain as a respectable place. I knew my mother worked her way up from being a domestic servant, to a nurse and then a senior nurse. Somehow she met my dad; he was a junior doctor at the time. I would imagine that would be the ultimate achievement for her, to be a doctor's wife; at the same time she might have thought she wasn't worthy of it, because of her background.

By hiring the detective agency I had found out about my grandfather, and his wartime experiences. However, I also discovered how my mother's family had disowned her. I believe this was because she had married a Protestant but, of course, there might be another skeleton in the cupboard that I don't know about.

As part of the *Tubular Bells II* tour in 1992, I played four nights at the Albert Hall. For the last night I got in touch with all my various uncles and cousins. I put them all on a coach and they came to see the show. Afterwards, I remember they were all up in one of the rooms in the top of the hall, having a drink, but it wasn't a particularly happy occasion for some reason. You would think it would be all hugs and tears but it wasn't like that, not from me or from them. It felt like I was in a room full of strangers. They didn't know me and I didn't know them, it was very odd. Almost all were real, Southern Irish people apart from the younger ones who'd come to live in Britain. I do feel a great affinity with the Irish, with all Celtic people, I always have, but these people didn't seem to have anything in common that I could feel. They didn't seem like relatives, and I didn't see any reason to keep in touch with them afterwards.

I had also invited my aunt from Leatherhead, but she didn't come. Strangely enough, she only lived for another few months. It was like she had been staying alive just to pass all that information on to me.

* * *

My father's family used to have a whole chain of pubs, around London. I think it was down to my great-grandfather: he must have been quite organised and intelligent, not just to run one pub but a handful of them; he must have had a little bit of money as well. My grandmother was a piano player, and she used to play 'Roll Out the Barrel' and that kind of stuff in the pub. I have since learned that she was not exactly gifted but she had a musical ear; like me, she could hear a tune and then simply play it.

I don't know much about my father's childhood, other than that he was a Londoner. He went to St Paul's boys' school; I know he had experience of the war, as he told me he'd heard the sound of the doodlebugs coming. He had an older sister who became a painter; while she's not very well known, she is pretty good at what she does. My father must have wanted a proper job, however, so he decided to train to be a doctor.

I think my grandparents must have been very proud of their son doing all that study and going to medical school, just a few years before the war. He started his training at a hospital in Blackpool, and learned how to do minor surgical procedures. I remember he once told me he was assisting in the operating theatre when someone had their leg amputated. He had to take the leg off somewhere, and couldn't believe how heavy it was. Then he went on to Guildford to complete his training and become a junior doctor, which is where I think he met my mum.

Towards the end of the war my father went to do his national service, at an airfield in Egypt where he carried out medicals on the pilots. He'd kept photographs of him flying his model planes on the runway. Somewhere around this time my parents were married and my sister Sally was born in Dublin. Maybe my dad was home on leave, then he went back out to Egypt; meanwhile, my mother went to stay with friends in Dublin. It could have been another thing that distanced my mother from her strict Catholic parents, I don't know.

When my dad came out of national service, I presume they went to some medical council and he was offered all these different practices. They decided Reading would be a good place to live, so that's where they ended up, and my brother and I were both born in Reading.

My father moved after my mother died; he married a German lady and lives in Stuttgart. He is now 83 and still playing tennis, which is amazing; he paints as well. I know my dad doesn't really understand my music; it used to really annoy me but it doesn't any more. There were two orchestral tracks on the *Millennium Bell* album that he told me he liked. I can see the way he thinks: to him, being a musician isn't really a proper job. That's just the way he is, and I've got tremendous respect for him.

It's all part of when I made my peace with him years ago; I learned during the Exegesis seminar how important it is to accept your parents just the way they are. Part of the training is to realise that we look at our parents like gods. If you don't grow up and see them in their proper place, as proper human beings, you can carry on your whole life looking at them through the wrong perspective.

Only recently, I've come to understand just how important family is, to a child. The family structure is obviously nature's preference, but somehow in our culture it is being destroyed. At this moment in my life, together with my wife and our child, I can see how important it is for a child to have two parents. My own son will react in a certain way when he is with his mum and in a different way when he is with me. I believe you need a father's authority, otherwise you could go off the rails and get the wrong values.

Through all my research I feel closer to the Irish side of my family these days. There are a lot of qualities of Irishness of me: it's absolutely brilliant to be spontaneously creative, as well as to be able to laugh and be joyful at the drop of a hat. Also with the Irish side comes the ability to drink too much, or to be unreasonable. There is a downside to everything, but I love the spark of unpredictability. My Irish qualities combine with a certain solidity, from my reasonable, down-to-earth English side, which I've got from my dad. If you get it right it's a great mixture, but it's taken all my life up until now to balance this chemistry.

While it's been a pretty volatile mix, it has given me a career, and some beautiful music has come out of it.

4. HAROLD WOOD – 1966

The feeling was that a move might be good for the family. My father was going to pieces, and my mum wasn't getting any better. Also, it was an opportunity for my dad to work in a new practice with a different partner, rather than his alcoholic one. He had found us a house in Harold Wood, which is in Essex, near Romford.

As far as I was concerned, my life outside home was finally coming together. All the feelings of not fitting in at school were in the past; at least, I'd made them a less important part of my life. Far more important was being with my older friends in the clubs, with my music. My friends would be playing chords and singing a tune and I would be playing guitar or piano over the top: for some reason my fingers flowed and I could play counter-melodies, harmonies, lead lines, counterpoints. I would be all over the place. The only way I can describe it is as a gift, though I didn't realise it at the time. I just knew it was something I was good at, it gave me some sense of purpose.

Just before we moved to Harold Wood, I went up to Edinburgh for the festival with a couple of friends, including my musical partner Chris Braclik. We travelled up in a

Morris 1000 pick-up truck and spent a couple of weeks there, playing at places like the Fringe and various folk clubs, wherever we could get in. There was something about that place. I was just turning thirteen at the time, and I could really feel the atmosphere. We didn't have any money so we used to busk on Princes Street, or we would go into the students' union and just play in the foyer. With a few shillings we could get a meat pie or two. Finally we moved into some terrible old ruined garret with a load of artists, actors and students. It was all pretty exciting. It was also in Edinburgh that I discovered the point of the opposite sex!

Shortly afterwards two of my friends were going on a 'Club 18-30' kind of holiday so I said, 'I look eighteen, I'll come along too.' We went along to somewhere on the Costa Brava, Blanes I think it was, on a little charter flight. Everyone was very much older than me, but I was used to that.

Then I came back to Reading and we all packed up, ready for the move. It was very exciting moving to the new place. The new house was on Redden Court Road in Harold Wood, number 8. It was all right, and I do remember it had a wonderful dawn chorus. We were all very positive about moving, and of course I had just come back from the festival and from holiday, so I was feeling pretty happy.

Unfortunately, the move didn't make any difference to my mother. It was the same cycle; the only change was that we didn't go and visit her at Fairmile hospital. Instead we went to the one in Brentwood, and of course we had a different doctor. You could see the stress on my father: he could hardly keep his face straight, he was always gritting his teeth. He started getting into funny habits, like leaving notes around for everybody about all sorts of things. I got the feeling, which I still have, that I could never relax and that things would never be permanently all right, only ever temporarily. I was constantly on my guard, looking around the corner for the next thing to go wrong.

More and more, I started to need a life of my own. I still had to go to school, which was just a chore, a real burden.

This time it was to an awful place called Hornchurch Grammar. While it was called a grammar school, it was more like how I imagine a comprehensive school is these days, a big, modern building with modern classrooms and facilities. Not that I cared much. Even on the day I arrived, I was just marking time to my fifteenth birthday, when I could get out of there.

It was at Hornchurch Grammar that I had my first ever music class. I'd never done anything like it at my schools in Reading. The music teacher would do things like he'd give us a top line and we would have to harmonise it. You weren't allowed to harmonise it so that it sounded beautiful, you had to do it according to the proper rules of harmony. So there could be no consecutive fifths or octaves, no consecutive active thirds or fourths, and so on. It was a purely mathematical exercise: once you worked out what to do, you would get ten out of ten.

There were a couple of people in the class who would be given the homework and they would have it done in five minutes. I would go back and work it out on the guitar or piano, and make it sound gorgeous. Just a boring little old top line, eight bars long, I would make a piece of music out of it. When we presented our homework to the teacher, he would play it in front of the class. I remember him playing the pieces from the people who had done it properly and saying, 'Ten out of ten.' When he came to my homework, he took a look at it, and then he crossed this out and crossed that out. Then he played it, and I could see in his face that he was thinking, 'Wow, that's beautiful,' but unfortunately he would give me three out of ten. I was so disappointed that I applied to go to the art class instead, but I was pretty useless at painting so I came back to music.

I also wanted to bring in my guitar to show the music teacher what I could do but he wasn't interested in that. Eventually I just learned how to do what he wanted, but it was mind-numbingly boring.

The music teacher did one very good thing, which was to introduce me to Sibelius. He used to play pieces of music in the class, on this single, quad-electrostatic speaker. I just adored the sound of this one piece. I didn't know exactly what it was at the time. The piece sounded like pine forests and mountains, it had such a feeling of enormous space and motion, huge and great in its momentum and intricacy. I later found out that it was Sibelius's fifth symphony (there is only one version that I have ever liked, though – John Barbirolli with the Hallé Orchestra; I listened to other orchestras, and other conductors' versions but they just didn't do it for me). In the last movement he has one melody going on the bass line, on the double bass, which is playing at the same time as the main melody but at a quarter of the speed. It just moves along so elegantly, it is just phenomenal that somebody would create something not just beautiful to listen to, but intelligent and clever as well. I knew I wanted to be able to do something like that for myself. I suppose the beginnings of *Tubular Bells* started from my wondering, 'How can I do something like that?'

As for friends, I had none. The other people in my class, I didn't want to talk to them and they didn't want to talk to me. That was fine by me. I had my music and I didn't need anyone else.

When we first went to Harold Wood, every month or two I used to go back to Reading for the weekend to see my old friends. I used to stay with a chap called Andy Holland, who was almost our next-door neighbour in Reading, and I would go and see my other musical friends like Chris Braclik.

One night we had been in a village just near Wallingford, and Andy's dad had arranged to come and pick us up from Wallingford, for the drive to Reading. Unfortunately, we couldn't get there in time. There were no buses to where we were going; we tried to call a taxi but that was no good; of course, there were no cellphones so we couldn't call his dad.

So we decided to walk from this little village, about five miles outside Wallingford. We walked like crazy to get there to meet Andy's dad, walking the five miles took us about an hour and a half.

We finally got to Wallingford, absolutely exhausted. Andy's dad went completely bananas: he drove us back to Reading in a complete huff. When we got back, my bag was thrown out on the doorstep, the door was slammed in my face and that was it. It was about ten o'clock at night. I didn't have anywhere to go, I only had a couple of shillings in money and my return ticket to Harold Wood. The only thing I could think of was to head home, try and get the last train from Reading, and see if I could get the tube across London from Paddington to Liverpool Street – otherwise I was going to have to spend the night in Reading station.

So there I was, this thirteen-year-old boy walking all the way into the centre of Reading, late at night. I had my guitar in its guitar case, which at this time was a huge, banana-yellow case all covered in graffiti. I remember all these drunk, weird people acting in strange ways, like dirty old men, 'Come here, little boy,' that kind of thing. I got very scared and went to the local police station as I thought a man was chasing me, but when I got there someone laughed at me when they saw my big, yellow guitar case. So I bolted from the police station and I got the very last train, which got into Paddington at about midnight. The tube had shut, but I wouldn't have had enough money to get the tube anyway. I certainly didn't have enough money for a taxi, so I had to walk across the centre of London through the night, carrying my guitar.

My God, was that a scary experience. Drunks everywhere, lots of strange people: it was the end of the 60s and London was not a nice place at night. I was trying to keep out of the streetlights, ducking and diving as I went. If I saw someone suspicious, I would hide.

It took me three or four hours to get all the way down Marylebone Road from Paddington, and up through the city. I was passing tube stops as I went, all of them were shut of course, until about four o'clock in the morning when the tube finally opened. I'd got to somewhere like Moorgate or Bank, one stop away from Liverpool Street, and I had just about enough money to go the one stop. It didn't save me much time, but at least I felt a bit safer for a few minutes. Once I'd got to Liverpool Street, I hung around until I could get the first train back to Harold Wood.

Although it was a terrible, horrible experience, it somehow made me grow up. There was nobody to help me; I had to find my own way home, across the centre of London in the middle of the night, at the age of thirteen. I was terrified, very afraid, but it was character building. However, I wasn't in much of a hurry to go back to Reading too often. Occasionally my friends came and saw me, but the distances were just too big, so in the end that all petered out as well; I was separated from my musician partner Chris and my other friends.

It didn't make me any less interested in music. I'd had enough of the clubs by then, which did leave room for me to get involved in other things. These were the late 60s after all, and the whole music scene was very exciting. The biggest thing for me at this time was when I started listening to the radio. Like many people of my age in those days I would listen to the pirate stations, with a transistor radio under my pillow, late at night. There was Radio Luxembourg to start with, playing progressive music, and later on there were Radio Caroline and Radio London.

The music coming out at that time had an enormous influence on me. The whole scene was different then, because it was all so new. While before we had blues, it was straight blues. The new music was based around the blues scale, but some of it was mixed up with other scales, like Indian scales. Pink Floyd were just starting out then, I do remember they had a piece of music that had that classic, Arabian semitone scale. I found that incredibly powerful. Indeed I still do; the sound of a muezzin calling the faithful to prayer from the top of a mosque is a very evocative sound.

At the time, it was the first time we had heard all these melodies. If we fast-forward to 2007, there are only a certain number of combinations of those notes in the musical scale – nice ones anyway – and they have all been done. So a lot of the songs which we hear nowadays are mixtures of music we have heard before: they get the response, 'That's the chorus from that song, that's a bit from that song.' Back then it was the first time for everything, there were lots of undiscovered things to be done. That's why it was so good, it was a really exciting time.

I remember coming home with *Sgt. Pepper*, which I had just bought in a record shop – Woolworths, I think – and I remember buying *Tommy* on the day it was released and things like that. The personalities involved were discovering it all, like Bob Dylan: he would have an idea and that would become his music. It was the same with every artist: they weren't trying to be a tribute band or copying somebody else, because it was all so new. Plus, nearly everybody was out of their brains on some kind of drug – that was all new as well.

These days it is quite well established that many musicians get stoned, or they are coked up or on something or other, when they are recording. Perhaps it's always been that way, at least for the last couple of centuries: the majority of the world's greatest works of art, painting or poetry are probably the result of either insanity or drug-induced mental states. It stands to reason: a calm, normal person who's quite at ease with life is unlikely to produce anything extraordinary. Van Gogh, the Beatles . . . think of the great poets – God knows what William Blake was on, laudanum or opium, perhaps. But look at the incredible things they produced – then they probably all went mad and went to an early death. It's just the way it works.

My sister was at Bristol University, and I remember visiting her on a few occasions. It was one such weekend that I met her boyfriend at the time, Nick Gregson. Nick was the son of John Gregson, who was quite a famous actor, he'd been in films like *Whisky Galore!* and *The Lavender Hill Mob*. It was around this time I first tried hashish.

It had an incredibly strong effect, I think more of an effect on me than it would normally have on people, perhaps because I was still quite young. I was really out of my mind – almost incapable of moving, walking even. What I do remember was that Nick was playing the piano and all the notes took on a whole new significance. Time slowed down completely and the music became a completely different reality, like a real world. You could almost exist in there: at the beginning I found that absolutely fascinating.

Thinking of Nick, he also got me my first ever time backstage. His father was in a play in the West End and I went with Nick and Sally through the backstage door. I can still remember the excitement of it. There was this perfectly normal man; the only thing different about him was that he was impeccably dressed, in a suit that was pressed to perfection, and a tie. He only had time to say hello just as his curtain call came, 'five minutes', through one of those little old speakers in the dressing room. You could hear the rapturous applause as he walked on stage. I kind of liked that, I thought, 'That's an interesting way to spend an evening.' I suppose that gave me some of the idea that I wanted to be a performer, possibly that I even really wanted to get to the top, so I could get that kind of reaction for myself.

It was back at home that I first tried LSD. It used to come on little bits of blotting paper. I don't think I had a whole piece, I think I had a half of one.

I already had all this musical ability, technique you could call it, but perhaps I lacked inspiration; then I tried that small part of an LSD pill. I just spent the whole night doing things like lying on my back watching the clouds pass by, or even watching the noise on the TV and seeing patterns. To me they were mystical visions, it was all quite extraordinary. The effect it had on how I felt about music, how I saw music, was profound.

My first proper LSD trip was on Hampstead Heath of all places. I remember time getting distorted, it was like putting your head inside a wormhole or a black hole. Everything went totally strange, and I found myself in the kind of world where the song 'Lucy in the Sky with Diamonds' makes perfect sense, it is completely logical. Of course, then I would go back to Hornchurch Grammar and the bloody music teacher with his mathematical four-part harmonies that all just seemed so pointless compared to these drug-induced, musical experiences. It's such a strong thing to take drugs, I don't know what to say about it. On the one hand I would say beware, drugs can be dangerous, you are never going to be the same afterwards; but on the other hand, I have to say that for me, things wouldn't have happened in the same way without the drugs.

Eventually I smoked hash to listen to music. It was the only reason for me to smoke cannabis, because with that, music became three-dimensional, it felt like every single note was communicating something to me. Obviously I didn't smoke all the time, as I couldn't get the stuff. I do remember once, my brother Terry and I read somewhere that you could get stoned by smoking roasted banana leaves. We got a whole load of bananas and roasted them, ground them up and smoked them; it didn't do a thing, of course. So it was difficult to get such things at that time; it was only later on, when I was playing music full time, that I was able to get a regular supply.

That was my introduction to drugs. These first experiences might have flipped a few switches in my brain that led to the utter paranoia I experienced later which left me feeling incapable of doing much at all, for years and years. Through all of that came my life as it is, *Tubular Bells* and everything else. I wouldn't put it all down to my drugs experiences, but they made me who I am, and made the music the way it was.

I remember once, I went to see Sally play at a folk club in Bristol. To accompany her songs she would play a little bit of guitar, lots of little submelodies and harmony lines. There's the act of strumming your guitar and singing a song, and then there's our way of doing it where you really use the guitar. For example Paul Simon's 'Homeward Bound', that's a proper guitar part: it's nicely played and has some lovely little melodies in it. I seemed to be able to do that without even thinking about it, because I practised until it became natural. I'd started getting experimental; my fingers knew where to go and I knew what sounded good for whichever key I was playing in.

Sometimes, Sally would visit Marianne Faithfull, who at the time was living with Mick Jagger, in a flat on somewhere like Pont Street in Chelsea. I would go there just to see my sister and Marianne; I remember Mick popping in and out. The first time I went to see them, Mick and Marianne had this peculiar thing in the middle of the living room. It was a large black octagonal table with a great big plastic dome in the middle, which was a sort of milky-yellow colour. I think you switched it on and it had a light – it looked something like the middle of the Tardis in *Doctor Who*. I asked Marianne what it was, and she said it was a sculpture by some very famous artist. It was probably worth an absolute fortune.

One time I remember staying the night there when I was about fourteen. As Mick and Marianne were away I was sleeping in their spare room with a huge, great bed covered by an enormous, grand bedspread. They had two entire sides of the room full of clothes, these massive wardrobes with incredible exotic jackets, dresses, feather boas, going on for ever. When Marianne was back in the flat, I remember how I was downstairs and I put my cup of tea on this sculpture. Marianne came screaming out at me, 'How dare you put your cup of tea on that statue!' or words to that effect, and with that, I fled out of the flat. So I was standing outside this place with my fluorescent-yellow, graffiti-covered guitar case, thinking, 'Oh, my God, what have I done?'

I didn't have any money so I found a phone box and reversed the charges back to my dad. I said, 'I've just been chucked out, what should I do?' My dear father obviously rang Marianne up and gave her a bit of a talking to on the telephone, because ten minutes later she came down the road, looking for me. She took me by the hand, back into the house, and gave me a cup of tea and a bar of chocolate. Then she got her purse and gave me about thirty shillings, which was more than enough for my fare home: it was a fortune for me at the time. My father was always prepared to stick up for me like that.

I liked Mick Jagger a lot. Not because I was in awe of him, he was just a really nice person. He was the first very famous person that I had met; before that, I thought famous people were meant to be in a class of their own and act like gods, but he didn't at all. I was very surprised later on, meeting famous people who did act like gods and who thought they were somehow different from everybody else. Mick Jagger was a special kind of person, and there are very few of them, who actually deserved to be in the position he was.

One evening Mick was there with Marianne, Keith Richards was there with his girl at the time, Anita Pallenberg I think it was, and we were all sitting there at this Indian table, smoking joints and stuff. I wanted to impress them so I sneaked round the corner and picked up Keith Richards' big Gibson J-200 guitar. I started to give it a good old thrashing, which unfortunately Keith didn't like at all. So I shut up and skulked in the corner behind an afghan cushion, until they all disappeared off to some club or another.

As Sally played the guitar, and as I was already a very good guitar player too, we had the idea of me playing along to her songs. When she came back to Harold Wood we tried playing together: we used to practise the songs at home, then go out and play them at folk clubs. We didn't really get close until that point, although as things had been falling apart for our mother, in some ways Sally, being the oldest, had taken the role of being head of the family.

My first experience of recording came when Mick decided to give Sally and me a chance to make a demo. We went to this recording studio called Sound Techniques: the tape operator was a man called Gus Dudgeon, who later became a very important producer, working with people like David Bowie and Elton John. Sally found this Indian tabla player called Rafiq in the local Indian hippy shop, and she invited him to come and play with us. Mick Jagger was up in the control box, and all I can remember of the recording is Mick pressing the intercom button up in the box, saying, 'Rafiq, Rafiq, shut up!' I don't think he liked his playing very much. I've no idea what happened to the tapes from those sessions.

Back at Hornchurch Grammar, I was just marking time and waiting for my fifteenth birthday, after which I could leave. At that school they were always telling you to get your hair cut. It was just after the session with Mick Jagger and my sister, and my hair was starting to get long, when the sports master said, 'Oldfield, go and get your hair cut.' I said no, I wouldn't, then he asked me another couple of times and I just flatly refused. So I was dragged off to the headmaster's office. The head gave me this lecture about how the necessary qualification for the average supermarket manager was seven O levels and two A levels.

I said, 'Sorry, sir, I have just been in the studio with Mick Jagger and I'm going to be a musician.' He said something like, 'I'll let you off, but don't worry if the girls laugh at you.' I assured him that I wouldn't worry about that, thank you very much.

Shortly before I left school I took an O level English oral, which I passed with a B or a C. That was my only qualification, in English. A few months later, on 15 May 1968, my birthday arrived.

I had finally turned fifteen, and my sister had decided she was going to make a record. Something had spurred her on – strangely enough, she'd had a life-changing experience not far from Bristol, at Portishead. She'd been watching the sun set, and she says her whole life ever since has been about that moment.

Soon after, Sally started going around the record companies. It was the end of the hippy times, and she would float into a record company's offices in a wispy dress and say, 'I want to make a record.' So my sister wafted into the Transatlantic Records building, the company that had Pentangle, Bert Jansch and John Renbourn. 'By the way, my brother is a very good guitarist,' said my sister to Nathan Joseph, the managing director. So she brought me into that.

You didn't send demo tapes in those days; you actually went in and played, in the manager's office. We went and sat in front of Nat Joseph and played, and obviously he was sufficiently impressed because he wanted to make a record for us.

Nat was not only the managing director but he also produced all the records. That was the first time I'd been in a studio properly. They had a four-track machine the size of a big, old-fashioned fridge, with very big meters and knobs, it was all very exciting. I loved the atmosphere and tension in the studio – when everything is ready, they switch on the tape machine and you have to give your very best.

After we'd done our bit, Nat brought a little orchestra in, with a string section and a flute. We weren't allowed into that session for some reason: I think in those days, the artist was invited to do the performance then the producer and engineer did all the work. When we were allowed back in, we heard our music with these beautiful strings, there was a harpsichord on one track and a flute on another. It was magnificent to hear our music with proper, professional accompaniment, especially when they had put effects like echo on it. It was mind-blowing, it sounded just like real music you would hear on the radio or watch on TV.

Until then the only music I'd done had been in the clubs, which is just being in a room singing and playing. So to hear it back was astonishing, to my ears it sounded amazing. I was overwhelmed. I thought, 'My God, I'm doing something professional here.' It was like the first step of a career, and it felt magnificent.

As well as the music, I just loved all the technology. It was very primitive compared to nowadays but I adored it, things like the different smells, of the tape and all the cleaning fluid they used to clean the tape heads. There was the smell of ozone from the electronics, I think it was from the transistors (whether they still had valves then, I don't know).

It was Nat Joseph's idea to call us Sallyangie, the name coming from my sister's name and the instrumental 'Angie', composed by Davey Graham and made famous by Bert Jansch. I didn't like the name but I was just along for the ride so I had to put up with it.

Once we had done the album, Nat found us an agent called Roy Guest, who was part of the Epstein organisation, NEMS. Roy got us various shows, little college gigs up and down the country; we would often have two or three shows a week. Our brother Terry was our driver, and we had a minivan which we sprayed orange. Our father must have bought that for us. Dad was always helping out like that, but we knew that for my parents' generation, being a musician was not a serious job. That would be a doctor or something, where you study for years to get to where you are. All the same, our parents were too involved in their own problems to worry too much about what any of us were doing.

We would think nothing of driving all the way up to Lancaster University, or Leeds and Bradford, or Cornwall, or to Scotland and Wales. We travelled thousands of miles in that minivan. Sally would sit in the front with Terry driving, and I would sit in the back with the two acoustic guitars, on a big rug with cushions. It's amazing what you can put up with at that age.

I remember some of the concerts. They were just little gigs at colleges, student unions and clubs, with a couple of hundred people. I would do guitar solos off the top of my head: sometimes I would be just flying, it would all be improvisation. Then the album came out – it was called *Children of the Sun*. Suddenly it wasn't just me and my mates at the folk club any more: we were a proper, signed recording act. The feeling of satisfaction and prestige of having our own album was just magnificent. I felt like I really was somebody, it didn't matter how well it sold – just to have something out there was enough.

We toured around for about a year. Gradually I became more and more of the feeling that I was in my sister's shadow as this was her thing. I do remember a photoshoot when we had these horrible clothes made. They were hippy clothes and I really hated them; I wanted to be a rocker, in jeans and a leather jacket. Once that shoot had happened, I just wanted to get out of there.

We did a few sessions in the studio for a follow-up to the first album. I was doing various acoustic guitar improvisations, based on what I'd been playing on tour. Instead of improvising in the moment, you can build on the same piece of improvised music over a series of dates. Unfortunately, that never worked quite as well in the studio. When I was off in my own world on stage, it was wonderful; in the studio I never really captured it in the same way. I remember playing what I thought was a really rotten improvisation in the studio, but looking back it was incredible. The speed of the playing was mind-bogglingly fast and technical, and I'm not sure I could play like that now.

Just afterwards, I told Sally I wanted to do my own music and didn't want to play with her any more. For some reason Transatlantic didn't carry on with just my sister; perhaps they saw me as part of it. The follow-up was never released, but I don't know why. I had become quite close to Terry by that time, and I wanted to have an electric group. Terry played a bit of bass, so we found a drummer and called ourselves Barefoot.

Barefoot was a very primitive affair. We cobbled together some tunes with a bit of an instrumental here, a riff there, and we went to see our agent. As Sallyangie, we had been passed from Roy Guest to his assistant, a lady called Julia Creasy, who became the manager of Barefoot. Roy got hold of an electric guitar for me, a Fender Telecaster that used to belong to Marc Bolan. I still liked my Lawrence pick-up, so much so that I spent a whole afternoon with my father at Redden Court Road, drilling a hole in the scratch panel and fitting the pick-up on to the Telecaster.

We needed a bigger van now, and we needed some amplifiers. I remember how Terry and I went to see Dad in his surgery, in somewhere like Chadwell Heath (not far from Harold Wood), and asking him for some money. We needed something like eight hundred pounds for a couple of amps and a bigger van, trading in the minivan for something like a Transit van. Dad agreed to buy them on hire purchase, on the understanding that it was up to us to earn the money and pay him back. I don't know if we ever did, not back then anyway. I do remember at the time, he said to us, 'You'll have to get a proper job one day!'

We only did three or four gigs, but it wasn't really working out. Before long, it all fell apart. The best thing we achieved was when we had a gig at a place called something like Shades, or some other speakeasy, in London. We had a review in a music paper the following week: it said something like, 'The power cut at the Speakeasy last Saturday meant the music was turned off, which was a relief to everybody there.'

So that was the end of Barefoot.

5. PIMLICO – 1969

When Julia Creasy joined Blackhill Enterprises as an associate, she took us with her. Blackhill were agents for the Edgar Broughton band and, at one time, Pink Floyd: one of their directors was Peter Jenner, who'd been instrumental in the Pink Floyd story. After a couple of months, Julia rang me up and said I should come in to the office. So along I went, with my guitar.

I don't think Pete Jenner liked me very much. As I arrived, he said to me, 'I've got this audition you can go to at EMI.' The trouble was, it was for a bass player and I wasn't a bass player, I was a guitarist. I said I only had my guitar, but Pete told me I should go anyway. He said, 'They'll have a bass there, but you'll have to borrow an amp from here.' In the office they had this massive amplifier, a Sound City 100-watt top and a four-by-twelve speaker cabinet. I'm not sure exactly how much they weigh but a cabinet that size is a substantial thing. It's got four twelve-inch speakers with heavy magnets in them, and is made of very hard material; if you're carrying one of those you can't see your feet, it's as wide as you can reach, you're like a walking square. The amplifier top was full of valves and transformers, and that weighed a ton as well.

I also had to take my guitar, so I had a big heavy guitar case, a big heavy amp and a cabinet, all of which I had to get from Blackhill's offices in Westbourne Grove to Manchester Square, which was EMI's office. Pete Jenner obviously knew how hard it was going to be, and he knew I didn't have any transport. He just looked at me and pointed with his thumb out of the door and said, 'Well, you'd better get over there.' As I headed for the door, I remember one of the secretaries was looking a bit dolefully at me, obviously thinking, 'You're not going to enjoy this, young Michael.' That was what everyone called me.

So I had these three things to get down the road. When I carried the massive speaker cabinet I must have looked like a huge spangle with my feet sticking out from the bottom. It's hard to describe adequately just how heavy and awkward it all was. I could just about carry the guitar in one hand – that was a big, heavy case as well – together with the amp top. I took them to the top of the road, plonked them down and then came back for the four-by-twelve. Back in the office, I picked up the cabinet and took it to the top of the road to go with the guitar and top, and so on. All the while, Pete was probably trying not to gloat as he watched me going back and forth. No doubt he was having a good old laugh at this, but there was nothing else for it. If I'd said, 'Can I get a taxi?' he would probably have said, 'Get off with you!'

I must have looked like a caterpillar, going backwards and forwards to get to the tube station. When I got there, even getting through the ticket barrier was a nightmare. I had to explain to the ticket collector, 'I'll have to go out and come back in, go in, out, and come back in again.' Then I had to get the lot down the escalators: that was worrying. I had to carry this huge cabinet down to the bottom of the escalator, get it off and leave it, then get the up-escalator to pick up the other things. I was worried about the cabinet being stolen, but then I thought to myself, 'Who'd want to steal that?' And even if they had, they wouldn't have got very far. I don't know what I would have done if I'd seen someone walking off with it, but luckily no four-by-twelve cabinet thieves were around that day.

When the train actually came and the doors opened, I had this mad rush to get the cabinet in, then back out for the amp top and my guitar before the train went off. Of course, I had to do the whole thing in reverse when I got to Oxford Circus. Then, just to get from Oxford Circus to Manchester Square, halfway up Oxford Street, with thousands of shoppers, was nearly impossible.

Finally, somehow, I ended up at the reception desk of EMI's offices in Manchester Square. I was a complete, slithering ball of sweat. Out came this cowboy-looking chap with long blond hair, who introduced himself to me as Kevin Ayers. I was struck immediately by how charming he was. I decided, 'That's a nice man, I want to be part of this.'

Kevin introduced me to a couple of other people, both of whom looked a bit weird. There was a very sullen-looking person called David Bedford: I learned he was a proper, recognised, avant-garde classical composer whose music had been performed at the Proms. I was a bit overwhelmed with the thought of working with a classical composer. There was also a funny little bald chap called Lol Coxhill who played saxophone.

Then it was time for my audition. Kevin started playing these songs, I didn't think they were that great at first but I picked up the bass and joined in. It was one of the first times I'd ever played bass: instead of just going 'dum, dum, dum' for every chord, I made a little melody around the bass line. It just seemed to work: the bass became something you could listen to on its own, I was playing little tunes as well as holding down the bass. Kevin said, 'Yeah, I'll give you the job.' So that's how I joined Kevin Ayers and the Whole World. I think he realised it had been like doing the London Marathon, getting that amp and top all the way to Manchester Square on the tube: so, thank God, he said I could leave my stuff there.

Kevin Ayers was the first person I met who had real character, real charisma. I guess he was a bit of a star: he was a good musician and had a lovely way of being, of moving. He looked very comfortable in his body, and in the character he had taken on. His band, Soft Machine, had been on tour throughout America as the backing band for Jimi Hendrix, so he had seen what it was like to be a real superstar.

Kevin took me under his wing, in a way: instead of wanting to teach me about music, he wanted to teach me about life. It's hard to explain why this was so important to me. Since the fight I'd had with my dad just before we left Reading, I felt I had lost an anchor. I wasn't exactly looking for a new father figure but I needed someone to trust, somebody I could look up to and rely on for guidance. In a way it was, 'I think I can learn something from you, and you're not going to attack me or go crazy.'

So, I became a young Robin to his Batman. I was sixteen; when I joined Kevin Ayers, that's really when I became a proper musician. Music became everything.

We started rehearsals in a little cul-de-sac in Shepherds Bush. We got straight down to work: Kevin's music was largely songs, and I had to play bass to them. The bass can be one string, really, you can just follow down, along, and over the chords with one note; or you could try to make a little kind of melody, very deep down, in the bass part. That's what I wanted to do with Kevin's songs, just to have the bass part and listen to that as if it were an interesting piece of music. I remember he had this song called 'May I', where I played in that way.

Working with Kevin, I quickly learned you didn't have to have a vocalist standing there, howling 'baby, baby, this' and 'baby, baby, that' all the time; you could have instrumental music, which was much more interesting. It was also the first I heard of nonstandard time signatures. It was very fashionable to play things in 7/8, 5/4, 15/8, 11/8 and so on: I saw for the first time that pop or rock music didn't have to be plodding along in 4/4. The other people in the group did it so easily, I was quite impressed. I remember when I first started I couldn't feel the beats at all and kept falling into 4/4 time, but eventually I learned how to do it.

From that point on, music took on another dimension – it became mathematical. When you're making music that is interesting, it gets your mind involved on another, mathematical, level. This was later to develop into my interest in these complex musical cycles. I was already into complicated instrumentals, and that's where the other musicians interested me. I remember watching Lol Coxhill playing jazz, and trying to work out what the hell it was that he was doing. Although I respect jazz I don't understand it, some of the rhythms and chords are so complicated. It doesn't move me emotionally, but that doesn't mean to say I'm not fascinated by it; there's something strange and mathematical about it.

As for David Bedford's music, that was off the scale in its weirdness. David didn't turn out to be standoffish at all; he was a charming man and I quickly became friendly with him, I felt it was great to be in the same band. He did things in this incredible, avant-garde way: he used to play his Farfisa organ with a brick in certain sections, and sometimes with cricket gloves – they were proper notes, but with his gloves on, they came in and out of tune.

When I went over to David's house and looked at all his musical scores, I couldn't believe somebody could write these huge, great books full of crotchets and quavers, all in multiple staves with zillions of violins and percussion, pages and pages of manuscript. Sometimes there would be strange things like a whole page of written music and then, on the next page, a picture of an elephant, then there would be more notes. I remember thinking, 'That's odd.' He played me a tape of one of his Promenade concerts and it was real avant-garde, classical stuff. It wasn't always melodic but I started to think, 'OK, why not, this is another way to make music.' I didn't want to be like David as a musician, but I did decide to do something that wasn't just pop or rock music. I wanted my music to have some kind of lifetime, to be important enough, enduring enough to last beyond the first few months after its release.

David was later to become quite a strong influence on me. He had one piece of music called 'Star Clusters, Nebulae and Places in Devon'. He'd looked at the Stone Age and Iron Age settlements in the West Country, places like Dartmoor and Devon; because he also studied astronomy, he'd worked out that Hercules was the closest cluster of stars that existed at that time, and that the light that had come from that cluster had taken about three thousand years to get here. So, when those settlements were populated and civilised, existing, that's when the light from the star clusters in Hercules that we see now started its journey. I thought that was wonderful, to be inspired enough to write a piece of music that connected not just ancient civilisation but astronomy and the speed of light, making it all into a big musical loop. That kind of thing was fascinating. It was a far cry from the pop music that was around at the time, bands like the Sweet and that kind of stuff. David's music was a hell of a long way from all that and I found it very, very interesting.

Once we started playing live together, we quickly got into a routine. We were a working band, playing three or four gigs a week up and down the country. In the beginning we had two roadies and didn't have to carry the gear ourselves, which was a real step up. We also had a six-wheel Transit van. I was used to travelling in a Transit with my brother, but I was impressed by this one. There were double-wheels at the back that could take lots of weight, whereas our old van only had four wheels, like a normal van. I thought, 'I'm in big time now, with a six-wheel van!' All the same, we didn't have back seats, because we needed the space to get all the equipment in. We would just sit on the four-by-twelve speaker cabinets, we didn't have any cushions or anything. There were no windows, so all you could see was out the front. We would have to travel incredible distances crammed in like that.

When we were on stage, most of the time it was quite eclectic but occasionally we would come together like a normal group and sound quite reasonable. Mostly I played bass, then Kevin might want to swap over and play bass for some of the set, so he would give me the guitar slot. I wasn't the front man; it was much more relaxing being the background person, as an accompanist. But still, it was good to be able to play guitar from time to time.

I didn't think our drummer was that good. In those days you'd be playing almost acoustically, you didn't have any stage monitors, so the bass player would stand next to the drummer. A live drum kit doesn't sound nice at all up close. Once you mike it up in the studio and EQ (equalise) it, put effects on all the different channels, it can start sounding quite good, but an acoustic drum kit, right next to you, just sounds loud and horrible. I was plonked right next to the hi-hat, with my amp behind me. So all I could really hear was a hi-hat and these terrible, acoustic drums. I had that hi-hat about four feet away from my head on every gig. I hated the sound of it, this clattering, thunking, plunking, bashing noise, right in my ear. I can still feel the pain of it.

Meanwhile Kevin's vocals sounded like they were down the end of a bathroom somewhere, repeating back off the far wall of whatever hall we were playing; add a bit of squeaky saxophone and that was that. So I very much got into my own sound. I loved the vibration in the bass: it was almost comforting, like a deep massage.

Apart from David and Kevin, they all used to treat me as 'young Michael'. I didn't know anything, I was very green and just did what I was told to do at the beginning. Of course, that was to change later. I was only sixteen or seventeen; these people were well into their twenties, and David Bedford was in his thirties. I was very much the young boy, and I didn't think they took me seriously at all.

They kind of tolerated me but, of course, I wanted to be thought of as being as good as them.

It was a good time for the first year or so. The 1960s really was the music decade. It was a fantastic time to be into music, there was just so much going on. We saw some great other bands: Wishbone Ash, Pink Floyd, those kind of bands. Genesis were around, weird groups like Black Sabbath were around – but it was a kind of 'natural' weirdness, it was just what they did, they didn't have this mystique of being weird like such bands have today. I never got to see Cream, although I would have loved to, or Jimi Hendrix. There was another strange band called Hawkwind that I could never understand, and we were often on the same bill as them. Sometimes we were on the same bill as Free, and I remember being gobsmacked by Paul Kossoff's guitar playing. The sound of his guitar was so much coming from him, from his personality, he wasn't just posturing. It somehow sunk into me that his guitar was his voice, like my guitar was my voice. It was just spine-tingling listening to him play; it wasn't incredibly complicated, but the emotion in it was electrifying.

We often used to be on with the Floyd, which I think was originally another Blackhill band. I remember we played a festival in Canterbury with them, along with the Faces, Rod Stewart's band. I remember how skinny they all were, they were stick men, but they were bloody good.

The sound at a Pink Floyd concert was brilliant, before its time: they were the top of the tree in terms of live music. This was before they had these great huge monster shows like *The Wall*: they didn't have a lightshow that I can remember. It was just the quality of the sound, they had this magnificent sound engineer and PA system, you could really hear everything. Years later I went to see *The Wall*; it was a great show with megabucks spent on the production, but it didn't have that basic essence, there was a lack of theatre. To this day I don't like any lightshows really: why do you need a lightshow, anyway? Back in those days it was just four musicians playing the atmospheric music and that's what was exciting about it. That was the last time in my life I can remember wanting to go and listen to a band and sit up front. Later on I tried to, but I would get bored to be honest, I don't why. These days I feel I belong backstage rather than out front. Perhaps it is the same for theatrical actors who sit in the audience, when they are aware of what goes on behind the stage.

The music was so different from what had come before. There was a great feeling of optimism everywhere. You would go to a college gig and there would be amazing musicians there, all the musicians would just be doing the same thing, there was no rivalry at all. Everyone had the same kind of PA, a standard four-speaker system on either side; we all had the same kind of van, a six-wheel Transit, and we all had a similar type of roadie who would hump in all the gear. I think a couple of people had a smoke machine but it wasn't a big deal, and nobody had a lightshow. If you were higher level you wouldn't travel in the van, you would most likely drive in a Range Rover. Pink Floyd wouldn't travel in the van; they obviously had a bit more money than we did.

I remember there was a big buzz about this huge, orchestral, jazz-rock band called Centipede, which was the brainchild of Keith Tippet; we were on the same bill as them a couple of times. Robert Wyatt was in that band, and so were Zoot Money and Julie Driscoll; they had a whole string section, brass, percussion and everything. Now, there was a band. When you went to one of their concerts, people would leave, saying, 'Wow, that's the most amazing thing I have heard in my life!' It was fun, it was rocky, it was dynamic, with loud bits and quiet bits. It really wasn't this 'classic rock' business, where you've got the orchestra looking at the band thinking, 'You arseholes', and the band thinking they are the superstars. It wasn't like that at all; it was just a whole load of musicians, with everybody totally into it.

Centipede was a little bit more jazz than I preferred. As I've said, I am not really a jazz person, more folk and classical. While I didn't understand it, I did try to learn from it. I started to experiment with all these strange jazz chords, which was not something I took to naturally. At the time we couldn't wait for the Centipede album, but funnily enough when it came out, I was disappointed. It wasn't like the live show, which was one of those things that is impossible to record. All the same, Centipede was a really big inspiration for me. I wanted to have my own Centipede, or make some music that had the same kind of effect. It was totally brilliant and I haven't seen anything like it since.

At some point, Robert Wyatt – who had played with Kevin Ayers, in Soft Machine – suddenly decided he wanted to join us as drummer. Of course, Kevin agreed straight away. Once Robert joined us, playing live became a completely different experience. He was the world's most innovative drummer, he was astonishing. I actually *hated* drums up until that point, but I loved to watch Robert play. For example, he would be playing along with a song and, suddenly, it would be like he was having an epileptic fit. He would just start making sounds with his drums, whining away and doing strange things with them. I would have to keep the rhythm going and we would build it up to a big crescendo. Somehow, magically, we would come crashing right down on the beat at exactly the right moment, and then we would float away again.

Robert was also quite a star at the time; he played drums like nobody else before or since. Soft Machine were almost like the gods of jazz-rock music. It didn't really come over on their albums, but to see them live, there was all the complexity of jazz but with all the rawness of rock about it. If you went to see them at a concert, you'd see the audiences so into it: it was something you could get involved in emotionally, and also intellectually. I respected them so much, and to have Robert in the band, to be playing bass to his drums, was fantastic. I looked up to him tremendously; he was my hero. The downside was that he was always so depressed and unhappy, and so full of angst and misery. Occasionally he would perk up, but not very often. Being on tour with him for a few weeks at a time, I've never seen such an unhappy person. As a drummer, however, he was simply fantastic. When he left we got our old drummer back again and it was like, 'Oh, God . . .'

Kevin loved his wine. He didn't smoke hash as far as I can remember. He would start drinking at the beginning of a journey and all the way to the gig he would be swigging from a bottle of wine. He explained to me once, 'As soon as I open a bottle, I feel all these little men coming around in my body, waving flags, going, "Hurray, here comes the wine again!"' He would pass the bottle to me and, of course, I would join in, we would both be half-plastered by the time we got to where we were going. When we arrived we would go for a very hot curry – Kevin taught me all about curry and how to dip your chapatti in your tarka dhal. He was brought up in Malaysia; I don't know his exact history, but he really knew about curries.

Kevin could handle the drink, but by the time we got on stage, I would often be completely sozzled. I would try to play my part as best I could. I eventually got a guitar solo, which, when aided by the alcohol, became one of the wild points of the gig. I really lived for my guitar solo: it was my big moment in the set. I was like Angus Young, that little chap in AC/DC that rolls around on the floor. People don't think of me like that, for some reason they think of me as a hippy, but I wasn't like that at all. I used to do all kinds of things, like somersaults round the stage, literally. At some point I picked up a mandolin and managed to work out the 'Sailor's Hornpipe'. It became my thing in the Kevin Ayers set and it never failed to get the audience happy and stomping around.

I always remember coming back late at night, watching the speedometer being stuck on 84 miles an hour (that was as fast as the van would go), for hour after hour, driving down the motorway from places like Tenby in Wales, or Preston, or Lancaster. We would often travel overnight, getting back at the crack of dawn. The poor old roadie, I don't know how he used to do it. He used to drop off Lol Coxhill in Luton, then David Bedford in Mill Hill, and then Kevin somewhere in London. Then he dropped me at Liverpool Street station. I was the last to be dropped off, normally at about six or seven in the morning.

From there I would get the train to Harold Wood, where I would have to carry my two heavy guitars (a bass and an electric, I always had my guitars with me) from the station to home, which was about another mile. I would get home about nine-thirty in the morning with a horrible hangover from all the drinking the night before. This was happening three or four times a week, which was punishing: it really was a good apprenticeship into the rock and roll lifestyle.

Quite regularly we would get the ferry over to Holland. It was exciting to get off the ferry, as the sun was coming up normally; then we'd be driving through the countryside, looking out of the windows. It was funny listening to the banter in the back of the Transit. Someone would say, 'windmill', then thirty seconds later, 'oh, windmill' and it would be windmills all the way to Amsterdam. In the end we would all be laughing uncontrollably.

Holland was a comfortable place, which became like a second home. When we were in Amsterdam we would always play at the Paradiso club: we played there many times. We'd stay in the same hotel each time, just across the canal from the Westerkerk – a very famous church, even more so these days because Anne Frank's house was on the corner right next to it. It's got these wonderful bells with beautiful melodies, called a carillon. I would hear those bells all the time, from my little room. It was in Holland that Kevin introduced me to Indonesian food: you get about twenty dishes, which I thought was wonderful. David Bedford used to smoke roll-ups with Samson tobacco, but when we travelled to Holland he used to get Van Nelle tobacco. I decided that I liked the feeling of rolling them myself rather than taking them out of the packet, so I started smoking roll-ups as well.

I don't remember meeting many local people, as we generally kept to ourselves. I don't remember any fans at all, really, we didn't cause that kind of reaction. We were a very odd group and would have avant-garde bits and silly songs as well as more normal music. We certainly didn't have anything like groupies! Sometimes Kevin would get a female interested in him, and he had a Dutch girlfriend that he always wanted to go and see, but that was about it.

Sometimes we would fly from Heathrow to Amsterdam or Rotterdam. I hated that, as I had become terrified of aeroplanes. I was in agony, not just panicky but completely fearful of being in a metal box with wings, in a big, empty sky. It was a mixture of claustrophobia and agoraphobia, shut inside a small place in such a big space. Nobody could understand: they said, 'Oh, don't be silly,' but that was the first I experienced of panic attacks, although I wasn't really aware then of what was happening. Unless you've actually had an attack, unless you've experienced it, it's a terrible thing but it's very hard to explain. I just thought, 'OK, I'm afraid of flying,' and left it at that.

We spent some time in Paris as well. Once we were on the same bill as Pink Floyd in the middle of the student riots. I remember walking out from the Métro right into the middle of it all. On one side of the street was a row of riot police and on the other side were all the students. I was walking in between the two, and in my naivety I didn't realise what peril I was in. I sauntered through, looking left and right between these people, and then wandered off to my hotel. By the time we played there was tear gas coming into the hall.

In my early time with Kevin's band I was still living in Harold Wood, but around the time I turned seventeen, I moved down to London. I had a girlfriend who was studying at the Architectural Association; she lived in this very small, second-floor flat in St George's Square in Pimlico, which she shared with a crowd of other people. That whole area around Vauxhall Bridge Road was full of different clumps of teenage flats, people would swap and change all the time. Somebody would move in one week and then move out the next, a bit like squatters, but somehow the rent was always paid: there must have been someone there who had got it together. It was like a village of different flats, full of people at a loose end, some of whom worked, some didn't.

I stayed with my girlfriend in that flat for a short time, but then we split up and she moved out. It was a horrible, dirty place. When I moved in it looked reasonable, with some furniture, but by the time I left it had been completely wrecked, the furniture destroyed. It's weird how teenagers tend to do that. While it became a complete hovel, at least I didn't have to do that train journey back to Harold Wood. It was the first time I had really lived away from home: once, my mother and father came to visit me and took me out in their car, an MG by this time. We went to Clapham Common as it was just over Vauxhall Bridge, and had tea there. It was probably once my mother had decided I was doing reasonably well that they left.

It was in that Pimlico flat that I got more heavily into drugs. It was easy to buy drugs then. The people in the flat would wake up in the morning and start smoking dope straight away: they'd smoke the entire day away. I started smoking hashish regularly, just whenever I felt like it, but after a few weeks I started feeling like a vegetable. I looked at the other people in the flat – they didn't ever do anything but smoke dope and I just didn't like it. I felt, if I carry on doing this, I will become just like them. Luckily for me, I got taken away from the flat on a regular basis. I would be summoned to the van and sit in there for ten hours on my way to somewhere. Nobody else in the band smoked hash, or only very occasionally.

Mainly I smoked hashish because it made music sound different and I could explore my musical world a lot better. It was like putting on high-focus glasses: I could see almost down to its atomic structure, at that level of detail. This is not unusual: I have worked with several musicians who have to be stoned to work at all. Suddenly though, when I smoked a joint I felt a horrible sensation in my spine: not a minor tingling but more like my whole spine was over-loaded with electricity. I felt I was being fried by electrical signals, from the top of my head and all the way down my back, burning me. It scared the life out of me so I stopped smoking hash at that point. I did start taking LSD more regularly, but it was like something was brewing, like a tornado was getting stirred up, about to be unleashed.

I didn't listen to music on LSD. With LSD you were more out in the streets, experiencing things or having hallucina-tions. I once saw fascinating halos around everything, people and objects. I still don't know if it was really a hallucination, or whether I was seeing things in a different way. Perhaps drugs can open up doors of consciousness artificially, which maybe will take us another couple of thousand years to develop. In any case, we are not ready for such experiences; we don't have the mechanisms to deal with them.

One night our flat was raided by the drugs squad. The drug squad police were horrible around that time, they were really heavy about it all. It just so happened on that particular evening that we had finished all the drugs: we had taken all the LSD and smoked all the hash. The police did a search, then this policeman came into the room with a piece of hash, and said, 'What's this, then?' We knew it was a setup, we could see it was the wrong colour for the hash we were getting at the time. Luckily one of our number was still sufficiently in his right mind to say, 'You planted that, that's nothing like the hash we do; yes, we do drugs, but we've done it all already – if you had come half an hour earlier . . .' Luckily this policeman backed off; they all slunk away, grumbling and saying, 'We'll be back.'

Living in that flat wasn't particularly pleasant: there were all these weird people, drunk and crazy. I remember once I was due to fly out that afternoon to Paris. We had been booked for a festival in a big hangar at Le Bourget airport, and Pink Floyd were playing on the same bill. We'd just been on a little mini-tour, a string of gigs in colleges up North somewhere.

The night before the festival I went to sleep back in the flat, and I had my takings from the mini-tour (which was only about thirty pounds) in my pocket. One person in the flat was very strange and effeminate, and he walked around in a dressing gown all the time. I didn't trust him, so when I went to sleep I put my money under my pillow. When I woke up at two o'clock in the afternoon, it was gone. Of course he was gone too, so I was literally penniless. Somehow I managed to get to West London air terminal, the place where you could catch a little bus to take you to the plane.

I went to Paris with no money at all, but we were staying at the Hilton hotel. It's difficult when you're staying in a luxury hotel, but can't afford to actually eat anything – it didn't occur to me to ask anyone else in the band for money. I can guess what they would have replied if I had! So, I decided to go begging, to buy a plate of chips. I went out onto the Boulevard St Michel and I asked people for a franc here and a franc there. That was the first time I had real *pommes frites*, and they were magnificent – I remember dipping them in mayonnaise. Eventually, someone had the bright idea that you could order things from room service, so I would always manage to get something to eat even when we had no money to pay for it. You paid when you left, and I never did find out who settled the bill.

6. THE HORRORS – 1970

I was still living in Pimlico when Kevin Ayers asked me to get involved in his next album. It was my first visit to Abbey Road, and I was absolutely joyous when I arrived. The studio was Abbey Road Studio Number Two, the famous one, full of things like a Mellotron, some tympani, vibraphones, harpsichords, glockenspiels, and beautiful Steinway pianos. The mixing desk was completely new: it looked massive then, although it was actually very small compared to the really big mixers that were installed in studios later.

When he was writing material for the album, once Kevin asked us to each contribute a verse to a song. He had this thing about health food: he introduced me to vegetarian and macrobiotic food. I remember I had to make up a verse about the dangers of preservatives and the chemicals in food: his verse was 'I'm an 'orrible orange', my verse was 'I'm a lamentable lentil' and David Bedford's (I think) was 'I'm a chemical kipper', things like that. Later on, in each country we went to, we'd perform the song in the local language, so we translated it into Dutch and into German: that was fun.

Kevin's agent Pete Jenner was also the producer; the engineer was called Peter Mew – he's still working at Abbey

Road, amazingly. I found out that if our session began at one o'clock, I could come in early, before anybody else arrived, and hang out in the studio and play all the instruments. From then I arrived as early as possible, so I would have two or three hours on my own, just smelling the place and looking at the equipment. I'd go down into the studio and try to understand how the mixer worked, or I'd play a real concert Steinway, or I'd fiddle around with the vibraphone, the Mellotron and the harpsichord.

Perhaps my favourite things were the tympani. You had to tune them with pedals: I would go to the piano and find A, B or C and set up the little meters on the tympani to be in tune with that. There were three tympani, so I could do a three-note melody with them. By moving the pedals, I could change the pitch of the drum to make a more complicated melody. I discovered that if you hit the tympani right, it would make a lovely sound and the hammer would bounce right back up, ready to hit the other one. Gradually, I practised enough to do cross rhythms and I was having a whale of a time. I didn't play them brilliantly, not like a proper percussionist, but I loved whacking these huge drums with sticks and hearing that fantastic sound vibrating everywhere. It was just magnificent, spending time with all that gear. That's where I really got the idea of creating a piece of classical music but recording everything, doing everything myself. There was one piece of technical wizardry that I couldn't master, though. In the canteen was a microwave oven that I didn't understand and I managed to reduce a large hamburger to the size of a Smartie.

Around that time there was a rumour that Paul McCartney was in Studio Number One, which is the big orchestral studio. We heard he was making an album all on his own and he was playing everything: drums, keyboards, the lot. I thought that was fascinating and I kept trying to peek in through the door, but I never got the courage to go inside. I didn't even pass him in the corridor – I never actually met him there – so I was never sure if it wasn't just rumours.

CHANGELING

So for a few months I was working almost every day at Abbey Road. The recording sessions were absolutely great. I didn't really write anything: they were Kevin's songs, I just played the bass. A good thing was that halfway through a session, a man would appear with an envelope full of pound notes. I got the incredible sum of something like thirty-four pounds and ten shillings, which was a fortune to me at the time for a day or two's session work. I remember the exact size of the envelope, these were the big, old pound notes, they really felt like something. Then we had to sign a release form, to relinquish our rights to any royalties from the resulting album.

All the same, some things were starting to bother me. We worked incredibly hard during that period, but after a couple of years I started to feel really dominated and not listened to. I had so much music in me that I wanted to get out; I sometimes felt like I was being prevented from contributing. As I'd joined the band as a sixteen- or seventeen-year-old, everybody still called me 'young Michael'; they didn't really listen to me. By the end I had become an important member of the band, almost an attraction, but that wasn't how I was being treated by the others. I felt frustrated.

Later, I wondered how much of *Tubular Bells* I did just to impress those other musicians from Kevin Ayers' band; as if to say, 'Look, I can do it as well as you, and maybe even better.' That was one of the advantages of being thrown into a band like that at such a young age. I saw it as a challenge, to understand what it was all about, and to create my own compositions. That may have been why I took such care when I was composing *Tubular Bells*. I wanted to show these people that I was capable of more than they thought.

But then, disaster struck.

One evening, I was to have the last LSD trip in my life. I'm not sure exactly what happened, but I do remember walking down Vauxhall Bridge Road, where we were tripping. All

92

of a sudden, something simply switched in my body, almost like switching on a huge electric current. It felt like I was being electrocuted.

The effect on me was immediate. I felt a veil was lifted off, from where I was and what I was, and from what everybody was. The people around me, they weren't people I knew any more, everybody was stripped of anything I had ever learned about them. They looked to me to be just like biological machines, almost like robots, but made of flesh and blood. I saw into their bloodstreams and down to the molecular level; I could see that all their movements were dictated by electrical impulses and chemical reactions. They were inhaling this gas which we call air into their lungs, they were somehow processing it into energy so they could move around. Even their mouths, the way they spoke – they were making these weird, strange sounds we call language. It wasn't that I had a hallucination, that I *imagined* that humans were machines, but I knew, I saw it, and indeed I can still see it. We are machines. If you see that in its harsh reality, it's horrifying.

Then my consciousness expanded even further. It became a hopelessly lost, weird thing, floating in the middle of an eternal void. It was like, quite suddenly, somebody had told me the secret they had been trying to cover up for my whole childhood. I faced the harsh reality of looking at our existence in its purest, most physical level, without the foggiest idea how we got there, or how we came to be conscious, or why, for what purpose. I felt I had unlocked some terrible Pandora's box, that somebody had told me life was not really how I imagined it, that I was lost in a completely bio-electromechanical world without a clue as to how I had got there or why I was there; what was more, I was going to disappear from it by dying, without finding a single explanation for anything. At the time it just seemed such a terrible truth. I felt I was the only person who knew it. I wanted to go up to everybody and say, 'Don't you know, don't you know, this is real, this is how it really is!'

I'd always been sensitive to the world around me, with my emotional 'antennae' that could tune into the atmospheres of places. I'd sometimes wondered how I could get closer to what it was all about, if I could only find the doorway to the wider understanding I knew was out there. Suddenly it was smashed wide open, like the huge doors of a cathedral being ripped off and hurled away, and I was thrust outside. I could see physical objects down to the atomic level, and I could see our whole planet as a great, big sphere hurtling through space, all at once. I felt overwhelmed with dizziness, just being on our planet. I was conscious of the massive size of it, of the fact it was going round and round, that the entire thing was hurtling through infinite space at an enormous speed, pushed and pulled by incredible forces. I felt I was going to fall off at any second; I was seasick just from standing still.

It completely terrified me. We grow up, we are indoctrinated, we live our lives, we die and that's that; but with this thing it was like a rocket going up, 'ssshheeooooee!' It felt like I didn't belong here, I felt I was a fish completely taken out of water and I was lying on the shore, gasping for oxygen. I'd always felt like I didn't belong, that I was a person apart: well, it was like that feeling, magnified a million times.

That was the beginning of it. It was like seeing the other side of the coin. One side was, 'My name's Michael Oldfield, musician, I'm living in Pimlico, I went to St Edward's School in Reading,' and the other side was, 'I'm a nameless organic machine, lost and existing in an incomprehensible world, an incomprehensible universe.' I tried to deal with it, but the panic I felt was indescribable. It was a real sledgehammer blow. I'd experienced normal panic attacks before, but this was totally different, like letting off the Hiroshima bomb compared to a little firework. It's all very well panicking when you're about to take off in a plane, but when you have that same experience on the ground, in a garden with butterflies flying around and birds singing, there's something seriously wrong. I couldn't communicate what I was feeling to anybody; I tried, but nobody could understand me, which panicked me even more. Indeed, people still don't understand me when I try to explain it all.

Of course, I now know I'd got what they call the horrors. There must be something about LSD that fundamentally changes and expands how your brain works and perceives things. I have never touched another LSD pill in my life and I've only ever had the occasional puff of a joint. I am still terrified when someone is rolling a joint and passing it round, and I would certainly never go near LSD again.

I must have fallen asleep that night, eventually. When I woke up I tried to shrug it off as a bad dream or a nightmare, but it wouldn't go away. It started coming back: I would switch in and, suddenly, I would be seeing things in that way again. It was terrifying beyond belief. I would think, 'It's not like that, it's not like that,' and try to fend it off, but it would develop into a panic attack. My heart would race and I would run around the place trying to hang on to something, just rushing around in circles going, 'Argh, what can I do? What can I do?' It didn't matter where I was, I could be in the middle of London, in a shop, or I could be out in the country, or in a garden. I do remember that I didn't like neon lights – they really affected me.

That's when it started, the whole period of panic attacks that lasted up until the end of the 1970s. From that moment on it used to happen all the time, no matter where I was. It was an abrupt, harsh discovery of my place on planet Earth, not just physically but spiritually, in terms of human existence. From early on I'd loved watching the sky, I had a love of what's out there and a fascination for what is here. Suddenly it became excruciatingly scary, as it finally sunk in what our existence really is. On top of this was the stress I was still feeling because of my mother. From beginning life as a child who didn't know what fear was, I suddenly became afraid of everything.

I'd experienced nightmares in the past; this was like my worst nightmare come true.

I ran home to my parents, back in Harold Wood, and stayed there for a while. I was spending whole days at home, listening to a lot of classical music. I listened to everything from Sibelius to Beethoven and Bach, and religious music as well. I found things like Bach's *Mass in B Minor*, or Fauré's *Requiem* comforting, perhaps because they had a spiritual dimension, but in a nice, soothing way. When I listened, they gave me something to cling on to.

I was also listening to strange composers like Bartok, Delius and Stravinsky. Their music would often start off in the first movement with a chaotic sound, which would eventually evolve into some kind of theme. That theme would usually develop and get to some climax, where it might change slightly, for example from a minor key to a major key, or it might go into a softer section. They obviously didn't all do that, but I really liked the idea of taking themes, developing them, modifying them and blending them with other themes. To me it was like reading a book: it starts with a bit of a story that grows up, then another character comes in and so on. It's just what classical music does: I loved the way that happened and I found it very comforting. I wanted to do the same with my own music, to create a space where everything was just comfortable and pleasant, relaxing and safe.

At home we had the little upright piano that used to belong to my grandmother – we'd inherited it after her death. Gradually I started playing around with it, picking out tunes of my own. The feelings of frustration I'd felt with the others in the band had not gone away, and here I was, sitting at home for days on end, listening to music and with nothing else to do. As I tinkered with the piano, I started mapping out some ideas in a notebook. From the teach-yourself books and music classes I could write enough musical notation such that if I had an idea, I could remember it; over the top I developed my own notation, more to do with the timing of different parts. I hated crotchets and quavers so I thought there must be a better or easier way of writing music. Instead I would write things down as block diagrams, counting out the beats. In bar notation I'd note after how many sequences the bass would come in, 'The guitars are going to go at this point,' I'd write, butting up against the next sequence, and so on.

I had some of the improvised, acoustic guitar instrumentals that I used to play with my sister, and some bits and pieces I'd done with Kevin Ayers. I put those in as well, and over time, a piece of music started coming together. To me it was a mathematical thing; I worked it all out properly in my notebook, in my own way. The mathematical idea came directly from Sibelius: it was a useful way to occupy my mind and if I could make it sound good at the same time, so much the better.

Meanwhile, I was still playing with Kevin when he went on tour. I was no longer living in Pimlico so it was back to being dropped off at Liverpool Street station at six o'clock in the morning, having to get the train and do the walk. Even in those days Liverpool Street was a really unpleasant place, with tramps and other people hanging around – it was like running a gauntlet just to get on a train. Sometimes I was so tired I couldn't face waiting, so I would get a taxi from outside Liverpool Street. It would cost about eight pounds, which would be just about what I had been paid for the gig. I spent my entire earnings on the taxi to get home.

I wasn't enjoying playing with Kevin any more. It wasn't just the panic attacks; I felt I was kind of carrying the band, holding it together. The whole thing was very disjointed, from where I was standing. We had Kevin with his guitar, Lol Coxhill who was playing the saxophone but almost in a different world, David Bedford on keyboards, and somebody keeping the rhythm. There were all these little bits that didn't really relate to each other. I can remember standing there and trying to glue together all the bits and pieces with my bass. If I heard a little bit of saxophone I'd respond to it, and if I heard something from the drums I'd respond to that. There was obviously Kevin's personality that people liked, but in terms of the music, I felt that if I had stopped playing it wouldn't have sounded so musical.

That was my view at the time, anyway. I don't know if I was right or wrong. Something in me was uncomfortable, though, I felt so unhappy. I don't know how I was perceived by others at the time, but I do know it affected my picture of myself. Coupled with my subordinate status in the band, being so scared of everything made me feel like a coward. I was really dreading going to gigs, that would mean having to join in with the band, hold things together. I wanted more say in things and I tried to suggest things we could do, but I was still 'young Michael', who people didn't take seriously.

I knew more than ever that I wanted to make my own music. At one of the recording sessions at Abbey Road, I turned up a bit early, as usual. When everybody was supposed to arrive nobody came, so it was just me and the engineer, Peter Mew, sitting there in Studio Number Two, twiddling our thumbs and waiting. I said, 'Well, look, nobody's going to turn up, I'll make a track,' and so he said, 'All right then.' In about an hour and a half I made an entire track: all the overdubbing, the percussion, the guitar and bass – I did three harmonised electric guitars. I was really getting carried away, it was all a bit megalomaniacal. I got the entire staff of the studio in at one point, just to sing some lyrics I made up. I was having a ball, and it sounded bloody good as well.

Eventually, Kevin rolled in. I said, 'I've done it, I've done a track!' He was a bit put out, I think, that I had taken over his studio time, so my track got taken off the machine. Funnily enough our tape operator at the time was Alan Parsons, he was quite young at the time. Somehow, something must have taken off in his imagination, as he's had quite a career. Anyway, my little effort was taken off and Kevin took control again. He did keep it as a backing track: he put some different words to it and it was put on the album, I think it's called 'Champagne Cowboy Blues'. It was my first solo effort: I had finally been unleashed in the studio, just because nobody else had turned up.

That was the one ray of sunshine in an otherwise bleak period.

Somewhere around this time Kevin's album came out, it was called *Whatevershebringswesing*. I remember my first review, in *Melody Maker*. It was Phil Manzanera, from Roxy Music, giving his commentary on things. In this piece he said he really liked my guitar solo, he called it 'snakey'. That was the first review I remember (apart from the one from the speakeasy, about the power cut). I had heard of Roxy Music, but I hadn't really listened to their music; I knew they had a good reputation, though, so it felt like a kind of validation. I actually bumped into Phil many years later in Barbados, and I thanked him very much for writing that about me.

I was still having recurring panic attacks; they would come without warning and weren't getting any easier to deal with. I knew I was on borrowed time. It all culminated on a trip once again to Holland, when I just collapsed mentally. We were in Amsterdam in our usual hotel, just over the canal from the church with the beautiful bells. I remember the bells were chiming, but I was panicky and unhappy. I was sick to my stomach, I couldn't eat and was really upset. I was panic-stricken and completely freaked out. I just couldn't go on.

Somehow I got back to England and I just retreated to my parents' house. Funnily enough, like when my father had taken the tranquillizers, my sickness gave new resolve to my mother: she looked after me very well for the few weeks that I was there. I think my father spoke to Kevin, and he explained that I didn't want to do it any more and was no longer available. I spent most of the time in bed, completely incapable of doing anything, comatose; looking back on it, it must have been a nervous breakdown. I remember it was springtime, because eventually I was able to get up and I would walk around Harold Wood, looking at the crocuses and wild orchids in the gardens, all the signs of new life. Every spring I remember that time – seeing the flowers coming out still reminds me of how awful I felt.

When I was going through my worst times, I thought I was possessed. I had this thought in the back of my mind that whatever had been exorcised from my mum had come back and attached itself to me, somehow. I couldn't eat or sleep, and when I wasn't in that panicky state I was worried that I was going to get into it; I felt like I was holding on for dear life. I stuck it out for a week or so, but I wasn't getting any better so I went to see the doctor. I didn't want to take any drugs but I didn't think I could survive with nothing. He gave me something like Valium, but I didn't like the mental fuzziness it gave me; I was also terrified of such things because of what had happened to my mother. One night I tried drinking a bottle of cider and that helped, so I drank another one. That began a long period of alcohol dependency, but it was better than the alternative. If I drank a bottle of wine, though I didn't feel physically well, at least I had anaesthetised the avalanche of emotions and fears.

My parents were still holding it together but it wasn't long before my dad decided to leave home and my mother. I think he said he wanted a divorce: he was desperate, out of his mind by this time. He had bumped into a lady just round the corner, and they became friendly; I don't think they had an affair, I think she just took pity on him and took him in. Her husband was there as well, but I don't think there was anything weird about it. My mother was devastated. Funnily enough, after he left she didn't ever go back to hospital again, but she was at home, alone.

I'd been told the band were carrying on doing gigs without me but people had been saying, 'Where's Mike Oldfield?' so after a few weeks Kevin came to see me at home. 'I really want you back in the group, what would it take for you to come back?' he asked. I had nothing to lose and I'd been working on my own material, so I told him I wanted to do the arrangements, not only for his songs but I wanted to put some of my own music in there. 'I want to add some more instrumental music, call it progressive music,' I said. Also I didn't want to play bass any more, so I told him I wanted to play guitar. Finally, I said I wanted us to get a new drummer and a new bass player.

Much to my surprise, Kevin agreed. 'You can have it your way,' he said. I was suddenly almost the boss of the band and we held auditions for a new bass player and drummer. I set about doing the arrangements, there were even pieces of what would become *Tubular Bells* in that version of Kevin Ayers and the Whole World. It was great for me – suddenly I had taken over.

As part of the new setup, Kevin suggested we moved to a new house. 'I'm going to rent a house, we can all live there,' he said. 'I'll do the cooking, you've got to do the washing up, and you all can pay me a certain amount of money per week for food and all that.' The house he rented was in Westbourne Gardens in Tottenham, just off the Seven Sisters Road – a few years ago I was doing some rehearsals in London so I went up to look at the old house, but it's a bit of a slum now. Each of the musicians had a room: Kevin lived downstairs in the biggest, and I had a small room on the first floor, overlooking the garden. It wasn't even a bedsit – there was space for a bed and just enough room for my guitars and an organ at the end. Our new drummer, William Murray, was in the basement; I got on well with him immediately. Meanwhile Kevin would do the cooking, we would contribute a little bit of money and have communal dinners.

It all started with such great intentions, but unfortunately it didn't last very long. It just didn't work out. We only did a few gigs before the other people in the band seemed to get miserable and grumpy. To them I was acting up, getting a bit above my station, and they became resentful of that. I arranged all their parts, so that rather than being free to tootle away like they had improvised in the past, I gave them parts to play. I think perhaps they thought I was too young to have all that power and was becoming too big for my boots.

Kevin decided the band shouldn't exist any longer, as he didn't feel it was his band any more. We were doing a gig at some college like Loughborough, and afterwards he asked me into his dressing room and said it just wasn't working for him. 'We can't do this any more,' he said. 'I'm going to split the band up.' To be honest, I didn't mind. By then I hated being in a band, I just wanted to do my own thing.

ON SPIRITUALITY – 2006

We are living in an intelligent universe. I sometimes sit back and wonder at what force made it all come into existence: just to ponder on the mystery is magnificent. Looking out at the stars offers the slightest inkling: the distance, the scale of it all, how tiny we are, how amazing the universe really is. Somehow it grew, or it was created; nobody really has any idea but it is the most incredible thing. In nature as well, looking at a single human being or an animal, a horse or even an insect, the design is amazing. As much as I adored Concorde, and I love the Internet and the technologies we have, the designs in nature are light-years ahead of anything we could create.

There is so much we don't know. There's that wonderful quote from Hamlet: 'There are more things in heaven and earth . . . than are dreamt of in your philosophy.' I have these feelings that I couldn't even start to explain: I often feel like I'm just a slightly advanced monkey or chimpanzee, able to think but not to understand. Whatever is going on, I don't think we have the capacity, I don't think our brains are evolved enough, to understand it logically. It is not a question of having enough brain cells; I don't even think we have the right *type* of brain cells. I believe there will be a completely new science that we have yet to discover: it will have the same importance and structure as the rules of physics, but will be along the lines of the occult. Once we can get into that realm, we will start to evolve a little bit beyond the slightly intelligent Neanderthals that we are today.

It was explained very well during the Exegesis seminar. The only proof we've got that the world exists is what our five senses tell us. Everything that goes into our ears, eyes and so on through these physical mechanisms, the little bits of skin and tiny bones, is translated into electrochemical signals. They're just signals, like the radio or TV – all of reality, to us, is made up of these signals. They can be faked, they can be corrupted; our senses are only designed to pick up those specific things which are useful to keep us alive, to help us eat, and to stop us from bumping into things.

There is going to be an incredible breakthrough at some point in the future. We keep hearing tantalising little snippets from people like Stephen Hawking about quantum physics and superstrings. In physics, something like 98 per cent of the universe is made up of dark matter – well, what's that then? I find that fascinating; I hope somebody invents a dark-matter sensor, so we can find out what it is actually composed of. Perhaps our whole existence might be a simple manifestation of the universe looking at itself: we might be some little sensors that were popped up to look at the whole, big thing. Who can say? Whatever it is, I just hope I live to see the beginning of when we start to find out.

What we do get are symptoms, indications of everything that we don't understand. Some are the simple effects of synchronicity – coincidences that seem too impossible to be a coincidence. Some factor has intervened to make them happen. For example, you're thinking about somebody you haven't seen for ten years and then, suddenly, there they are in front of you, in the middle of the road.

Other experiences are deeper, scarier perhaps. I remember how we used to play with a Ouija board at the house of one of my brother's friends, Paul Rose. It really would move on its own and say extraordinary things. One evening we got the message that someone had just had a terrible accident. We asked, 'Were you hurt?' and they said they'd died. We asked their name – I can't remember it now – and it just so happened that Paul knew the girlfriend of this person, so he rang them up. I'm not joking, he said, 'Can I speak to . . .' and he gave the name. They said, 'We can't talk, something terrible has happened . . .' He'd been killed in a motorcycle accident. That actually proved right in front of us that it wasn't somebody playing a joke; it was real, serious stuff.

Everybody must have had these experiences, from déjà vu to seeing ghosts; there are nice ones and there are nasty ones. You could be just about to say to somebody the most important thing you've ever said in your life, and a wasp lands on your nose. They're the bad ones, the gremlins. We live in a universe that has lots of different strata. We might not be able to see them directly but we're able to visit them in different ways, for different reasons, at different times. We can have experiences of good and bad things, call them evil if you like; our inner senses can tell us what's happening, if we only listen to them.

I remember on 11 September 2001 I was working away in my studio in Chalfont St Giles, where I used to live. Suddenly I felt uncomfortable and physically sick, really awful. I just thought, 'Oh, I'm getting the flu.' Suddenly my assistant rang me up and told me, 'There's been a terrible occurrence in New York, a plane has crashed into the World Trade Center.' I'd had the feeling before, like when I waited outside a patient's house for my father, and I would know someone had died: this time, I felt really peculiar and ill. It's not that I have dreams or premonitions, it's more like a sixth sense; I can just feel that there's something wrong.

I worked quite a few years ago with Jon Anderson from Yes, who told me he believes totally in fairies and little beings. That's his reality, and it's fine by me, and who's to say there aren't little forces around everywhere, good and bad, that there aren't guardian angels. We just don't know. Just because an idea is illogical, the thought that it should be dismissed as heresy or witchcraft happens less and less these days, which is encouraging.

Clearly, it's not just me that thinks there is something out there. Our whole planet is covered in shrines to a spiritual dimension, whatever religions they represent. I suppose the best word for it all is 'god', in its original sense. There is a fundamental force around us that we don't understand. The answer to it has historically been religion, which is quite a good answer really, but for some reason we have separated it from the rest of our existence – 'I've got a life over here and spirituality is over there.' We need to be able to bring them together, somehow.

Back in the olden days everybody would go to church on a Sunday: religion was locked into a theology that everyone was content with. We are not content with it any more and we have to find out more about it, because that's the real reality; all we can see with our eyes is a small, local, physical reality. Perhaps we need that; we are going through a cultural dip at the moment but I am fully confident that we have come this far and will progress further. Either that or the scientologists are right, we are all exiled Thetans. Perhaps L. Ron Hubbard was right all along!

If any of the possibilities are in even the slightest way true, they give a deeper appreciation of so many things. Once you start to realise how things work, you can step out of yourself, almost in wonder, and appreciate all that is going on. In a funny way you can let it happen, but you don't identify with it, you just observe it.

It was when I was having my panic attacks that I first had the idea there might be something else other than the physical, mechanical, biochemical robots that we are. I

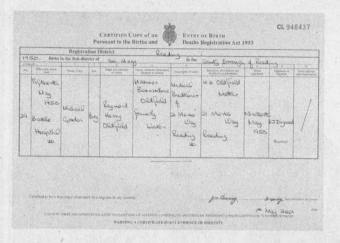

Above: Battle hospital, where it all began
(Picture: Mike Oldfield)

Right: Mum on the beach
(Picture: Mike Oldfield)

Above: Happy family, but it wasn't to last
(Picture: Mike Oldfield)

Above: Finally traced our Irish roots
(Picture: Mike Oldfield)

Above: And some relatives
(Picture: Mike Oldfield)

Above: With sister Sally, at last I'm out of school (Picture: Brian Shuel/Redferns Music Picture Library)

Above: The face of concentration, recording *Tubular Bells* (Picture: Brian Shuel/Redferns Music Picture Library)

Above: The dear old manor
(Picture: Simon Heyworth)

Left: Richard larking around
on a moped
(Picture: Simon Heyworth)

Virgin 'twins' logo
designed, drawn and
(c) Roger Dean
rogerdean.com

Above: What do all these knobs do? I was determined to find out
(Picture: Simon Heyworth)

Left: The manor studio, an old squash court decorated in mystic runes
(Picture: Simon Heyworth)

RECORDS

Below: The multi-track tape monster
(Picture: Simon Heyworth)

Tubular Bells
Mike Oldfield

BY PAUL GAMBACCINI

An unknown English teenager playing over 20 instruments has produced the most important one-shot project of 1973. It is a debut performance of a kind we have no right to expect from anyone. It took Mike Oldfield half a year to lay down the thousands of overdubs required for his 49 minutes of exhilarating music. I will be playing the result for many times that long.

Oldfield has assembled the sounds of a wide range of musical instruments both in succession and on top of each other. At times there is a solo passage; on other occa[sions] generates an orchestra[...] Tempo and dynami[...] There is no predicti[...] he will be doing th[...] utes hence. Yet there[...] stant unity as strand[...] section of the piece [...] the next. The transi[...] as impressive as the t[...]

Some of Oldfield'[s] ments speak plaintiv[...] ers aggressively. Ther[...] lyrics to *Tubular B[...]* human voices do oc[...] appear. The only tal[...] is that of the master [...] monies, Viv Stansh[...] figures in the work'[s] fective segment. Pea[...] and a church organ [...] a babbling undercurr[...] struments. Stanshal[...] ly utters, "Grand p[...] which point said pia[...] with a clear stateme[...] shall names another i[...] and it solos. Ten[...] creases simultaneous[...] the crescendo of t[...] Viv's phrasing as he [...] fully announces the [...] of each guest instru[...] tributes to the buildi[...]

When he finally [...] "Plus—Tubular Be[...] bells strike out tri[...] It is a moment of e[...] rare to recorded music, a tri[...] umph over the recurring bass line that conveys a spiritual release. A female chorus "aaaha" away to supplement the semi-religious atmosphere. Just when one fears Oldfield may take the easy way out and end with a crashing din, he drops the [...] side one [...] that is extr[...]

WITH MICK Taylor, David Bedford, Kevin Ayers, Viv Stanshall, Steve Broughton and — of course — Mike Oldfield playing the music, and Mick Jagger, Edgar Broughton, John Peel and other luminaries in the audience, last week's performance of Mike Oldfield's "Tubular Bells" at the Queen Elizabeth Hall was as much an Occasion as a concert.

It was one of those things where although the actual performance wasn't quite as stunning as you expected or hoped, you're really glad you were there because the whole event had such a good feel to it — almost like a family party at which even local strangers are made to feel at home.

As you'll have gathered from things

● MICK TAYLOR

Below: An early Virgin megastore
(Picture: Simon Heyworth)

Above: The Bells were even a smash down
under (Picture: Simon Fowler)

Above: At last I could afford my own
instruments (Picture: EMI)

Above: Polly the Afghan taking a rest from chasing the sheep on Bradnor hill (Picture: Mike Oldfield)

Left: After the seminar it's off on tour (Picture: Tom Sheehan)

remember thinking that was just what was going on inside me. The entity that is me is physical most of the time, with all its electromechanical sensors and the electrical activity that results from it: memories of past experiences, thoughts and worries, making plans for the future. But I can be somewhere else, *outside* the physical me looking at myself – and if I am somewhere else, where am I? Maybe there is something beyond, something spiritual, pure and beautiful, in another dimension perhaps. All the physical, paranoid stuff can exist in its own place, and I can in some way exist outside and distance myself from it.

Such things get laughed at because they are not scientifically sound, but we have these instincts – dogs and other animals have them as well. If we acknowledge that we are descended from animals, we need to recognise that the instincts must be there; but we suppress them somehow, because science deems it unscientific to believe in them. Luckily things are changing: it seems to me that people trust less in traditional science than they used to and are becoming more open-minded to less scientific ideas. In fact, what used to be laughed at as 'hippy, New Age rubbish' has actually crept into our civilisation, so that most of the daily newspapers write about meditation, spirituality and so on. It has become acceptable, mainstream.

That's why art is so important. You can say things you can't understand logically in art and in music, in painting, poetry and writing: it just has a mood, an essence, a soul. I have no problem at all talking about my thoughts, and describing sequentially what has happened in my life; but if somebody asked me to talk about my actual music and what it is, I can't do it, because music is the only way I can express such feelings.

Spirituality definitely influences my music. There is even a name for it now – it's called 'being in the zone'. It can happen to a sportsperson, an artist or whatever; when you are there, you are completely plugged in to the whole power of nature, God, the universe, everything.

You are functioning in tune with all that, you become not just a musician making an album, you really are connected to whatever energy it is. We don't really know what it is exactly. One day we will find out. It won't be totally logical and it will have some connection with creativity.

It's probably going to take a few thousand years before we are developed enough to appreciate what's really going on. Nature might not be able to advance us enough, we may have to do some of it ourselves with genetic engineering; or it might be a mixture of things, allowing us to make that big step in evolution, at the same time, I suspect, as space travel. I believe we'll find the way to do it will not be to build an actual, physical machine to take you where you want to go, but there will be a completely different way of going.

We don't know what's coming in the future. It is possible that if there is some kind of human disease that wipes most of us out, the great apes could overtake us in intelligence. Perhaps we will emerge from the embryonic state of the human being and become able, maybe, even to join a galactic community of beings. I don't know, but I'd like to think we'd achieve something like that, one day.

7. THE MANOR – 1971

S tress is a kind of mental disease. You don't have the
ability to logically understand what's going on inside
you, so you can't deal with it properly. When things got
really bad for me, there were only two things I could look
calmly on: one was alcohol and the other was music. I
remember listening to one of George Harrison's albums,
there was one track I loved called 'All Things Must Pass',
which really helped me. It made me think, 'This is all going
to go away.' It didn't, of course, not for years and years.

When I wasn't making music I felt so totally like a fish
out of water, it was like I was living in an alien world – I
just didn't seem to fit. The normal world was scary: I had
to anaesthetise myself with alcohol just to get through each
day. I started reading science fiction around that time, and
would often read all night. I remember this beautiful story
by C. S. Lewis, about somebody living on a completely alien
planet made out of liquid, floating on this watery landscape.
I read that in an entire night; it pretty much summed up
how I felt.

When I was in the worst of it, I used to feel like I was in
a living hell; sometimes I felt possessed by some kind of

devil. At the time I didn't relate it to my extra-sensory feelings, or to whether there was something inside me genetically that predisposed me to have such strong perceptions. All I knew was that I felt I would rather be physically tortured than have to suffer the mental anguish I was feeling.

Tubular Bells gave me a way out. I was so completely into it, the music became the sole, solid purpose of my existence, the focus for my entire life.

Kevin told us he was moving out of the house in Tottenham, not straight away but in a couple of months. He was (and is) very kind; he knew I'd been working on my own material so he said, 'I'll lend you my tape recorder, so you can get your own demos done.' It was just a simple, two-track Bang & Olufsen machine, and I took it from his downstairs room and up to my room. I also had David Bedford's Farfisa organ up there, and a few little extras like a toy bell set. With all that I set about making some demos of my own, up in my room in Tottenham.

Obviously bands like Centipede had influenced me, and I had heard pieces on the radio by the minimalist composer Terry Riley. He had this repetitive riff called 'A Rainbow in Curved Air', a keyboard sequence that was almost like a round because the second part was the same as the first, but played half a bar later. I challenged myself to be able to do that: I wanted to see if I could get the right hand going, then the left hand with the same thing but two beats after. It was hard, and I was very proud of myself when I could play it. It was a bit like being able to pat your head and rub your tummy.

Repetitive riffs were a hip thing at the time. Kevin had this thing about repetition and there was one track we used to play called 'We Did it Again'. We would play the same riff over and over again, for the only reason that we were playing it over and over again. I asked Kevin, 'Why do you keep going round and round?' and he said, 'Exactly, why not? That's what you're supposed to do, it's a thing that just repeats. Like the seasons, they repeat, clocks do that, they're supposed to do that.' I did understand, in a weird way. I related it back to Sibelius with his cycles, such as the sequence of music where one melody is half the speed of the other, or to Bach's *Toccata and Fugue in D Minor* with its seesawing melodies.

I loved the whole idea: I thought, 'If I am going to make my own piece of music, I want a repetitive riff at the beginning.' Up in my room, I fiddled around for a few minutes on the Farfisa and came up with a riff I liked. I thought of it as one bar in 7/8 time and one bar in 8/8 or 4/4; I wanted to make it slightly different from 16/8 so I thought I'd drop a sixteenth beat. I probably chose the key A minor, because it is the easiest minor key to play on a keyboard: it's all white notes. To be honest, I didn't think about it for very long, it just sounded right to me. I found the record button on the Bang and Olufsen and played that riff for about five minutes or so. I listened to it back, and it stuck. I thought, 'That's it, I'm happy with that.' In the last 35 years I've tried to find a better riff but I can't, so I've given up trying now!

There it was, the *Tubular Bells* introduction riff, the one that was to become the *Exorcist* theme. It is quite amusing when I listen to people who have sampled the 15/8 riff, people like Janet Jackson. I can see the person with the sampler saying, 'Oh, where is the extra sixteenth beat?' and somehow sticking it in, or only using the second half. I can't quite work out why they do that. If you tap your foot to it, you find your foot tapping to the off beat, then there is a repeat and it comes back in again. That's how it's supposed to be.

I knew I needed to have two tracks, so I found a screwdriver and had a look inside Kevin's tape recorder. It wouldn't have been in the manual but I worked out that once I had recorded one track, I could change the record head into a playback head on one side, and change the function of the two heads. 'I can pick that wire up and stick it on there, and wrap that around there, and block the erase head off with a piece of cardboard,' I thought to myself. It all meant that I could use the tape recorder's sound-on-sound facility, and then bounce what I had recorded from one track to another. I could play back the first track from the playback head, at the same time as I overdubbed another instrument using the record head, and they would be in sync, or nearly. In other words, I could primitively multitrack.

With this worked out, the second instrument I put on was the bass. I had borrowed a bass guitar from Kevin, a cut-away Precision. Bass playing was very natural for me at that time, so I just played this little, melodic bass part on top. The two things sounded good together, repeating over and over. I thought it had to stop somewhere, I couldn't just keep going. A bit later I tried to develop another section that went just beyond the first one. I used the little toy bell tree to make the bell sound on the demo; this turned into the glockenspiel when I recorded it properly.

For the start of part two I had six melodies, all playing in different times. After two minutes they would come together to make one cycle, then two cycles; that was just the backing. I don't know why it was, but it just felt right at the time. It wasn't so much the music, more how I felt when I was making it. As I gave it life and meaning, I somehow felt I was reaching out, through those doors that had been blown open, bringing back something from that other place, the other side, that I had felt existed since I was a child. It was a wonderful feeling, and it doesn't happen very often. A lot of music is not like that at all, it is very much from the dimension of humans, human civilisation; perhaps that's why some groups of people absolutely hate my music. It's weird when I see such a negative reaction, the indignation. It's not like, 'That's not my cup of tea' – it's really, 'Turn it off, it worries me and bothers me, turn it off!' I think some people find it threatening. I accept that now. It used to worry me and upset me, but it doesn't bother me these days.

THE MANOR - 1971

By this time I had about three tracks and it sounded OK, but they were only in mono; the tracks were all on the left channel. I wanted to change the sound on the Farfisa and have the tracks in stereo. I worked out that I could block off the erase head on the tape recorder so it didn't erase on the right-hand side (I probably just cut the wires); then I could swap over the cables from the record and playback heads to get them to play in sync. There didn't look to be any difference between the record head and the playback head anyway, so I swapped them round. That meant I could also get three tracks on the other side of the tape.

I had the other bits of music pretty well worked out, so I worked on each section in turn. I managed to get them all down somehow: 'I'll put that there, I need another link bit there,' and so on. I had a good few months with all these ideas to put them together really, beautifully well. I had a flute tune in the middle, some jazz guitar chords as well, and the end riff was a fast bass guitar. I didn't think about it too hard; I just churned away and went for it. I had so many ideas at that point, it wasn't a problem to just keep going.

By the end, I had the beginnings of a stereophonic demo with six or seven overdubs, all done on a two-track machine. It was twenty minutes long and a lot of it was pretty reasonable, fairly respectable I thought. For me, it was my own piece of classical music: I think I was going to call it 'Opus One' at the time. Above all it was a sanctuary, a refuge from the panic attacks, which I had created for myself. I could listen to it and feel safe.

As for Kevin's tape recorder, I twisted the wires back together before I gave it back and he never complained.

Even though Kevin didn't want the band to continue, he did want us to work on another album. By then I had my demos on a tape and I felt really proud of them. I remember taking my demo into Abbey Road before the sessions started; Pete Jenner was there, he was producing again. As I played the beginning of my tape to everybody, they all looked terribly bored. The band, Pete and the engineers, even the tape op, they all looked at me in a 'What's young Michael up to now, hasn't he caused us enough grief?' kind of way. There was a general, uneasy silence, like they were thinking, 'Get this rubbish off the bloody tape recorder, quickly!' Someone pressed the stop button and rewound it (as later on, most of the record companies did). The rest of the band were still not happy with me.

I couldn't understand it at all. The only person who said he liked the music was David Bedford, but he had to creep up to me and whisper in my ear, in case he was thought of badly. I also played it to our roadie, Pete. He thought it was great; he even offered to take it around some record companies later.

I must have got the tape copied somewhere, and I started sending it round to some people. John Peel was my big hero, he was a superstar then. Somehow I got the number of the BBC, so I gave them a ring and asked to speak to John Peel. Funnily enough, the phone went 'bbrrrr' and there was John Peel. It was in the days when you could do that. I said, 'Hello, this is Michael Oldfield, I'm from Kevin Ayers' band.' He obviously knew me, so I said that I had a demo and he said to send a tape to him at the BBC. I sent it off, but it was lucky that I had had some copies made because he said many years later that he never received it.

At the same time I went to see Nick Mobbs, who was in charge of the Harvest label for EMI, the same label as Pink Floyd. I took the demos into the EMI building and played them to Nick; he did think about it for a couple of weeks but then he turned me down. I took them to CBS, where the tape lasted about twenty seconds on the machine before it was rewound and I was shown the door. They thought it was unmarketable, as did Pye, and several others. After about three or four rejections I became totally despondent. Pete, the roadie, took the tapes round to the companies I hadn't been to, but he came back dejectedly, saying, 'They all said it's no good, it's not marketable.'

Things were not going well. Once Kevin had left the house, the whole thing fell apart there as well. Willy Murray was left in charge for a while but it just didn't work out. I wasn't working and I didn't have any income at all; I didn't have money to pay rent, or even eat. I remember calling my mother and she sent me ten pounds, but that only lasted a week or so. Every now and then I'd creep down to Willy's room and steal a piece of bread. Once, I stole a potato from one of those open-fronted greengrocers, which I then took home to bake.

I was still regularly suffering panic attacks so eventually I went back to Harold Wood to stay with my mother. She was just the same, depressed and despondent, but she didn't have the terrible night-time crises, when she would howl and be carted off to hospital. I don't know why, but I presume it was because my dad had left. She even managed to get her job back as a staff nurse: for a while she worked in the local hospital. While she was out at work I worked on my 'Opus One' some more, at my grandma's upright piano in the living room.

When my mother came home every evening we drowned our sorrows together, sitting there in the front room of the house and getting completely plastered, just the two of us. We would go and pawn all her jewellery and buy alcohol with the money: I remember how we would get a couple of bottles of wine, or a bottle of vodka. It was actually the closest I'd ever been to her; we were finally bonding in misery and booze. One of the last Christmases I had with my mother, we had the most awful time. She was losing it badly, and my father was no longer there; it soured all those happy childhood memories of Christmas a bit.

One day I was at the house and the doorbell rang. There on the step were these two nurses, propping my mother up between them; she was completely drunk and drugged. They carried her in and put her in a chair; she was still in her uniform, poor thing. She had got drunk at work and that was that – she'd been sacked and would never work again as a hospital nurse.

In the back of my mind I knew that it was pretty tragic for my mother, because she had made an effort to try to do something. It wasn't really her fault at all; medical science in psychology and the human understanding of the psychological state was not like it is now. The medical world was, at that time, of the opinion that people were just like that, or became like that; there were addictive prescription drugs to deal with the symptoms, but to see a psychiatrist was a big deal. Nowadays, it seems that everybody can see as many therapists as they want. Neither did I have a clue about anything to do with my own psychology at the time: I couldn't help my panic attacks, I didn't know what to do about them and nor did anybody else.

Meanwhile, I was looking around for a job, something to do. I just wanted to earn some money, so I did whatever came along. My agent at Blackhill got me in touch with Alex Harvey and he really liked my playing so he asked me to join his band for a while, as guitarist. He was a real gentleman, this was just before he became successful. Around this time I finally passed my driving test. I had been driving illegally without a licence but I had persuaded my dad to pay for lessons. My first car was a clapped-out old Mini, which cost sixty pounds from a car dealer around the corner. It was a complete disaster but I liked it because it had spacers on the wheels, washers that attached to the hub to make the wheels stick out a bit further.

As well as playing in his band, Alex Harvey said he needed a musician for the musical *Hair* at the Shaftesbury Theatre in the West End. This was the original production, still running from the early days; the famous night when Hendrix got up on stage and all that was still going. I wasn't sitting in the orchestra pit but actually on the stage, around the side. It was good fun, I liked it, but I didn't fit in well with the other musicians at all. I started playing around with 'Let the Sunshine In' and doing super-complicated bits, but I was playing in the wrong time signatures and it was putting the dancers off. I would mess about with the music and get these dirty looks from other members of the band, especially the brass, they really didn't like me – I've hated brass players ever since. I think eventually, after about six months, they said, 'Either he goes, or we go.'

I didn't have much money, but by the time I left *Hair* I did have a girlfriend. She worked, and would give me money for my fags and food. When she was out during the day, I started working on the ideas in my demo, turning them into something really organised. I worked everything out in my own notation. I didn't record the parts but I had them all worked out, a few notes in one cycle then the bass part, how many cycles of each and how they came together. I had nearly the whole album apart from what ended up as part two of *Tubular Bells*. It was all in my head and in my notebook – all I needed was a recording studio and the instruments. I had the ability to do it, and I knew I would be able to do it if I was given the chance.

When I lost the job at *Hair* I got a call from Blackhill again, from Pete Jenner in fact. 'We've got a musician called Arthur Louis and he needs a bass player,' he said. First of all I went to meet Arthur Louis in Hampstead: he was a strange man who looked and behaved like a star. I thought, 'Well, it's a job, it's work.' I was going to get paid for it, although not much.

Arthur Louis described himself as a cross between Dylan and Hendrix; in fact he was untalented. He thought he had charisma, which I suppose he did; he used to drive around in an old Mercedes with leopard-skin seats and wear lots of beads, but he was a poor musician. He was getting together a band to rehearse, so they had booked into a house in Oxfordshire called Shipton Manor, in Shipton-on-Cherwell.

Arthur's roadie came to pick me up in Harold Wood and took me down the A40 to Oxfordshire. We drove up to this big house, and I remember pulling into the drive and having my first sight of the Manor, thinking, 'Wow, I'm glad I said yes to this.' As I walked in the door, I thought it was marvellous. I had never seen a big home like that before, such a huge place, with its big rooms and fireplaces, full of such interesting people.

There was a lot of building work going on. I could hear the sound of hammers in what used to be the squash court, they were still building the studio in there and leaving massive holes in everything. As I found out later, Richard Branson had just bought the house with a loan of about £20,000 from his dad. He had just been arrested for trying to smuggle albums in and out of Dover without paying the duty. So he was in a bit of trouble then, but he had this house and wanted to set up a record company.

We were allocated a room somewhere in the building and started rehearsing. The rehearsals were rubbish, but I enjoyed getting to know the other people in the house. I'd bumped into a couple of the engineers, Simon Heyworth and Tom Newman. Tom was kind of Celtic with fair hair, he was clean-shaven and quite well built. I remember him coming out of the door of the Manor with a proper bow and arrow, not a toy one – he used to make his own arrows like a traditional archer. He also liked making model aeroplanes, building them himself. I went up to his room and saw these planes and I thought, 'Oh, great!'

I realised I might have the opportunity to get some of these people to listen to my own music, but unfortunately I'd left the tapes at home. At some point I was talking to the roadie and said, 'I've got some really nice demos which I'd like to play for the people here.' That wonderful man, he drove me from Oxford back to Harold Wood to pick up the demos, then all the way back again. In those days, it was about a three-hour drive. I can't remember his name now, but I really do owe him everything; none of what came later would have happened if it weren't for him.

There was one room called the TV room where they had some old Ampex tape machines, so I put on my demos in there. I remember Tom and Simon sitting in the TV room and listening to them. For once, here were people who took the demos seriously; they didn't hit the stop button and rewind and say, 'Sorry, not marketable.' They actually liked them. Our time at the Manor was only a week or ten days or so, so I asked, 'Are you going to give me a chance?' They said it was going to be another year before the studio was ready, but perhaps there was something they could do. They said they would have to talk to Richard, which was the first time I had heard the name.

I saw Richard very briefly, when he came to the Manor. People were excitedly mentioning his name, 'Richard's coming, Richard's coming!' I remember seeing this enormous (for me) Bentley arrive and Richard climbing out, wearing a woolly jumper. He had this very glamorous lady with him, which was his wife Kristen, and he also had these beautiful dogs, two Irish wolfhounds.

When the rehearsals with Arthur Louis had finished, I went back to Harold Wood and carried on working on my piece of music, in my notebook. From time to time I would ring up Tom and Simon and ask them, 'Any news yet?' Nothing was happening. I didn't want to join another band, although I did go for an interview with Gun, who'd had a hit a couple of years before. In the evenings I used to go to places like the Roundhouse, I suppose that was the equivalent to a club or a rave now, and I'd just stay there all night. I was still trying to fend off my panic attacks; most of the time when I was at home I was drinking with my mother, as alcohol was still really my only relief from the attacks. As the weeks passed, I became more and more despondent: I felt rejected by everybody.

After several months, I had an idea. I had heard that in the Soviet Union you could be a State musician, so one day I looked through the telephone directory and found the number of the Soviet embassy in London. I was just toying with the idea of calling, but at almost the moment that I decided to call the embassy to say, 'I want to go and live in Moscow,' the phone rang. I picked it up and this voice said,

'Hello, this is Simon Draper from Caroline Records,' – they weren't called Virgin then. He said they had listened to my demo, and would I come along and have dinner with him and Richard Branson on his houseboat in Little Venice. I said, 'Yes, sure!'

Simon Draper said he would meet me at the Virgin shop in Notting Hill. I didn't know they had a shop there; apparently they had another one as well, a small place at the far end of Oxford Street. At the agreed time, I went to this little record shop. Upstairs were six or seven people in offices, which I learned were the start of the record company. Simon introduced himself and said to follow him in his car, so off we went. I can't remember what he drove but I still had my Mini, and I had difficulty keeping up with him. We went down to this little towpath, to a canal boat, and there, once again, was this strange, wiry-haired person with a wide grin. I was introduced to Richard but I didn't feel he liked me very much. I had the impression it was Simon who had decided it was worth giving me a chance, and somehow he must have persuaded Richard.

I felt completely terrified. Richard was a few years older than me but it was more than that, we were worlds apart. I was a different class to him (I thought he was quite upper class, although he would probably describe himself as middle class). His father and mother were judges or magistrates, and he had been to a public school. I didn't think we had anything in common at all. Richard didn't seem to be the creative, artistic type; but in any case, given my state of mind at the time, for Richard to understand that side of me would have been impossible. I didn't understand it myself, and I certainly wasn't able to talk about it.

Kristen had cooked dinner. I felt that Richard tolerated me for the meal, but Simon was quite friendly to me. I don't know why they wanted to have dinner with me: perhaps it was the social thing to do, in Richard's world. I've always been a lonely, outcast, outsider kind of person, I'm not very sociable. These days, if somebody asks me to go to a drinks party, I know I'll be completely out of place so I'll say, 'No, it's not really my cup of tea,' but when I was younger I thought I had to do that, to join in. I would worry that nobody would like me and I'd have a terrible time, probably get drunk and upset somebody. I'm honest enough now to say it's not really my thing. I've never been a Richard Branson, 'life of the party' kind of person, that's just not part of my nature.

So there I was, this paranoid, crazy guitarist, invited to a sit-down dinner on Richard's boat. I thought they'd probably got me down there just to see what I was like, and I knew I had to make an effort. Inside, I just thought, 'What the hell am I doing here?' I was quite happy hiding behind a pillar at the Roundhouse and skulking in the darkness, but here was Kristen making everything all nice, with napkins, candles and things like that. I hate fish, so of course she had cooked salmon. I forced myself to eat it because I was too terrified not to, and I think they gave me a glass of wine which disappeared in about half a second.

I don't remember saying much, in fact I don't remember much of anything. I think Richard finally said something like, 'What do you need to make an album?' so I started rolling off a list of instruments and he just wrote them down. He said, 'We'll get that lot for you, and we'll give you a week.' The studio time was arranged there and then, a couple of weeks in the future.

As I came off the boat I wasn't feeling elated exactly, probably more scared. Finally I was going to get a real chance, with the freedom to do something that really mattered to me: I was going to be able to record my own music. I can't remember much of the next two weeks, but I do remember getting in my Mini on the appointed day, driving down to Shipton Manor, and not really knowing what was going to happen next.

8. THE RECORDING – 1972

When I went back to the Manor for a second time, in November 1972, the place was completely different to how it had been a year before. I could hear music coming from the studio: there was a musician I had vaguely heard of, called John Cale, who was just finishing his sessions. The house was utterly organised: they had a chef, and in the main room there were people looking after this beautiful log fire burning in a huge grate. My bedroom was amazing: it had an *en suite* bathroom and everything.

Somehow I managed to sleep that night and when I got up the next morning someone had made me breakfast. I thought, 'Great, things are looking up.'

I went into the studio and had a look around. There were people from Maurice Plaquet, a musical instrument rental company in London, who were taking out the instruments from the previous sessions, and bringing in the ones I had ordered. I only had one guitar, my one old Telecaster that I had been given by my old agent Roy Guest. I don't think I even had a bass guitar, as Kevin had taken it back, so I had ordered one, as well as a Martin acoustic. Funnily enough I wasn't planning to use tubular bells at all, and I hadn't thought to order any. However, when I saw them taking back this set of bells, they just looked as though they might come in handy. I remember saying, 'Could I possibly keep those?' They said they would put them on the bill and I said, 'Thanks!'

So there I was, with all my instruments. The only thing I didn't have was an engineer; I didn't even know who it was supposed to be. It was like a ghost studio. I looked around the studio, then I looked at the mixer and the tape machine, but I didn't know how to operate them myself. I was completely helpless, which I didn't like much. I think I walked into the kitchen and asked, 'Any idea where the engineer is?' 'Oh, Tom will be along later,' they said. So I hung around there nearly the whole day, waiting for an engineer.

Finally, about four or five o'clock in the afternoon, Tom Newman (who I had met the year before) rolled in. He looked pretty annoyed, and I guessed it was because he had been lumbered with the job of recording with me. I later discovered that Tom was more into rock and roll, the Rolling Stones and so on; also in hindsight, he was perhaps more interested in getting his own music together. Then, another engineer turned up: Simon Heyworth, who had become the manager of the Manor, a very grumpy engineer called Phil Newell and another chap called Dave Hughes. It was like Richard or Simon Draper had said to them, 'You're going to have to give this Oldfield chap a chance.'

So we set everything up. I finally got to sit down at this beautiful Steinway piano and I started playing the opening riff. I was doing it completely wild, without any backing; I started adding a couple of things but it just wasn't working, my timing wasn't very good. By the end of the evening, everybody was getting miserable and Simon eventually said, 'We need to do a click.' He got out an old piano metronome, and we left it for the night. The previous time I'd been at the Manor, somebody had shown me that it had a wine cellar. There was a bottle of Jameson's whiskey in there: I had a big swig of that and managed to sleep that night.

The next morning we started a proper day's recording. We put the metronome downstairs with a microphone and played it through headphones: that was how we got our click track. It was all very straightforward and mechanical; technology was so much easier then. I really got myself sorted, with the two Farfisa organs and the piano. I'd had more than a year to work out all the pieces, on that little upright piano in Harold Wood, so I was very well practiced; with the help of the click track, it all went very smoothly. Before long the bass got onto it and we started slowing the tape down, doing double-speed guitar and dropping in a few pieces, added layers of music, things like that.

Halfway through the second day I had started overdubbing the Farfisa organ: I wanted the sound of a tinkly bell, like my toy bell in the flat in Tottenham. I said, 'Why not do it with a glockenspiel?' I was useless at hitting it, though. One of the technical engineers used to be a drummer, Phil Becque his name was. What he did was hit the glockenspiel repeatedly, while I was stopping and unstopping the notes with my hands to get the syncopation. With both of us and the click track, it started to sound quite good.

I didn't see much of Richard at the time, I was just aware that he was around. One of Richard's dogs was a big Irish wolfhound called Bootleg, who spent most of that week under the mixing desk. I really liked having a dog around for some reason, it made things feel homely. Bootleg was the first nice dog I'd met: he was friendly and relaxed, he just loved to hang around. When I arrived at the Manor, I had heard this story that Bootleg had had a partner and they had been out chasing sheep. His partner, I don't know her name, had been shot by the farmer, so we all felt sorry for Bootleg and thought he was lonely. Later, when I had enough money, I bought Bootleg another partner, I think we called her Beatrice. Bootleg and Beatrice had a long line of puppies, and I had one of the puppies eventually. Bootleg's descendants are probably still around to this day.

At the end of that very first part, the music changes key and builds to a climax, and this beautiful melody comes in. I do remember it was wonderful on the second day, as we worked on that climax section. I needed a flute in there so Tom went off and made a phone call; that afternoon, a flautist called John Field arrived with his flute, which he played beautifully. Later, someone turned up with a double bass, and that was great as well.

For the climax section, I wanted an organ chord to float up. They didn't have pitch bend in those days, so the technical department came up with this idea of changing the frequency of the electric motors on the tape machine. I recorded one chord, and we made a tape loop and stuck it together so it went round and round on the machine. The technicians went off into their workshop and built this great big transformer with a huge, switching knob, so you could make the sound go 'neeeaauuggghh' upwards by increasing the voltage on the motor of the two-track machine. They called it a 'voltage-control-amplifier-organ-chord'.

While Tom had been quite sceptical at the beginning, as the section took shape he really started getting into it. By the time it got to that climax, Tom had changed completely, he was over the moon. 'This is totally brilliant,' he said. After having been an irritating little guitarist who they had been lumbered with, I was suddenly everybody's big hero. Meanwhile I was watching the clock, thinking, 'My God, I only have seven days, I'm already into day two and I've got nearly twenty-five minutes of music to make . . .' I knew I had to be out at the end of the week because the Bonzo Dog Doo-Dah Band, Viv Stanshall's band, was booked in.

Gradually the other people there started to get into what I was doing, like Simon Heyworth and the technical engineers. I remember having a beautiful dinner in the dining room with a huge log fire burning in the grate; all around me were people who really took me seriously, for the first time in my life. Phil Newell was the only engineer who still didn't like what I was doing, and he objected to the amount of studio time they were giving me. I was having a great time but was still terrified that I wouldn't get it all done in a week. I thought it was the only chance I would ever get in my life to be what I wanted to be, a real musician in my own right.

The more time went on, the more everybody got into it, until I became very good friends with Tom. Most of the people I was recording with were really into what I was doing, but I didn't see much of Richard, or Simon Draper, or anybody else for that matter; the staff at the Manor listened to Rod Stewart and that kind of stuff, so they weren't interested. All I can remember is that the week passed in a blur.

Eventually, I did start to find out what Richard was like. I remember one afternoon he turned up at the Manor with Kristen. We were in the studio but suddenly we heard this incredible smash of glass, and there was this screaming noise coming from the downstairs toilet. We all rushed down just as Richard came staggering out. It looked like he'd suffered this horrific injury – his face was in his hands, and it was covered with what we thought was blood. As he collapsed to the floor, still screaming, we were all panicking. Someone said to call an ambulance, but as soon as we'd dived for the telephone, Richard jumped up off the floor with a huge smile. There was a first-aid kit in the toilet containing things like bandages, plasters, iodine and scissors. For some reason, Richard thought it was highly amusing to smash the toilet window, then pour iodine all over his head and come out pretending he'd had some terrible accident. While we were all recovering, as our heart rates were calming down, he was having the most hysterical laugh of his life. With that, still shaking, we all trooped back to the studio.

Every now and then we would take a break and go to the pub, or if we were too into what we were doing, we would send someone out to get some beer. We had this huge champagne bottle, a jeroboam or something. Someone would go down to the pub to have it filled with draught Guinness, and we would drink that while we were overdubbing. At the time I was smoking cigarillos, little cigars. The engineers would be furious with me, as all my ash would fall down into the faders and between the knobs. When they took them out to clean them, the insides of the mixing desk would be full of my ash. They really didn't appreciate that very much.

Eventually we got to the riff at the end of Part One, the bass riff. That in itself is a marathon to play – it lasts about five minutes, it's fast and it's difficult. I remember I did have an audience of a couple of people at the Manor, and I wanted to impress them. I tried playing it once and, I don't know, I must have had a few swigs of the Jameson bottle because I took off my shirt and really went for it. 'Here we go,' I thought, 'I don't care if my fingers bleed, I'm going to get to the end.' I also did it wild, without a click track. They just switched on the tape recorder and off I went, playing that bass riff for five minutes. Something must have happened inside my head, I was really focused, in the zone!

Once I'd got to the end of that, I overdubbed the guitar to go with it. That went on for five or six minutes as well. I had built up the bass part so it started all nice and gentle, then by the end of it I was slapping the guitar and getting into a sweat from the effort. I think you could ask any musician to play that riff for five minutes and it would be the same: it's a stretch for your fingers, and also, it has to be done with a plectrum to have the right level of drive and attack. We were on the last night by then, so I knew I had to finish it. Already the Bonzo Dogs with Viv Stanshall had moved into the Manor, they were having dinner next door at the same time as I was doing my guitar pieces.

Finally, we got to the last section. I said, 'What can we put on there next?' Then I remembered the tubular bells that had been left behind from John Cale's sessions, and I thought it would be a good idea to put them on as a finale. However, when I tried playing the bells, they didn't sound very impressive, so I asked if anyone had a bigger hammer. Someone found one, but it still didn't do it. 'Anybody got a *really* big hammer?' I asked, so someone went out to the garage and got a massive hammer. Meanwhile, Tom had been fiddling around with valve microphones and ancient compressors and things, he'd set all that up. I walloped a bell and made a huge dent in it, and it made this amazing sound. I thought, 'That's the one, that's more like it.' It was only because the bells were there that I thought to use them, but here was the perfect point to put them, right at the end. It was sounding bloody great. I've been trying to track down those bells ever since. Various people say they have the original ones but they don't have the big dent in them, so they can't be!

Finally I had the idea to introduce the instruments by name, in the order they appeared on the piece of music. The piano was the first thing, then the glockenspiel, then the pipe organ, just playing the tune, gradually building it up as they appeared. I suddenly had an idea. I knew there was a Bonzo Dog track with Viv Stanshall doing the introductions, so I asked if there was any chance Viv could introduce the instruments. I think Simon went off and asked him, and about twenty minutes later he rolled in. I couldn't believe it. He was kind of a superstar in those days, with legendary performances. He was pretty worse off for drink, which I think was quite normal for him, but he was charming, very respectful.

Viv Stanshall was like the master of ceremonies, he just introduced each instrument before it played. I wrote everything out for him and we both had headphones on. I had to point to each line and lead him in; it wasn't easy to sample and move things around in those days, so we had to get it right. When I pointed at the grand piano he said, 'Grand Piano', and so on. He really got into the spirit of it and we were all really excited, we did it in one take. When I pointed to the tubular bells, he said, 'Plus – Tubular Bells!' It was perfect.

Once he was done he tottered off back to the TV room; I think the Bonzo Dogs were playing snooker. By that time it was about eleven o'clock at night and we hadn't even mixed it yet. I think we sent out for another jeroboam of Guinness, and we sat down to do a rough mix that we could play to Simon Draper and Richard. It wasn't the final mix, just a mix you could listen to. The whole piece was 22 or 23 minutes long. It was very complicated and difficult to mix: we only had 16 tracks, so we had to cram everything in so every single space on every track was full with something. Almost every few seconds a track would change from one instrument to another, such as a bass to a guitar.

All the while I was picking up how to work a mixer. I didn't like the fact I didn't understand it so I was asking lots of questions, I really wanted to learn how to do it on my own, for later. Somehow we managed to complete the mix – we finally finished at dawn the next day. I remember coming down the steps around the back of the studio and heading back to my room. It was just getting light and I was pretty drunk at the time, but I was feeling quite happy as well.

I eventually found my way to bed, and that was the end of that week.

The following morning, I knew I didn't want to leave the Manor straight away. The Bonzo Dogs had gone into the studio and taken it over; there wasn't really a place for me but it was either stay or go back to Harold Wood, so I hid around the place, keeping out of the way.

I managed to be quite inconspicuous for a day or so. The tape must have got to London, as the day after that Simon Draper called and said he really liked what I'd done. I think that was genuine, I think he was impressed by it. I asked if I could speak to Richard and, cap in hand, I said, 'I like it here, I don't want to go, please can I stay?' He hummed and harred, and said something like, 'Don't make a nuisance of yourself. If you are any trouble you'll be out on your backside.' I said, 'OK, I'll behave, then.' Of course, a little bit of me was thinking, 'I'll do nothing of the sort.' My main thought was that I'd better start working out the second half of the album.

After a day or so I asked Simon if we could make a proper album. I said, 'I've got more here, I've got a whole second side.' As it happened, at about that time Virgin Records was planning to launch as a record label, and they were trying to decide what they should have as the first release. Initially it was going to be something called 'Manor Live': they'd got various musicians that were fairly well known at the time, and who had come in and done some jam sessions. For the cover they'd got this giraffe running around the garden, photographed against the background of the Manor. They must have decided it wasn't a good idea to make 'Manor Live' the first release, and perhaps 'Opus One' as it was then called would be better – so I was given the time I needed.

All the same, I understood they needed the money and they had bands booked into the studio virtually all the time. The only way for me to get any studio time was to go in when the other bands were not recording. There was the odd day off here and there when we could use the studio, but most of the second part of *Tubular Bells* was done at night. Simon Heyworth did a lot of the engineering: first we had to finish off the very end of Part One, where I wanted to hear some voices with acoustic guitar. The voices were provided by my sister Sally and Tom Newman's girlfriend; those two sang and did three overdubs, and that's the lovely choir sound. Then everything fades down, leaving the guitar, which is a really nice touch. I remember Simon and I spent hours trying to get the right acoustic guitar sound, with microphones down the corridor and up the stairs, all that kind of thing.

When I started work on Part Two it all came together beautifully. Unlike Part One, I was starting mostly from scratch with the arrangements. I had a long cycle worked out at the beginning, which I had been working on at Harold Wood. It was a piece with several melodies, all at different time signatures, which would cycle and then come together after about 38 bars before continuing. It took a lot of working out but I just loved it, I had been through it so many times by then, I could play it easily.

Apart from that, Part Two was more improvisational than Part One. It was made up of various, leftover bits and pieces: there was an acoustic guitar tune, and I had a bagpipes bit and the caveman section that I'd recorded years before, in the basement of the Blackhill agency offices. I didn't really have the joins worked out – I had all these pieces individually but I hadn't worked out how to put them together. It was a case of saying, 'I'll put that bit there, that there, and that bit dovetails into that bit,' and so on.

Perhaps it was quite a good thing that I had to wait for the studio time, as I couldn't record it all in one go. In between when I could go into the studio, I spent the time working out what should go where. I didn't have to rush anything; things were a lot more relaxed in the studio as well. Part One had to happen as a first take, but we had more time for the second part so I could say, 'I can do that better, let's do it again.' I remember Richard popping his head in occasionally, to see how we were getting on. He was becoming much more interested by that point.

The next section of Part Two was a beautiful, floaty piece of music that represented to me a real sanctuary, a refuge from my panic attacks, from my terror of being alive. I had created a restful, tranquil, almost spiritual place, somehow represented by this piece of music. To me it was like being back in the womb or a safe warm place, where nobody is going to attack you, you're comfortable, you're happy. I had always liked building things with my father, and now I'd built myself the ultimate, safe place, in my music.

I'd already made a beautiful demo of the piece, on a Farfisa organ, where halfway through I had to move a slider up and down to create the expression in the note. Unfortunately, on the Farfisa we had at the Manor, the slider crackled when we moved it. No amount of switch cleaner would do; we asked the technician to change the slider over but it still wouldn't stop crackling. In the end, instead of the Farfisa I had to use a Lowry organ, which wasn't as good. Perhaps that's the only bit of *Tubular Bells* that I couldn't get better than the demo. I was disappointed I wasn't able to get that right as it was a very important part to me, but the blossoming of that part, where the mandolins come in, we got that perfect. All those mandolins were done at half speed, and when we sped them up they sounded great.

At the end of that piece, all these guitars come in and wind down to when the tympani enter. This was my bagpipe guitar section. I was not a great tympani player but I could do it, I loved to play them. Then we put all the guitars on that. Strangely enough, a significant part of *Tubular Bells* wasn't really my natural way of making music. There were all these jazzy chords and syncopated parts, things that I learned when working with Kevin Ayers. They weren't really my cup of tea but I put them in there anyway for some reason – I just thought it should have them.

Then it went into the caveman part. When I'd worked with Kevin Ayers, we were often on the same bill as the Edgar Broughton band. I'd really liked the drumming of Edgar's brother Steve; I liked him as a person as well. We somehow got in touch with him and asked if he would come and do a session, so he came along and set up his drum kit. I was really thrilled. 'Wow, I'm finally playing bass with Steve Broughton!' We played together completely wild, there was no click track, no backing track, no vocals, nothing. From my simple bass playing he somehow picked out the entire drum part. He did it magnificently, in about two takes. It sounded just great, even now if you just hear the bass and the drums they sound fantastic. I can listen to that quite happily on its own, it's a great track.

I managed to wangle it so I could stay on at the Manor until Christmas, when this Canadian band was coming in. I wasn't in the big bedroom any more, just a little room at the end of the building, but that was fine by me.

I can't remember the name of the Canadian band, but I do remember that when they arrived they didn't want me hanging around. I was told I had to leave, so I went back to Harold Wood for a couple of months. My mother wasn't doing very well at all, though she had managed to get a job as a night nurse at some care home. She also had a lodger at the time, a student. I remember asking to borrow his tape machine so I could play my tapes.

So I spent Christmas with my mother; my sister had only been at home from time to time, and my brother had gone on a trip around the world, he'd been hitchhiking somewhere in the Australian outback. Mum had started getting suicidal and she was drinking a lot, more than she had been before. By then her whole physiology had been damaged by the years of prescription drugs. I remember she had joined some group-therapy session: she had a male friend there, just a friend, who had an addiction to a cough mixture called Chloradine. Incredibly, I saw he was almost a male version of my mother: both had the same kind of helplessness. That was quite a revelation, and I really feel they were both victims of the primitive state of medicine at the time. It was very weird.

Those were very sad, very difficult times. I couldn't wait to get away from there, back to the Manor, so I could carry on working on Part Two of my opus.

I finally got back to the Manor in about February or March 1973, and I had a decent run to finish the whole album off. As I wasn't under the same pressure of the clock in the studio, I felt I could take things a bit easier.

We built up the layers of instruments day by day. I remember the piano part: rather than playing, I was karate-chopping the notes, I wanted them to really 'cut'. When I was younger, I used to try and cut bricks with a karate chop but I don't think I ever managed to, mostly I just bruised my hand. On the piano it sounded really good, though.

I was improvising a lot by this point. I remember, towards the end of Part Two, the backing track just sounded fabulous but I had no idea what to put on it as a lead instrument. I wrote a bass line for that and then improvised on top with a double lead guitar solo, based on what used to be my guitar solo in my Kevin Ayers days. It became this ambient piece that just went round and round. That built up to the 'Sailor's Hornpipe', which I also used to do with Kevin Ayers and the Whole World. It was a traditional tune so I put it on the end of my album.

It was nearly done. The only thing I didn't have was a lead instrument for the caveman bit. Indeed, it wasn't called 'the caveman bit' at all, at the time. I did have a melody and I thought about writing some lyrics for it. I even had a few lyrics jotted down, but I was such a useless singer, I didn't know what to do with it. One night, we had been to the pub. I'd had four or five pints of Guinness and I was feeling pretty full of myself for some reason. I said, 'Have you still got that Jameson's in the basement?' I went and got it, and started drinking that as we recorded. We slowed the tape down to nearly half speed using the multi-control-super-gizmo thing the engineers had made; I took a microphone and made all these screaming, guttural, primitive, Neanderthal noises over the top of this track.

It was the most wonderful session. It was a real primal scream: it felt that all the angst of my entire life came out in those five minutes of screaming. We did it all in one take, then we played it back at proper speed and there it was, the caveman section. Trouble was, I'd screamed so loud that I couldn't talk for a week. I really damaged my vocal cords, and was completely speechless. I could only whisper, and wait for my voice to come back.

The whole thing was very relaxed. As time passed, I got to know Richard a little: for some reason I wasn't overawed by him like most people were. Though I liked him a lot, I wanted to wind him up, to tease him. One day at the Manor, there was a bright yellow Ferrari in the drive: I wondered who it belonged to. There were whispers of 'Keith Richards is here!' He looked pretty much like he does now, skull-and-crossbones ring and all that. Around that time he was going through a big ordeal – he'd been with this girl and her boyfriend had been chasing him, it was in the papers that a gun had been found in his car, I presume in the Ferrari. I certainly wasn't going to ask him about it. He didn't talk to me, or to anybody else really – he was Keith Richards, after all. Apparently they were trying to get him to stay the night, hoping the Stones would record there, and Richard was fussing around. He had done a good job on the house: it was beautifully clean, with flowers, the main master bedroom had candles and there was a bottle of Jack Daniels by the bed.

For some reason, I got it into my head to steal the bottle of Jack Daniels. Richard went bananas. He was chasing me all around the house trying to get this bottle, which I kept taking huge swigs of. I had drunk over half of it by the time he got it back, which kind of spoiled the effect: a half-empty bottle of Jack Daniels isn't quite the same as a full one. I don't think the Stones ever did record there, so it was probably my fault.

At one point I invited Kevin Ayers to come and work with me on a track, or just hang around. Much later on Kevin somehow got involved with Richard's wife Kristen, and they ended up going to Majorca together. I've always linked that back to me inviting Kevin to the Manor. I still feel a bit guilty that it happened, but there wasn't really anything I could do about it.

We finally got to the point of mixing the album. With only sixteen tracks to record onto, every track was completely full: at one point it would have a piece of guitar, then, as soon as this had finished, we would squeeze on a bass part, and so on. We worked out just how many pieces we had to mix. If you say every track changed 20 times, that works out at 320 pieces. Then there were the sub-mixes, where we had taken several pieces and bounced them down to two tracks, so including sub-mixes there were about 500 separate pieces of music on each side, about a thousand overall.

Tom Newman had kept various bits and pieces of track sheets, with what was on where, so we had this big pile of paper in the corner. It was Tom who decided we should get organised: first we needed a single, linear sheet of paper, so we stuck together lots of track sheets into a huge roll, about ten feet long. Meticulously, Tom drew out a line for each of those sixteen tracks, reading like a book from left to right. The other thing we needed was a sheet on top of the mixer, in columns, with sequentially what happened on each channel. Channel one would start off with a piano, and then a guitar, and so on. We toyed around with all of these ideas, to get them right.

It was horrendously complicated. We thought about doing it all in one pass but quickly realised it would be impossible. Everything had to change every ten seconds: sometimes the echo would fade in, and sometimes the EQ – the equalisation filter – would need to be switched on or off. Fader levels were changing all the time, so we ended up putting them on as marker points on the mixer, so the sliders would be in the right position at the right time. Back then we had two echo plates for reverb: great, big, resonant boxes with a vibrating metal piece inside. They kept them in a big metal shed and people were not allowed in there: if you opened the door, they could hear you in the studio. We had one of them set to two seconds or one and a half seconds, and one set to four seconds, so we had two different reverb times.

Then we realised we didn't have enough hands, so we had me, Tom, Simon Heyworth, one of the technical engineers and another person, all of us mixing at once. We were all over the mixer, we had to rehearse it over and over until we could run the two-track machine and record the mix. Each person had to do about eight jobs, to move this at this point and move that at that point. If somebody forgot to move one of their knobs or sliders, we would interlock hands over the mixer, getting in each other's way. We could only get up to a certain point because it was too complicated, after which we all stopped and everything had to change round totally. I remember when we got to the beginning of the fast guitar section, which was about four minutes long, it took about a week just to get the hang of how to do it.

Somehow we managed to get to the end of the first part. When we played it back it sounded great – apart from, just where there's a big climax near the beginning, we could hear a number of clicks. 'What the hell are those noises?' we were saying. Eventually someone identified them as the sound of the EQ controls switching in or out. The clicks took the space of about ten inches on the tape, so Simon started to cut them out physically, and join the tape together with sticky tape. Then, when we played it through, instead of a 'click' sound there was a 'thunk' sound. That ruined it, and we didn't have another copy, so we had to go through the hell of the mix with interlocking hands again. Eventually we said, 'What's it like if we just cut the whole bit out?' We listened to it and it jumped a bit, but there was no other way. We didn't think we would be able to do the whole thing again so that's why it jumps in the music, to get rid of all those clicks.

By this stage, I had picked up enough from Tom and Simon to operate the mixing machines by myself. My first production effort was when I mixed the caveman section on Part Two. I got in one night and spent from about ten in the evening to six or seven in the morning, just mixing that section. It was the first track I had ever mixed on my own. I loved it too, you can really make something come alive in the mix. There was no automation so I had to work it with several fingers at once, and probably both feet and my nose as well. I made it sound great, and that is still the mix on the album.

Eventually, we managed to get it all done and we sent the final tapes off to Virgin. When they had the finished product, they took it to a music-industry trade fair in Cannes and played it to somebody there. Whoever it was said, 'Argh! No, it should be remixed, it needs drums, it needs vocals, it needs lyrics!' One night I found Richard and Tom Newman in the studio trying to remix the album. There was nothing I could do about it, I didn't know what the hell they were up to.

As it turned out, they gave up after a day and left it as it was.

9. THE BEACON – 1974

O ne day, I went to Virgin's offices above the record shop on Notting Hill Gate to meet a photographer called Trevor Key. I'd first met Trevor on Richard's boat: he used to take black-and-white pictures of chromium objects. He loved chrome. I do remember he had lots of pictures in his portfolio, and they were works of art, though some of them were a bit weird. Richard was asking what we were going to call the album – Opus One was only ever going to be the working title – and everybody was getting very angry at me because I couldn't think of a name. One of the pictures was of an egg, which looked like it had blood coming out of it, weird but beautiful at the same time. Richard was exasperated. He was saying, 'I'm going to put this egg on the cover and call it "Breakfast in Bed"!'

I asked Trevor to come out to Harold Wood so we could talk about some ideas. I remember walking back down Redden Court Road to the station with him, saying, 'So, what are we going to put on the cover, then?' We still didn't have a title for the album at the time, but in my mind I was really happy with the idea of the bell. It wasn't just the sound of it; I remembered what had happened in the studio and I was imagining what it would be like to hit it so hard that it shattered completely. I asked, 'Can you get a picture of a bell being smashed to pieces?' He didn't think he could do that, but maybe he could get a bell and make it look like it had been destroyed in some way.

Back in Harold Wood, I thought to myself, 'Well, Viv Stanshall says "Tubular Bells" and it sounds wonderful, and if we're going to have a bell on the cover, how about we call it *Tubular Bells*?' I rang Richard up and asked him what he thought. Everybody said OK, so the name stuck.

A few weeks later I saw the actual cover idea. Instead of a bell being destroyed, it had been bent into this beautiful shape. Trevor was a very talented man. He'd obviously built a model of it: I don't think it ever existed in its entirety, only the front. He'd gone down to somewhere on the south coast, got bones from the butcher and set fire to them, then superimposed the two images together. From the first minute I saw the composite image, it looked exactly right. I couldn't find anything wrong with it, it was just perfect.

A few days later, Richard Branson and Simon Draper came to see me. They said, 'Look, we need something to launch this new album, you've got to do a live concert.' My heart sank when they said that. I didn't know how the heck I could do it all live: every second there were twenty different instruments, each doing different things. 'You *can't* get musicians to play that,' I said. They were very insistent. They didn't exactly ask me whether I wanted to do a concert, to me it felt like they weren't going to let me out of the room until I agreed.

I suppose there was one good thing – they were obviously taking me seriously, but the psychological pressure was enormous. I was also terrified by the whole thought of it: I'd been quite happy doing my thing with Kevin Ayers, standing at the back next to the drummer, or getting blind drunk and going wild. This was different: it was *my* music, and I didn't see how it could be done properly in a live setting. Initially in the meeting, I think I flatly refused, but the pressure became so great that I just couldn't say no. They had even booked the hall, the Queen Elizabeth Hall in London. Suddenly this thought occurred to me: I remembered that big, huge Bentley I had seen Richard arrive in, at the Manor. I said to Richard, 'I'll do it, if I can have the Bentley.' To my astonishment, he agreed!

So I set about writing the score for the whole of *Tubular Bells*, from scratch. For a proper, classically trained musical writer, it wouldn't be that difficult, but for me it was a major undertaking. I remember thinking to myself, 'Oh, bloody hell, how am I going to do this now?' There was nobody to help me and I was not very good at that end of it, so it took ages to write it all out in multistave form. Eventually someone came in and helped me write out the parts. I can't remember how long it all took, but one good thing about it was that it distracted me from my psychological problems. I was so busy writing the whole piece out, I didn't have time to get worried about the concert.

Once it was done, we had to find musicians and teach them how to play it. Richard wanted some well-known musicians in it, so he asked Mick Taylor from the Stones if he wanted to be involved. Mick used to drive around in a white Mercedes with an exotic-looking female chauffeur. I remember going to see him, he lived somewhere like Cheney Walk. I walked into his apartment, full of huge African statues and exotic-looking artefacts. It was the first time I'd met him and there he was, in a snakeskin suit and matching boots. I thought to myself, 'Well, can he actually play?' It turned out that he could, but he was more used to doing blues riffs with the Stones. I had to teach him to play a proper part, note for note; once I had, he was perfectly capable of playing it. He was all very superstar-like but he certainly did the job.

It was only really jazz musicians who could physically, technically play like I needed. We brought in people like Fred Frith from Henry Cow and a jazz guitarist called Ted Speight; we even managed to get David Bedford involved.

We eventually started rehearsals somewhere in London and there on the horizon was the date of the concert, just a few weeks away. I remember David Bedford was there, being very calm. I felt awful, I thought it was all going to go horribly wrong. I remember trying to explain to the guitarists how to play like me, but I didn't play like a normal electric guitarist because I came from the folk world. Everything was finger-picking but they were plectrum people and couldn't play in the same way. It really was agony trying to explain. Also, I used a different kind of vibrato. Electric guitar vibrato is up and down, vertical, and I played using violinist vibrato, which is side to side. Of course, they couldn't do that, either.

As the weeks passed, everyone started to get the hang of it, though. Then, the date was looming and I was terrified.

The signing of my contract with Virgin took place just before the concert, in June 1973. I really wanted a contract: before *Tubular Bells* was finished, I had absolutely no idea that it was going to be as successful as it turned out. Indeed, at the time, neither did anyone else. No one knew the album was going to be a massive success; Richard was taking a huge chance on it.

At the time Richard was unknown as well; nobody knew his abilities, but I knew I wanted to work with him. Richard is like a pied piper, a mythical character who can lead people along. He's charismatic, he can get the best people to do the best job for him. I don't know how he does that, but I do know that I became really focused on him. I wasn't looking for a father figure, but perhaps after Kevin I was looking for a captain, someone to follow. Richard became that for me.

Richard didn't have a standard contract. He came along to see me at the Manor with this scrappy document, which he'd based on the contract used for Sandy Denny, when she had gone solo from Fairport Convention. It was two or three pages of text, which I vaguely read. Although I wanted

142

to work with Richard, I still wanted to wind him up about things. He really wanted me to sign the contract so I playfully refused to sign it. He chased me around the Manor and eventually, not in a nasty way but in a joking way, he grabbed me and held a knife in front of me. We were just messing around: it was a knife-and-fork knife, nothing dangerous.

I signed the contract without any legal representation. To be honest, I would have signed anything, just to get some kind of security that my album would be released and I would be able to do another one. If I had known that signing that piece of paper would commit me to seventeen years and, in the end, thirteen albums with Virgin, then thirty-five years at a low royalty rate, I might have paid it a bit more attention ... I'm still receiving such rates from *Tubular Bells*; the album comes back to me in 2008.

At the time, it was everything I wanted, though. I remember Richard putting me on the payroll. I was to get £25 a week plus luncheon vouchers, which to me was a lot of money. It was regular, not like getting four pounds here and eight pounds there.

A couple of days later, the big day had come. The Queen Elizabeth Hall had a capacity of about 800 seats, and it was sold out: I remember arriving at the venue, feeling absolutely scared out of my wits. Backstage, I was a quivering and trembling jelly. To me the music hadn't sounded good at all in rehearsals, it seemed to me like a pale shadow of the work that went into the real album. Part Two had taken four or five people at a time just to mix it; I didn't know how we were going to get away with performing it live. I thought to myself, 'I'm going to get tomatoes thrown at me, I'm going to get stoned to death, it's going to be absolutely awful.'

Just before the beginning of the show, Mick Taylor came into the dressing room and said, 'I've brought Mick to see you.' Behind him was Mick Jagger. He was the only person there who could give me any confidence or courage. He looked at me as if he knew just how I was feeling. I don't know if he had heard the album yet; maybe he had, maybe Mick Taylor had played it to him. He was so supportive, and just to have him there made me feel at least like I had a chance of getting on stage without collapsing.

The moment came to saunter out onto the stage. I felt like a man condemned and my knees and fingers were trembling. Up I went, and the audience clapped politely. David Bedford gave me confidence by starting it off like a classical concert: I think he was wearing tails as well, which added a little bit of dignity to the occasion. Unfortunately David started it off much too slowly. Once it started at that tempo it had to stay at that tempo, so it dragged along and the whole concert became a horrifying, agonising torture for me. Everything went wrong; well, I felt it was all going wrong, I noticed every tiny mistake. When we got to the introduction of the instruments, Viv Stanshall introduced the piano when the glockenspiel was playing, the Spanish guitar when the organ was playing, and he announced the tubular bells two verses too early. Then we came to the tubular bells themselves: without the benefit of the huge hammer, the compressors and microphones, they just went 'dink' instead of that fantastic sound we had on the album.

I didn't allow a break between the first half and the second half: I just wanted to get the whole thing over as quickly as possible and get the hell out of there. The caveman part came and went without any cavemen, then we finally got to the 'Sailor's Hornpipe'. As we finished the final note, I was just waiting for the first rock to hit me, the first 'boo' or just the silence, the audience thinking, 'Why the hell did we waste our evening going to this concert?' I was physically stunned when the entire audience stood up and clapped, like I had never heard an audience clap before in my life. I couldn't believe it. They clapped and cheered and whistled, they went totally bananas, they were in rapture. I was just sitting there with a huge question mark over my head, thinking to myself, 'You liked that? You actually enjoyed it?'

I felt extremely confused. Richard tried to drag me off the stage and hoist me around the auditorium on his shoulders, in front of the audience. I was physically fighting him off. 'Leave me alone,' I said. You would have thought I would be happy but for some reason I thought I had done such a terrible job, I couldn't understand why everyone liked it so much. Somebody told me she had this strange image or vision at the premiere, where I looked almost like a puppet being controlled by some strange-looking figure, much bigger than me. That was exactly how I'd felt.

I could remember having seen Mick Jagger in the audience, and when I got back to the dressing room he was there. He looked at me and said, 'I told you so, I knew it would be all right. Now it all begins . . .' That was the last time I saw him; funnily enough, I haven't spoken to him since.

So that was the end of the concert, and I fled in Richard's Bentley.

I am very proud of *Tubular Bells*, but at the time I went through this strange rejection of it. The reviews were very good: John Peel even played both sides of the album on the radio, he devoted his whole programme to it. I still don't know why I lost interest in my first album, perhaps it was because it took such a lot of effort to make, followed by all the work I had to put into doing the concert. I was supposed to start promoting it, but I'd just had enough of it. Of course, in the end it didn't need any promotion. I couldn't have made it do any better than it did, but we didn't know that at the time.

After the concert Richard took out two pages of *Melody Maker* to make it look like it was a review. He'd hired somebody to write this rapturous description of the concert, with the word 'advertisement' written in tiny letters at the top. As it happened there was a genuine review in the same paper, which was just as rapturous anyway.

I also did my first interview with a man called Karl Dallas from *Melody Maker*, which at the time was a highly respected music paper – I certainly regarded it highly, anyway. I remember thinking that he didn't look like a Karl and he didn't come from Dallas – he was a bald-headed little chap with a very normal accent. I later found out it was an assumed name, a nom de plume.

That was a weird ordeal. I didn't like being interviewed at all. I found his questions very probing, and I naïvely thought that when giving an interview, you were supposed to give an honest answer. When he asked me something like, 'Why did you write *Tubular Bells*?' I literally thought about it for twenty minutes, but I couldn't give an answer, indeed I still can't. He kept asking me 'why' about everything, but I didn't have reasons. I just wasn't that way, I did things because that's what I did; there wasn't a 'why'.

The whole interview was agonisingly painful and I was really pleased when it was finished. I couldn't believe he would want to know all these personal details about me. It had been a painful experience and, after that one, I was determined to avoid interviews at all costs, for the foreseeable future. Later, it was really strange reading the *Melody Maker* when it was all about me. That put me off even more.

We recorded another performance of *Tubular Bells* for the BBC, at the television centre in London, which was quite a strange experience. We actually had Mike Ratledge from Soft Machine on keyboards, but somehow by then, the whole bubble about fame had burst in my mind. The kind of awe I used to have for such musicians had dissipated, perhaps because I'd achieved something myself and become very successful with it. I don't know what happened, just that it was all very confusing. In a couple of steps, I'd progressed through what would normally take someone a lifetime: from being an unknown, young person, I was quite suddenly at the top of the pile.

Apart from that, my mind's gone blank about that time; it's all quite hazy. It was a very strange time for me, a bit of a whirlwind. I wasn't really paying attention to what was going on at home, in a way I'd moved on. My parents hadn't come to the concert; parents were one world and kids were another. That's how people were at the time.

I do remember how I'd finally been able to swap my clapped-out old Mini for what turned out to be a totally clapped-out Bentley. I took it to Jack Barclay, the Bentley dealer on Berkeley Square, who said it would cost more to fix than what it was worth. It looked beautiful, it had this lovely carpet but if you pressed too hard on the floor on the passenger side, your foot would go straight through.

By this time, I had a girlfriend who I'd met at the Manor and we wanted to live somewhere out in the country. We set off in the Bentley looking for a place, somewhere to live. I remember how we headed west, over the Severn Bridge, through Ross-on-Wye, then up to Monmouth and Hereford. Just on a whim, we carried on north of Hereford to a little place called Kington, right on the Welsh border. I remember seeing a big hill there and a golf club at the top, and just down a bit was a little house with a 'For Sale' sign on it. It had a beautiful view looking down upon Kington, and you could see the Black Mountains in the distance.

The house was called The Beacon and it was on Bradnor Hill, about eight hundred feet up and on a forty-degree incline. It was only a little place, flimsily built and a bit run down, wedged on that hill surrounded by bracken and sheep. It was all quite lonely up there and the wind was blowing all around.

The house cost twelve thousand pounds. I hadn't even looked inside it but I rang up Richard, saying, 'There's this house, can I buy it?' I think he just bought it and deducted it from my royalties. Richard was my manager at the time as well as my record label, so I never thought about anything to do with business. I just let him take care of everything.

The Beacon was really meant in the summer for golfers. The golf course was known for being the highest in England and there were always some fanatics up there, even in the fog or snow they would be playing golf. God knows how they found the ball. I would park on the top of Bradnor Hill, in the car park of the golf club, then I would walk down this incline to the house. Climbing back up again was a hell of a slog.

As you came in the back door (it didn't have a front door) there was a kitchen on your left. It was very basic, it didn't even have a fridge, but instead it had a special box that evaporated water, and the evaporation kept the box cool. For the first year or so I didn't have enough money to buy a fridge so I had to keep pouring water into this box.

From the kitchen you carried on along a little corridor; at the end there was a double-storey room with a high ceiling, almost like a hall. Off that there were several tiny bedrooms. They were all made out of cheap wood and seemed really rickety, like they would fall apart at any minute. My bedroom was up some attic stairs, on top of the kitchen. It was cramped but the view was just spectacular. You looked straight down onto Kington, and the Black Mountains were in front of you. I can remember looking out at the clouds, rocketing and rolling over the hills, in a storm.

The house itself was thinly built, not exactly a wooden shack but when the wind blew the carpet used to billow up in the living room. You could literally walk about and flatten it down as you walked. There wasn't any heating at all apart from a little log fire that I had to go and get logs for, so the first winter was agonisingly cold. I wore three pairs of socks and four jumpers; I remember buying a couple of electric bar heaters and sitting huddled next to them, as the draughts blew all around me.

What with the carpet billowing up and the roof rattling, it was quite a place. I wasn't exactly happy there – it's certainly strange looking back on it – but for some reason I felt secure. It was good not having to live in Tottenham or Harold Wood. I was able to go and open an account at Barclays Bank in Kington; there weren't any restaurants, or proper ones, so I used to travel into Hereford to have a curry. I remember Hereford Cathedral, which I loved. I have always loved any place that has got that kind of spiritual energy: it could be a cathedral, a mosque or a temple, or even a stone circle for that matter.

After a while I discovered this little restaurant down the road called Penrhos Court. It had a medieval, olde-worlde feel, with big flagstone floors and wooden beams, candle-light and a huge, great log fire. It felt like it had been there for hundreds of years, which, of course, it had. I found that homely and comforting. I felt vaguely safe there; to me it was a place I felt I could fit in, like home.

The owner was a big man called Martin Griffiths. He was a bit like your favourite barman, you could really talk to him. Martin was an interesting character, quite a bit older than me, and he had been a parachutist in the army and also a pilot. I couldn't believe I actually knew somebody who could fly a plane. I didn't believe him at first, so the next morning at nine o'clock a plane went right over The Beacon. I remember watching this blue plane doing mano-euvres over the house and being tremendously impressed. I had always wanted to be a pilot and part of me would have loved to have gone flying. Martin offered to take me up but I was much too scared at the time.

I made friends with a local musician called Leslie Penning. He was a medieval musician who played the hurdy-gurdy, the recorder, the crumhorn and so on, all those early instruments. We used to play in the restaurant by the fireplace, folk tunes for free wine. At the time I didn't want anything else apart from that. The safest I'd ever felt was sitting in front of the fireplace at Penrhos Court, having drunk most of a bottle of wine, playing these simple, undemanding medieval tunes with my strange, recorder-player friend.

It was also at Penrhos Court that I first heard the legend of the black dog of Hergest. Five hundred years before, there had been a very bad man, who sometimes appeared as a huge, black dog. When he died, his spirit was captured in a snuffbox and buried somewhere, but the spell was only supposed to last for five hundred years. Of course, that happened to be the year I moved to The Beacon, which was good timing: I was constantly looking for this black dog. He supposedly lived in a manor house called Hergest Court, which is sometimes open to the public. I remember going there once: it was a strange, weird place with lots of atmosphere.

Back at The Beacon, I started to think about how to set the place up, to make it my own and build a studio. I wanted to have some sound-absorbing material and I'd heard egg boxes were pretty good. I went and got masses of egg boxes from somewhere, and glued them all to the walls. That was my acoustic design, egg boxes everywhere. They actually worked fine, they made very good acoustic tiles. It's right, what they said, I thought.

There was a snooker table in the downstairs room which I didn't want: by chance I had become acquainted with the person who renovated Clearwell Castle, which is not too far from Kington. I got in touch and said, 'I've got this full-size snooker table and would like to use the room as my studio, do you want it?' So he came and took it all to pieces – it was a massive great thing full of huge slates. He had some little sledge device with him, so he sledged the slates down the hill and took them off to Clearwell Castle. It's probably still there, as far as I know.

Tubular Bells was a big, bold instrumental. I wasn't trying to be pretentious, I just wanted to make rock music using the forms and structures of classical music. While the result turned out just as I had wanted at the time, it wasn't an instant success. The popularity of the album grew slowly, by word of mouth; in the meantime I was still on £25 a week plus the luncheon vouchers I would get in the post. That was just about enough, but I often had to go and see the bank manager in Kington when I had gone a few pounds overdrawn. I would be lent money until mine came in, the following week.

I was quite cut off from everything. It was a strange feeling; I was aware that on the other side of the country the album was doing well, then it was doing very, very well; but my only contact with the outside world was through Richard. On occasion I would go over to the Manor to visit. I would hang around a bit there and then I would come back home again. It kind of suited me, to be an outsider.

As time passed, all the big cogs began to turn. *Tubular Bells* started to get some recognition and was appearing in the lower end of the charts. Gradually the phone started ringing and after about five or six months it was going nonstop, people saying, 'Let's do this' and 'Let's do that'.

Before I knew it I was hanging on for dear life to my sanity. Richard wanted me to take *Tubular Bells* on tour but I just couldn't imagine it, I was fending off panic at every second. He could perhaps have got me to do it with my own, full-time psychiatrist, who could come and spend the six months with me on tour; who could somehow give me some confidence, sort me out psychologically. Perhaps he could have wrapped me in cotton wool and let me out when it was time to go on stage, with blinkers on or something. Without that, I felt I just couldn't do it.

Richard was also pushing to get the Americans interested. He started to get a little bit fed up with me – well, not quite fed up, but frustrated. I would get phone calls from him saying, 'They *really* want you in the States!' I was getting requests from just about everywhere to go and perform concerts, but I just wasn't psychologically capable of doing that. I had difficulty enough just going down to Kington, let alone getting on a plane.

As well as the requests to tour, to do publicity, interviews and so on, Richard wanted another album, a follow-up. Obviously I'd had one incredibly successful album, they must have thought, 'What do you do – aha – you do another one!' I knew my contract was for ten albums but the trouble was, at that point, I didn't feel I had a follow-up in me: there was going to have to be something, some time, but I didn't want to make another album yet. My whole life – short as it had been – had gone into *Tubular Bells*. I didn't know what the hell I was going to do next. I just wanted some space.

I felt that I was under pressure from Richard to make another album, but in that way only he can do. Richard has got this infectious enthusiasm, so when I was with him I didn't panic for some reason, I just wanted to do what I could for him. It is a great catalyst for people to have that kind of enthusiasm, and that's Richard's gift, you just feel full of energy. He manages, with his smile and with his manner, to get talented people around him who will do their absolute best for him.

I do remember one phone call in particular. Richard was saying, 'Do you need anything to help you to start writing music again?'

I said, 'Er, well, there was this organ that David Bedford used to have, in Kevin Ayers and the Whole World?' Richard asked what it was called. 'Er, a Farfisa? Not a Continental, a Professional Two or something.' I could remember it was a big old thing, all the knobs were painted these different sugar-coated colours, in pink and yellow. The next weekend I looked out of my window and saw Richard staggering up from the car park at the bottom of the hill, actually carrying this monstrous, ugly Farfisa organ. Of course, I went down and helped him bring it up. I thought it was quite charming, he could have got somebody else to do it, but he brought it himself.

In the end, I agreed to start work on a second album because I felt obliged to. Richard wanted me to do it, and on the other hand, by that point I didn't know what else I was going to do with my life. I'd never really felt like a musician; a musician was somebody different, somebody who plays in orchestras, or clubs or something. I'd just ended up doing that, but I'd never felt like I belonged there.

I later came to believe that Richard wanted me to get on with another one, not only because he wanted to hear another piece of beautiful music, but because he wanted another successful album. That was the reason but I didn't realise it then, I thought he was only into the music.

Along with the Farfisa, I had been given some recording equipment, some four-track tape recorders and a mixer. It wasn't very good, but at least I could do more complicated demos than my sound-on-sound demo of *Tubular Bells*. I also had a couple of pieces of music left over from the sessions for the last album.

With all of that, I started working on some ideas.

Above: Wow they really do like the music
(Picture: EMI)

Left: I hate having my picture taken (Picture: Fin Costello/Redferns Music Picture Library)

Below: Victor Juliet, my Beechcraft Sierra (Picture: EMI)

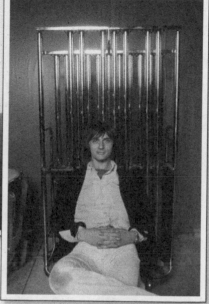

Above: The proud owner of a helicopter PPL
(Picture: EMI)

Below: Clyde the lion
(Picture: Mike Oldfield)

Above: Those Bells follow me everywhere
(Picture: EMI)

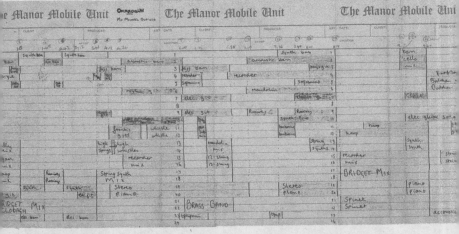

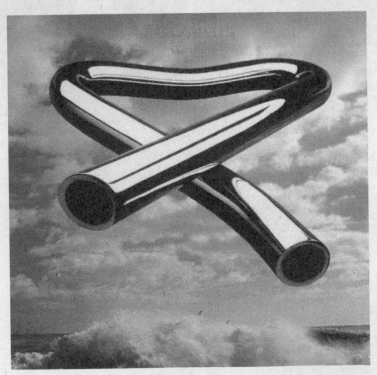

Above: The powerful cover
by Trevor Key
(Picture: EMI)

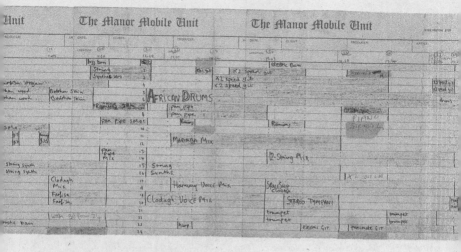

Above: Finally! The finished
tracksheet of part one *Ommadawn*
(Picture: Mike Oldfield)

Left: Memories of our flight to hell and back
(Picture: EMI)

Below: Always burning the midnight oil
(Picture: EMI)

Below: Let's have a look into this dimension
(Picture: EMI)

Above: Lost in Tubeworld
(Picture: Mike Oldfield)

Right: Scenes from Music VR
(Picture: Mike Oldfield)

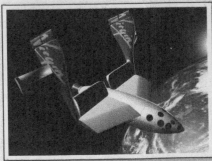

Above: Hmm... turned 50
(Portrait by Andy Carne
www.andycarne.com)

Left: Who'd have thought it in
1972?
(Picture: SpaceShipOne in
the feathered position/Virgin
Galactic)

ON FAME – 2006

Being famous is very weird. There's nothing else I can really do in this life other than my music; it wasn't my first choice of what to do, and I *still* don't feel like a musician. It's very strange, I have just been given that purpose, I haven't chosen it. I was certainly not well prepared for the success of *Tubular Bells*, but it was only later I started to understand the real, terrible drawbacks of being famous.

As I became more and more successful, I found that fame wasn't all it's cracked up to be. The worst thing was friendship – I had to say goodbye to that. After a few years I realised that many of the people I believed to be friends were actually employees, they worked for me. I was paying people to be my friends; when I talked about it to people of similar status I found they were going through the same thing.

People seemed to think that if they were associated with me, especially if they shared some of my private thoughts, they would be entitled to large amounts of my money; sometimes even their relatives want money. They were friendly towards me just because they wanted something: if it wasn't money, they'd want something else. Eventually I realised that I couldn't have any true friends any more, because I couldn't trust why they were being friendly. People can be ever so devious in terms of how they get on your good side. Perhaps they feel some of the success will rub off on them and they will become successful, by magic or something. It wasn't just my paranoia at the time: there are examples throughout the music industry and elsewhere, where previous 'friends' hire lawyers or go crying to newspapers: at the end you've got to have an army of lawyers to fight them off.

It's horrible, but I couldn't see any way of avoiding the feelings of mistrust. To succeed in the music business you have to be very savvy, worldly wise. If anybody can rip you off they will, without a second's thought. I'm sure it was like that before for Beethoven, Bach and Mozart, they had their own businesses and entrepreneurs around them, and they were probably ripped off as well. The paradox is, if you became strong and tough enough to deal with it, you could lose the sensitivity needed to create whatever it is, the music, the art. That's why people have managers; even then, it sometimes happens that the manager will end up doing their own deals on the side.

I found it very difficult to be suspicious of everybody the whole time, it added to my feelings of isolation and anxiety. I think that's typically what happens when some people win the lottery: they end up terribly miserable. I did have my family, but even there, success would get in the way: I know it was quite difficult for my sister and brother, as I became more and more famous. It's a terrible thing that can happen to families if one child becomes more successful than the others. It got worse over the years, until I just didn't see them any more: I felt like I was holding them back. It was in the years that I didn't see them, that they carved out careers for themselves. We get on very well now.

You might get somebody who says, 'Doesn't he sound such a sad, bitter person, what's he complaining for?' but they've not gone through the same experiences. Most people in my position would agree, that's just how things are.

Still today sometimes, when people find out I've got a famous name, suddenly they act very differently. If I write a cheque for such a person, when they see my name on the cheque, they start trembling. I went into a motorcycle shop recently, to buy a helmet: the person recognised my name and started physically shaking. It's incredible, and very unnerving. The other thing of course is, unless I am using a trusted company, when somebody is doing something like building work for me, I make a point now of remaining anonymous. As soon as they hear my name, the quotation miraculously multiplies by three.

There are some good things, though, like when on holiday recently in the South of France. I was riding my rented Harley Davidson through Monte Carlo dressed in my tatty jeans and ancient leather jacket when a very prim Monégasque policeman flagged me down and was about to throw me in jail for not having the right documents. When he recognised the name on my driving licence suddenly it was 'MYCOLLFEELD! MY COLLFEELD! I LURVE MOONLIGHT SHADOW!'

When I stopped being quite so successful in Britain, things became very hard. I had to put up with the vilification in the press, and I really could not understand all the criticism that *Tubular Bells* got later, as some kind of concept album. 'Concept of what?' I wanted to ask. They've given up now: I don't know if the people who were in charge of the media got so old that they retired. Even now, there's always some cynic somewhere, saying, 'Mike Oldfield, rubbish, yeah, whatever.' When I tour, no matter how carefully I audition the crew, there'll be someone who turns out to be a Sex Pistols' fan and tries to put a spanner in the works.

I'll never understand all that. Surely everything in entertainment, every movie we see, every book we read, every piece of music, has some kind of concept, but I don't get why people need to stick labels on things. Maybe it helps them remember where everything fits: 'I like to remember where I put the butter and the orange juice, I need to stick a label on every drawer.' But then people have to make judgements – like, 'Butter isn't any good any more, everyone should eat margarine.' None of that makes any sense to me. Besides, they could never find a category for *Tubular Bells*. They've got all these different boxes, but it won't fit in any of them. You can get addicted to categories, which then stops you making any new ones and you can't really advance.

10. HERGEST RIDGE – 1975

I was still struggling with the panic attacks. All the guilt, the emotional anger, the loss that I'd experienced in the past, it was all there inside me, like a ball of emotional energy. Many situations would bring back memories of my childhood: key moments like the fight with my dad would be triggered by certain things, like if I felt physically threatened. If I felt an injustice, that was a big one, it plugged into lots of things. I would often feel completely out of control, almost working on automatic due to my deep-seated fears and psychological conditioning.

I am sure anybody who has looked after, or lived with, a sick person for many years is the same; you start to resent them. Over time the resentment builds up and you find yourself hating them for causing you so much stress. At the same time, another part of you thinks, 'I shouldn't do that, I should be kind and giving.' That makes you feel guilty. For me this connected with all the other things, such as my childhood experiences and how I was indoctrinated by my Catholic upbringing, when I was taught that guilt is sinful. It all becomes a vicious circle.

Mostly I kept it down with alcohol; I was drinking too much, but it was to suppress the attacks. I didn't like to take drugs of any kind but I always carried a Valium in my wallet: occasionally, when I got into a panic, I would have a little nibble of the tablet. For some people, the only way out is to use tranquillizers but I didn't want to end up like my mother, who was dependent on prescription drugs.

I loved it up there on Bradnor Hill, and being out in the middle of the countryside kept the wolf from the door in terms of my panic. In front of the house there was this beautiful, long, ridged hill called Hergest Ridge. On the top was this strange boulder called the Whet Stone, a famous landmark that was supposed to date back to prehistoric times. I started making model planes, with the same kind of meticulous attention I had learned from my father. I got really into it. I felt at peace up there on the ridge, alone with my gliders.

I found animals very calming, so at one point I decided to get two dogs, Afghan hounds. I thought they were pretty but, my God, they were awful. I got into terrible trouble with the farmer, because they chased all the sheep on Bradnor Hill and killed a couple of them. I had to get rid of them, so I bought a couple of Persian cats instead.

When it all became too much, I could retreat into my musical world. It was like a cocoon around me, everything inside was just beautiful and safe. I could imagine every single instrument saying something – the bass wouldn't just be a bass guitar, it would be a big, deep personality. Music was as familiar to me as the human voice and human language, with proper words and sentences. It all made sense, in its own musical way.

It was as if I was an alien, remembering what it was like being on my home planet, where people didn't talk, they sang and emitted musical sounds as a way of communication. If I turned off my 'language translator device', all I could hear was fuzz and gobbledegook. An actual human voice talking is not a nice sound at all, most of the time. Different languages have some horrible sounds in them – the strange, guttural sounds of various European languages, for instance – it is not a very elegant way of communicating at all. Whereas the wonderful, musical world was much more graceful, a kind of nirvana in music, a place of safety that I lived in and that stopped the panic attacks from coming.

I gradually collected my ideas together and actually started making a demo of a second album. I didn't want to do it, but I didn't really think I had much choice. It's happened more than once in my career that I haven't felt like working but I do anyway, because really, what else am I going to do? I had Richard calling me up and asking me how I was getting on, but if I hadn't been doing something musical, I don't know what I would have done.

Hergest Ridge was a real struggle to begin with, but having pushed myself to get started, it was like piling twigs on a fire. It took on a life of its own, with its own momentum, and it became self-sustaining. Musically, it was nothing like *Tubular Bells*. It had trumpets and tin whistles, all different kinds of influences that were in some way echoes of the place I was living in, I suppose you would call them New Age sounds in today's terms. I was running on nearly empty tanks when I was putting it together, but I managed to cobble together some kind of album.

After a while I really started to get into it, or at least some of it. There was a piece of music that ended up on Part Two of *Hergest Ridge*, just acoustic guitar and organ, a simple, beautiful melody. The actual sound of it, to me, was like somebody talking: they weren't using words but music, musical notes and musical tonality. The voice was just really friendly and comforting, it was telling me, 'I'm safe, I'm comfortable, nothing's going to hurt me, I'm not going to have a panic attack, I'm not going to get lost in the gigantic, monstrous world where my nightmares are.'

Once I'd finished the demos, the time came to record it all properly. I had asked Tom Newman to help with it again because we had got on so well with *Tubular Bells*. The Manor was all booked up, so to start off I was put into the studios in Basing Street, an old cinema. I hated it there, I didn't want to work there at all. It made me not want to make a new album, but I could feel this pressure to get the thing finished. Then we were booked into a studio in somewhere like Chipping Norton. I hated that place even more, and in the end we didn't even use the studio time. I couldn't be bothered to work in there, so Tom and I would go out flying model aeroplanes instead.

My heart just wasn't in it. I had to squeeze it out, it was like getting the last bit out of the toothpaste tube. Whatever pent-up musical energy I had in me, I had let it all out with *Tubular Bells* and there was only a little bit left. Somehow the album got finished, which felt more of a relief than anything.

Trevor Key, the photographer who did *Tubular Bells*, came to Hergest Ridge to do the cover. He came up with Bootleg, the Irish wolfhound from the Manor: he's on the cover, up on Hergest Ridge. I didn't like the result, to be honest. After the *Tubular Bells* cover, which was so powerful, this one was just a bit weird.

Virgin had taken over a suite of offices in Vernon Yard, off Ladbroke Grove. When I was up in London I used to drift in and out of Vernon Yard, and Denbigh Terrace round the corner, where Richard lived with his wife Kristen by then (though he'd kept his houseboat). One day Richard was in the office and he was looking all funny, grinning and raising his eyebrows. He said, 'I'd like to introduce you to Ahmet Ertegun, the head of Atlantic.' I didn't really know who he was, so I just said hello.

Twenty years later, someone told me that Ahmet Ertegun was almost like a godfather to the music business, the man who signed Ray Charles and all that. Presumably I should have paid appropriate homage to him. He probably found my ignorance quite an insult. I did bump into him many years later at the Grammy awards in 1998, when I'd got a nomination for my album *Voyager*. My manager at the time, Clive Banks, introduced me to him. Ahmet said, 'Hi there, it was me who got you *The Exorcist*.' I thanked him. I knew who he was by then; I thought he was a lovely man.

I didn't know anything about this at the time. I wasn't really paying much attention, I was too bound up in my own problems. Shortly afterwards, I got a phone call from Richard, saying, 'There's a film company who want to use your music for a film, it is great news, it's going to be really big!' That was *The Exorcist*, of course. It has now become a cliché for a scary movie, but it was never really a horror film like *A Nightmare on Elm Street* with Freddy Krueger, all blood and gore just for the sake of it; *The Exorcist* is about demonic possession, the supernatural.

Why did my music become associated with what was possibly the scariest movie ever about the supernatural? It's just one of those synchronicity things, I think. There are musicians that make music purely for entertainment, be it rock music or ballads. I can, and sometimes do, make that kind of music, but when I feel I have really fulfilled my purpose of being a musician, my music doesn't turn out like that at all. In my mind, for music to really work it's got to be something completely different; it's got to have something like a spiritual connection. Obviously, that piece of music from *Tubular Bells* must have had that dimension, otherwise the director, William Friedkin, wouldn't have seized on it.

As it happened I didn't see the film until much later; at the time I had I rejected everything to do with *Tubular Bells*. When I did finally see it, I had heard so much about it, I was a bit worried it might give me nightmares or something. As it happened, the scary bits tended to make me laugh; there were bits I thought were close to the edge, and made me uncomfortable, but I wasn't terrified. I thought it was a very well-made piece of film. I later learned that the director would scare the living daylights out of everybody on the set by doing things like firing revolvers without warning. It was weird to see my music in it, but somehow it seemed appropriate.

By the time *The Exorcist* was released in December 1973, *Tubular Bells* switched to turbo in terms of sales worldwide: it seemed that it was number one in just about every country in the world. I remember I used to go up to Richard's office and he would have the Billboard charts on the wall, following the progress of *Tubular Bells* as it went up the American charts.

I suppose there might have been charts for other bands that were on the Virgin label at the time, bands like Hatfield and the North and Gong, but they weren't selling particularly well. I wonder whether that had something to do with Richard's exasperation with me – shared by the whole music business, it seemed – that I wouldn't go on a world tour and become even more successful, a big star. I can imagine Ahmet saying to Richard, 'Get Michael to come on tour in the States, we could really make something happen here.' But all I was interested in was flying my model aeroplanes on Hergest Ridge, and covering the telephone with a pillow. It was all I was capable of at the time; if I could have fast-forwarded my personality by ten years, I probably would have been overjoyed to do what they wanted. After some time, several months or a year, they gave up and the phone stopped ringing.

It became really difficult, particularly for Richard. It was obvious to him that when you had a worldwide hit, going on tour was what you did. Well, no, it wasn't for me, not at all. I just wanted to be left alone. He couldn't understand that I just wasn't capable of it, I was tortured beyond belief. At the time I wasn't particularly interested in the film, indeed I wasn't interested in anything to do with the record business. I didn't want to do any interviews after my experience with Karl Dallas, and I particularly didn't like the fact that people only liked me because I was a famous name, not for myself. I was terrified at the thought of all that attention, but Richard couldn't understand it – he still doesn't, probably. To him, I just wasn't playing the marketing game; I was on top of Bradnor Hill with my sheep, being difficult.

Somehow I was persuaded to do another interview with some reporter, from either *Melody Maker* or the *New Musical Express* (*NME*), I can't remember. I think his name was Steve Brown. I did the interview at the Manor and didn't enjoy it much. Then *Hergest Ridge* came out and this person tore into it, like a wolf into a lamb. He really savaged it; he said something like, 'If this had been Oldfield's first album, no one would have bothered; I didn't like *Tubular Bells* anyway, why does he waste our time?' Indeed, all the critics savaged *Hergest Ridge*; it was a complete reversal of the reviews of *Tubular Bells*.

The reaction to the second album was absolutely horrific but it didn't seem to make any difference, it was successful anyway. *Tubular Bells* was still near the top of the UK charts when *Hergest Ridge* went to number one. The two albums jostled each other for the UK number one spot, with *Tubular Bells* knocking *Hergest Ridge* off the top spot after one week in the autumn of 1974. They became number one and number two.

There was a superstar film-maker called Tony Palmer; he used to drive around in a Citroën Maserati with TP22 written on the side, in pink. At the time he was making a documentary series about the history of rock and roll, and he travelled all round the world and interviewed everybody from the very beginnings up until what was then the present day, which was 1974, I think. It was seventeen episodes on the TV, and I was the last chapter in the story. So at the time, *Tubular Bells* was thought of as the zenith of the achievements of rock and roll, where it was all supposed to be heading.

By then, though, I was not happy with *Tubular Bells* at all. To me it represented nothing but stress and hard work. I couldn't bear to listen to it. I thought it had been rushed and was out of tune, and I wished I could re-record it. It had its moments, but it sounded scrappy to me. However, it was voted the number one piece of music to make love to, in *Penthouse* magazine. I remember once speaking to Esther

Rantzen on the phone. 'My husband and I had a wonderful honeymoon listening to your music,' she told me. I suppose that was quite a compliment.

With *Hergest Ridge* out, I retreated back to my place in Herefordshire. The relationship I was in had dissolved, so I was on my own there, paranoid and neurotic. My brother was around for a while, and it was the first time I really got to know him. Terry really tried to help me but when somebody is in that panic-stricken state, it is difficult to explain to somebody who hasn't experienced it. We even went driving around Southern Ireland and back. I was terrified of flying, but I could sit in a car and be driven, or drive, for hundreds of miles.

Richard was always in and out of The Beacon, still trying to get me to do promotional work. Already I was starting to think about what would become *Ommadawn*, and I didn't really want to go on tour. Richard was saying, 'You've *got* to go,' but I told him, 'It just won't work,' which is when he got the idea to do orchestral versions of *Tubular Bells* and *Hergest Ridge*. He came up with the idea that if we got it all orchestrated, we could take an orchestra around the world instead of me. So he hired David Bedford to write the scores.

It was probably a reasonable idea, but in my state I didn't like the sound of it. I couldn't imagine my music working with an orchestra, following my experience with them in the past. When I played, it had been me playing: I loved every note, the passion and power, that's what made it work. I just didn't think it could be done with other people. I thought, 'It was me playing everything, how on earth can these classical musicians do it?'

Then they told me it was all going to be televised. They'd booked the Albert Hall, they planned to have live TV cameras there. It was a grandiose plan for a massive production, live on BBC2. A BBC director came over to The Beacon and said they would hire a helicopter, and film gliders flying over Hergest Ridge. They were bullying me to appear on it, to play guitar, but I said, 'No, this is nothing to do with me; this is what you want to do with it, I don't think it's right to orchestrate it at all.'

They went ahead anyway, with Steve Hillage, a member of Gong, playing my guitar part. It wasn't exactly done without my consent, but it was being done regardless of what I thought. I wasn't even aware that I could stop them, even if I'd wanted to. All the same, one small part of me did hope it was going to work. I was flattered that I was going to have an entire evening on BBC2 to myself, even though I couldn't quite work out how it could possibly happen. Also, I didn't want to annoy Richard. I trusted him. He was my anchor, my protector, and I didn't want to lose him.

I can remember sitting in my little house in Kington, watching the TV as it was broadcast live on BBC2. I watched, first of all with anticipation, then with horror, squirming in anguish at how it just didn't sound like I had imagined. It wasn't *bad* as such, I just didn't think it should have been played that way. I remember thinking, 'You just can't play that bass riff with a string section!' The timing was all wrong, it was agony watching it, and I didn't think it worked at all. I felt I had been proved right. As much as I like David Bedford, and he did a good job, to me at the time, it was not supposed to be played in that way.

I didn't completely reject it. A few weeks later they asked me to play the acoustic guitar solo, as an overdub. They hired Worcester Cathedral and we had Manor Mobile, Virgin's live studio in a container on the back of a truck, recording me playing guitar. So at least I was able to put something on it.

By this time a bit of money had started to come in. Instead of my £25 a week, I had a few thousand pounds in the bank. I remember with the first money, I bought a Mercedes Sport 500SL, which was fantastic after my old Mini and the Bentley. It cost about £8,000, but I wasn't thinking too much about the money. I remember one time when Kevin Ayers came to the Manor, I picked him up from the station. I was enthralled with my new car but he looked down his nose at me and called me a 'plutocrat'. I had no idea what a plutocrat was, but I got very annoyed with him, I thought he was insulting me. I later realised he was actually joking, but I was feeling very sensitive, hypersensitive in fact, at the time.

Around this time, the old drummer of Kevin Ayers' band, Willy Murray, came to visit. My girlfriend had gone and he was of no fixed abode, so he moved in as a friend, a housemate. It was nice not to be completely on my own. During the day we would get on with our own things, and in the evenings we would go down the road to Penrhos Court, where I was still playing in the restaurant with Les Penning, the recorder player. It made a great difference having Martin Griffiths and his restaurant, because I had somewhere to go, to hang out. Martin was rebuilding this ancient house and that became our second home.

Sometimes we would walk all the way from the beginning of Hergest Ridge to the end and back, through a village called Gladestry. It was a wonderful walk. From time to time we would go pony trekking together with Les Penning: there was a little place around the side of Hergest Ridge where we could hire ponies. If we had particularly bad hangovers, we would go clip-clopping around the place and up to the ridge. I could never get over the feeling of actually being on an animal; it wasn't great horsemanship, just three hung-over guys on little ponies.

When I had a bit more money, I bought a Range Rover and I would drive to the Brecon Beacons and the Black Mountains. It was really wild and beautiful: these huge, rolling hills had a dramatic, almost lunar landscape. I loved the mood of that area. I also bought a motorbike: in those days you could have a 250cc bike without a test, so I got this great 250cc trials bike. Whenever I could I would be on my bike, rocketing up and down, all over Bradnor Hill, down to the town and up to the top of Hergest Ridge. There was always plenty of thick, deep mud around: I used to love going through it, down a huge incline, through the mud and up the other side. Willy tried it once; unfortunately he fell off, straight into the mud, which was quite amusing.

On occasion I used to go over to Steve Winwood's place in Northleach, which was more or less en route to the Manor. He was a cool but amiable character, very much in a world of his own, and in the early days he took an interest in what I was doing. He was into all kind of things. He used to have ferrets, horrible little animals, that he'd get out and show me, wriggling in a sack. He had a whole garage, a barn full of cars: Ferraris, Bentleys and everything, about twenty of them.

Steve also had a stable, with a couple of horses. On one occasion I was persuaded to go for a ride with the person who ran the stable: I discovered that, if you could sit on a horse and you were following another one, it was just going to do whatever it was going to do, and you just have to hang on. I didn't have a clue how to ride, but eventually I went to a gypsy market and bought two horses myself. It was a total disaster: me and horses just don't get on. I like horses as animals but these felt more like pets, which made me unhappy for some reason. I also didn't feel particularly safe, even though I could happily ride a motorbike way over the speed limit and feel completely at home. I suppose you are born with some abilities and not with others.

Back in London, there were signs that Virgin was running into trouble. I was once at the offices in Denbigh Terrace, just hanging around. I went down to the basement and there were all these chairs laid out. In front of each chair was an agenda for a meeting, which I gathered was going to take place that evening. I was horrified when I read the agenda, it said something like, 'Out of all the artists we've got, it's only A, B and C, D and E [my name was one] that are going to make us any money, so we have to get rid of F, G, H, I, J and K.'

Until then I was a naïve musician in my early twenties who thought they liked me because of my music, but of course it was not like that at all. There I was, with proof that seven or eight artists were going to be told they didn't have a contract any more, that Virgin was only keeping a few. That was the first inkling in my mind that maybe these people aren't really my friends, or maybe they don't really like my music. They were civil to me because I was making them money. Equally obviously, it was my albums that were paying for everything. It didn't sink in then, it took a lot longer; indeed, it took many years before it really hit home.

I think *Hergest Ridge* was selling really well, and *Tubular Bells* was still doing fine, but financially there were warning signals – Richard would ring up and say, 'We need to get you sorted out,' but I didn't really understand what that meant. At that time, the top tax rate was 86 per cent on earnings and 98 per cent on interest, something like that, but I just said, 'Ummm . . .' I didn't know what tax was, I never thought it would be a problem and so I brushed it aside. Richard being my manager at the time meant he was taking 20 per cent of my income as well as paying me that low royalty.

As long as I had some money, none of that bothered me at the time. Finally I had enough money to get a heating system. I had night storage heaters, which are full of bricks, heated up on time clocks to be warm all day. God, that was a luxury.

Of course, it wasn't long before there was pressure again for another album. This time, the good thing was that I was stoked up again, I'd had a few more ideas. With *Hergest Ridge* getting such a terrible reaction in reviews, I subconsciously said to myself, 'Well, I'll bloody show you lot.' I wanted to show that *Tubular Bells* wasn't just a complete shot in the dark, a one-hit wonder, a lucky chance. I really had the energy, and there was plenty of angst to fuel me by then.

I'd hated working in Basing Street Studios, and I'd hated working in Chipping Norton, so I must have said to

Richard, 'If I'm going to do another album, I want my own studio.' At some point Virgin delivered me a proper recording studio, complete, which arrived by truck at my house in Kington. There was an old Neve console (it was probably new then, in fairness), a proper, very nice-sounding desk, plus a 24-track tape machine, loudspeakers and all the bits and pieces. I even had echo plates. It was my dream come true, I had everything I needed. It was magnificent.

I remember the engineers coming from the Manor to install it all in the bottom room, which used to be the billiard room. The equipment was all on loan to me: I presume by that time Richard had some money. I don't know if he deducted it all from my royalties, but I wouldn't have noticed even if he had.

The only problem was, at the beginning they provided me with an engineer who started to take over a bit. I said, 'Look, I don't want anybody, I know how to operate this equipment, I just want to be alone.' I didn't want to use Tom or anyone else any more, I didn't want to depend on anybody else. I wanted to do everything: musician, technician, engineer and producer. So I got rid of him. I was on my own, with this proper, professional recording studio.

It was just fantastic, looking down from the studio to Kington and seeing the mountains in the distance. It didn't bother me that in the winter, the carpet would billow up and the wind howled through the windows. I had everything I needed.

11. THROUGHAM SLAD – 1976

B y the time I started work on the piece of music that was to become *Ommadawn*, I had become quite dependent on alcohol. Most days, by mid-morning I would have got through a quarter-bottle of brandy, and I wouldn't let up as the day went on. Unsurprisingly, sooner or later my stomach gave up on me completely. If I tried to eat, I just couldn't keep anything down: my stomach refused everything, food or drink. Something in me said, 'You just can't go on like this,' so I stopped drinking completely until I could gradually start eating again. Since then, things have been more under control.

To begin with, the new album wasn't sounding that great at all. I remember working for quite a few months just getting my thoughts together, but when I started trying to record them, I was beset with technical issues. We were using tape, which at that time was going through a bad period chemically. It was not very high quality, and it started to crumble and drip lots of dust. I remember having to clean the record and erase heads every twenty minutes or so. I think it was a hot summer, which didn't help.

The more I tried to record that piece of music, the worse the tape became. Eventually I even asked Virgin for a copying machine. When it arrived I made a copy of the tape, but as I was working on the copy exactly the same thing happened. It was very frustrating. I had nearly finished one side of the album but the tape was literally falling to pieces and gradually the sound quality was dropping out. All my work had been wasted; I couldn't copy again, because that would just mean duplicating a bad-quality copy.

There came a point where I knew I'd have to start using completely different tape, even from a different manufacturer. We tried out lots of different sorts of tape, and finally found a batch that seemed to work. We set the tape machine to rewind hundreds of times and it didn't drop oxide, so now I could record. Trouble was, I knew that I had to do the whole bloody thing again.

At first, I felt really depressed. There had been a heck of a lot of preparation the first time around, and with all the tape problems I'd already recorded some of the music several times over. But once I got started, my God, was it a good job. Something clicked in me and I just went for it. All the previous efforts had been good practice: I had learned so much from my mistakes that I knew exactly what to do. In some ways it was like the preparation I had done for *Tubular Bells*, when I had worked it out and practised before I actually got in the studio. All the pieces fell into place again, and it sounded great. I really was able to organise things properly.

The situation in The Beacon was ideal: I was working downstairs, William was working upstairs (he was writing a book or something), then in the evening we would go out and see Martin Griffiths at the restaurant. Sometime around then we had gone for a curry at lunchtime with Martin, and we were talking about planes. I still had this fear of flying, but a fascination for it as well; I wanted to fly but was afraid of the consequences. That day I'd had five pints of lager, I felt calm and suddenly I plucked up the courage and said, 'I want to go for a fly in a plane.'

Martin said he'd take me up, so we quickly sobered up with cups of coffee and off we went to Shobdon airfield, which was about ten miles away. To my amazement, I was not a bit scared: I was still too drunk. We took off and I was able to take the controls. It felt fantastic to control this machine, even though I was only able to do it in a very primitive fashion. It was a lovely winter's day with lots of fluffy clouds and I remember saying, 'I want to go see that cloud, fly over it and dip the wing into it.' We'd fly through it and it would go foggy and then we'd come out the other side. I was feeling really full of myself. 'Do one of those things you did over the house, a "Chandell" where you go up vertically, then flip over,' I demanded. That was fun.

I was pleased I survived it: I could never have done it sober. Martin even let me help land it; I hadn't had a panic attack so I got a little bit of confidence back. I would have loved to do it again, and it became my dream to fly a plane properly. We'd seen these huge green circles up on Hergest Ridge; I didn't really know what they were so we'd taken some pictures of them. When we got down, we sent them off to the local archaeological society, who said they might be signs of an Iron Age settlement.

Back in the studio, in the billiard room, things were going well. If I needed anyone else on the album, I would ring up Simon Draper and he would arrange it. Simon really was the nuts and bolts of Virgin Records: Richard was the business brain and overall motivator, but Simon did the signing and the day-to-day creative side. I felt Simon really did have a good ear for music, but I didn't get on particularly well with him, I don't know why. I would ring him up and he would suggest people I could work with. I got Pekka Pohjola from that, he was an excellent, Finnish bass player; I got hold of Morris Pert, another avant-garde classical composer, who was also a rock drummer. In the middle of *Ommadawn* I wanted a brass band; I think Simon rang up the Hereford City brass band and they turned up a couple of days later.

I wanted some vocals, but I didn't really know what to do with them until I actually got started. One good friend from a long time back was a wonderful Irish lady called Clodagh Simmons. Willy Murray used to be the drummer in her band, before he was with Kevin Ayers. She had a raw way of singing, like a Celtic bat out of hell, so I got her along to do some vocals. I had this little melody at the beginning and I wanted Clodagh to sing it in harmony, but she had the idea to do it as a round, in four parts, like 'Frère Jacques': it worked beautifully.

I had all these strange instruments that I had got from a music shop somewhere, like a bouzouki, a marimba and a Celtic harp. I played the harp myself, it was a very simple melody so it wasn't difficult to play. I tried lots of different techniques, like overdubbing a twelve-string guitar a few times, to get a really stringy, rhythmical sound. There was an acoustic bass I just tried as an experiment. It took a lot of fiddling: it's not just a case of plugging in a microphone and recording it, you have to adjust this, change that, adjust the tone, even decide whether you play with your finger straight on or flick the strings with a little bit of your fingernail. I needed to take all these tiny subtleties into account.

That whole album just came together: the more I worked on it, the better it became. Everything seemed to just work. We added a bit of drums in a kind of reggae section, and then I had another singer who was part of John Peel's label, Dandelion, she was called Bridget St John. She had this deep, rich, dark voice, which worked really well. Around that time the first string synthesiser came out, the Solina. At some point the Edgar Broughton Band came to see me, I think they wanted me to play guitar on their album. They brought one of these along with them, so I stuck some of that on there as well.

To end Part One, I wanted to have a long repetitive piece, and had the idea of using some African drums. Back in my school days, the local record library had a section with music from different countries – it wasn't called 'world music' back then. I have always loved the sound of African music, in fact I preferred the sound of a stick on a skin drum to a drum stick on a drum kit. Simon Draper was South African and knew a lot of African musicians, so I asked him if he knew anybody; as it happened, he knew an African troupe called Jabula, so I booked them as well.

We had to record Jabula at the Manor, I didn't do it at my place because there wasn't enough room. Jabula was led by a truly wonderful chap called Julian Bahula, who arrived with all his friends. I didn't understand the ritual in those days but as we miked them up and they started playing, it just wasn't happening. Somebody suggested getting some beers, so we gave them a couple of beers each; they wanted more, so then we sent out for another couple of crates. They started smoking marijuana, and after a couple of hours of explaining the tempo and roughly the thing I wanted them to play, it started to come alive. It was very strange: they were getting into some kind of trance, like a ritual. They played all day and by the evening they were really cooking.

The only trouble was, they were doing the kind of thing that just goes on and on, without a beginning or an end. It wasn't that easy to cut and paste bits of audio in those days, so I needed them to start playing at a specific point on the track. I kept having to get them to stop and start again; eventually, I sorted it by going down into the room and saying, 'One, two, three and off we go!' By the end of it they shifted into overdrive, a kind of double speed. The chap who was doing the 'on' beat, was also doing a complete 360-degree turn between each beat, round and round. If you listen to the album it makes that shift unexpectedly, it's one of my favourite parts.

That piece was to go at the end of the first side. I took it back to The Beacon and listened to it, and thought, 'Wow, this is great!' I thought it would be fabulous to have a vocal chant on it, so I got Clodagh to come over again. I wanted to have some lyrics but I didn't want them to be normal, sensible English lyrics, just sounds. I thought, 'Clodagh's Irish, she could work out some sounds in Gaelic.' She wrote down the first thing that came into her head, which was:

> Daddy's in bed
> The cat's drinking milk
> I'm an idiot
> And I'm laughing

I think Clodagh rang up her mother or someone, who translated the words into Gaelic: those are the lyrics to *Ommadawn* at the end. 'Ommadawn' means 'idiot', but it's actually spelled 'amadán'; that's how I decided on the title for the album. We recorded several eight-tracks of that, which I mixed down to two and put the harmony on, so I was multi-tracking one vocal. I then added a thumb-piano kind of part, played on wooden marimbas.

It was all sounding great.

That Christmas, at the end of 1974, my sister and her boyfriend Rosie had brought my mother down to see us at The Beacon. At the time, Sally was living in the house in Harold Wood. My sister's boyfriend was a character: I liked him, although he was a rough diamond. I think he'd been in trouble for fighting, but to me he was as gentle as a lamb. She called him Rosie because he had this massive rose tattooed on his chest.

My mother had tried to participate, but she was in a terrible state. I remember how she had looked at me and she was obviously not feeling well at all. She said, 'You know what it's like, don't you, Mike.' And I did, I knew instantly what she was talking about. What I didn't realise was, that would be the last time I would see her.

Sometime in January, Willy came down the stairs to see me in the day, which was unusual. He didn't look well and he was very quiet, he'd had some kind of phone call. I didn't know him well enough to say, 'What's the matter?' – we were more like colleagues than soul mates – but I knew something was very wrong. Suddenly the phone rang upstairs, he was expecting it and I went up to answer it. On the phone was my sister saying, 'Mum died this morning.'

All I can remember is, it felt like I had been connected by a massive umbilical cord, big and snaking, like a huge python, and in that instant a huge blade had cut through it, chopping it completely off. I fell backwards, as if I had been physically knocked over by the recoil of this snake, this cord, I don't know what to call it. I could almost physically see the recoil – it knocked me completely on the floor. I was absolutely speechless. In an instant I totally lost everything. Willy had come upstairs with me, and he took the phone and said, 'We'll get back to you.'

I have lost my memory about the next few hours. I do remember telling my brother, who had a similar reaction. God knows how I got through the next few days. We had to go to the funeral, so Willy drove me over to Harold Wood in his sports car, an Austin Healey Sprite or something. I got back to the house on Redden Court Road and all I wanted to do was rush in and see her chair. In her last couple of years she used to sit there all the time, smoking with her long cigarette holder. I looked at the chair. It had burn marks where she had fallen asleep and the cigarette had burned through the arm. There in front of me was the chair, there were the holes, but there was no mother, and that really got to me. I realised it really was true, she really had gone.

Then we all went to the crematorium. My father was there, it would be the last time I saw him for quite a while. Richard had sent a thousand daffodils, they were all over the place. I don't think he had even met my mother, but it was a nice gesture all the same. The next thing I remember is driving back in silence on the motorway, back to Herefordshire. I can just about recall getting to Martin's restaurant and sinking a whole bottle of wine, quite quickly.

We later heard that the official coroner's verdict was 'accidental death'. In my mind it *could* have been suicide, but the official verdict was accidental so nobody really knows. I remember calling the crematorium and asking for a tree to be planted or some other memorial, just something to remember her by. The people at the crematorium were not that sympathetic, in fact they were quite rude to me, so I was pretty upset about that.

I was still only 21, my mother had died and I was barely communicating with my father; it was like my whole childhood had been lost to me. The panic attacks were coming a-plenty but I was all right while I was working: with *Ommadawn* especially, it was a way to forget about my mother dying, forget about my panic attacks. I immersed myself completely in my music: I remember having this idea to make a backing part out of three guitar parts, not just strumming but really hacking. With the three of them compressed together, it added a kind of stringed power to the African drums.

The whole thing built up to a tremendous intensity. One night I had this indescribable feeling, I wanted to play electric guitar in a way that would somehow reach out, release the tension that had been building up. There were the stringy guitars, the African drums, Clodagh's voice, which was kind of screaming, and on top of it all, I just put my whole power, committed all my energy to this one guitar solo. I don't know what the hell happened. I started to unleash this guitar solo and, somehow, got it all out. It still raises the skin on my neck to hear that solo. Of course, a sane, happy-go-lucky person wouldn't be able to do that: being so messed up had its advantages. It was hugely cathartic: the feeling of playing like that is just incredible, it's like a mouse suddenly stepping into a lion's body and roaring.

To finish Part One, I wanted to add some tympani. I invited Pierre Moerlen over, he used to be the drummer in

Gong. He worked out a part that was quite difficult to play, so he spent the entire day practising it, with these orchestral tympani, on the top of Bradnor Hill. There are houses all around there; eventually a delegation of the neighbours came en masse to tell me to shut up. That was it, really. If I didn't have the freedom to make as much noise as I needed, I knew I would have to find a new place to live.

The whole of the second part didn't take that long: I think I did it in just over a week. For the beginning, I had this idea to have a mass of overlaid electric guitars, not like ten or so, but hundreds. That was done by overdubbing eight tracks down to one track, then overdubbing and mixing them down to a single track again, stacking and stacking them up until I had this enormous, buzzy mass of electric guitars. I ended up with 1,984 of them.

My brother Terry came over and played some pan pipes; then I wanted a bagpipe part, so I thought I'd really like to work with Paddy Moloney from the Chieftains. I can't remember how I got hold of him. In those days I was probably so famous that I could have got anybody, I could just click my fingers and in a couple of days there they would be. Paddy Moloney flew into Shobdon with his manager and I met him there. He was a lovely man, like a living leprechaun. We sat down in my living room in The Beacon and I played him this track while he took down some music. He didn't write music as notes, he wrote, 'Do, re, la, la.' Once he started on those pipes it was like magic, it was such a privilege to play with such a wonderful musician.

Following all my pony trekking experiences with Willy Murray and Les Penning, I decided to write a song about it all; it's the song called 'On Horseback' at the end of the album. It's like having the 'Sailor's Hornpipe' on *Tubular Bells*: I wanted to finish off on a lighter note, like a dessert course.

I had all the space and time that I wanted. By then, I had completely unplugged the phone, so that had stopped ringing altogether, it was the end of the summer and there was a lovely view out of the windows. I wasn't lonely because Willy was around, and we had a little bit of a life as we would go down to Martin's restaurant in the evening. With that, I finished off the second half of *Ommadawn*. I was very happy with the album when I had finished it, and when people heard it, they seemed to love it as well. Phil Newell helped me to mix it all. He'd changed his tune by then: he was a lot more into it than he had been with *Tubular Bells*.

Back at the Manor, it was a different story. When we went to take the photographs for the cover of *Ommadawn*, Willy had called them up to make arrangements. I think he thought they would bend over backwards and help us, but when we got there, the people working at the Manor were not like that at all, they were behaving very strangely. Some of them had been there when I had been making *Tubular Bells*, and they'd always been quite friendly. This time they were not exactly aggressive but they were cold and irritated. Their attitude seemed to be, 'We don't want you here, get out.' It was a bit of a mystery, almost as if they had realised that *Tubular Bells* was paying their wages, and they resented me for that. It was horrible, and I couldn't wait to get out of there.

Looking back, it couldn't be good to have one artist supporting a whole company. It might have felt for them that they weren't much good on their own, they had to depend on me. If that was the case I didn't realise it at the time, I presumed they must have been making money from their record stores or something. Obviously, there were bands coming to the Manor to record, and the fees must have been quite reasonable, so they were also earning money that way.

When I thought back on it later, I realised it must have been quite difficult. Virgin had Gong, they had Hatfield and the North, Henry Cow and so on. They were all similar kinds of bands, kind of jazz-rock. Steve Hillage, the Gong guitarist, had a one-off hit with a version of Donovan's 'Hurdy Gurdy' – it got into the top twenty I think – but that was the only thing I can remember being successful until the Sex Pistols and Boy George. I don't know why they didn't sign any more popular acts; perhaps they just didn't look in the right places. Maybe they should have gone looking at talent-spotting contests, to see if there were any more sixteen-year-old, half-Irish, manic depressives. That would have been much more creative.

At the time I didn't really understand all that, but it might explain what happened later, when the opportunity arose to move me to the back of the shelves in the record shops. Maybe there is something in that, but it wasn't just Virgin, it was the whole music world.

It was October 1975. When *Ommadawn* came out it was like *Tubular Bells* all over again – everybody loved it. A journalist called Robin Denslow from the *Guardian* wrote an ecstatic review.

Obviously, I was still hearing warning noises from Richard about needing to sort out my finances. He had somehow got around his own tax problems by keeping his money offshore and building new businesses. He was saying to me, 'You must get an accountant, you must get a tax lawyer and, blah, blah, blah.' I listened vaguely, but I didn't really know what to do about it. People were saying there was no way I could stay in the country: I would have to leave and be a tax exile, either that or I was going to lose all my money, but the thought of leaving the country was impossible. I was so insecure I could hardly leave my own house, let alone live in a foreign country; I knew I would not be able to handle that. Once or twice, after our first flight, I had managed to pluck up the courage to fly with Martin down to France, to a house in the Dordogne somewhere. I probably had to be tanked up with alcohol, I was obviously scared, but he would still let me take the controls. When I was holding the controls and flying it I felt less panicky, but the idea of moving abroad altogether, that was just impossible.

At roughly the same time, funnily enough, Kevin Ayers asked me what my royalty rate was. I told him, 'I get 5 per cent of 90 per cent, with 20 per cent deduction for management.' He went, 'What!?' and said I should speak to his lawyer, Robert Allen.

Robert came to see me: he told me it wasn't right, or perhaps even legal, that Richard should be taking 20 per cent of my income as a manager, at the same time as being my record company and publisher. He said my royalty rate was really low and it should be much better, and that he could sort it out for me. I asked him how I would do that and he said, 'You would have to sue Virgin – take Richard to court.'

I really didn't want to do that. I didn't think of Richard as my friend, nor was he exactly a father figure; he was more my 'captain', someone I trusted, a big brother kind of person. I wouldn't have dreamed of upsetting him: I depended on him. When I felt panicky and insecure, I could speak to Richard on the phone and for the next couple of hours I would feel reasonably normal because he was so confident and full of positive energy. The thought of losing him and becoming his enemy by instigating some court action was horrific – I couldn't imagine doing it.

At the same time, we looked at the looming tax issue. I hadn't paid any tax up until that point, and I was going to have to pay a hell of a lot, in fact nearly everything I owned was going to have to go in tax. By then, Richard had provided me with two financial advisers, but they later turned out not to be very helpful at all. 'You're going to be in trouble unless you do something,' said Robert. It didn't help my sanity and my state of mind, people telling me that the person I trusted more than anyone in the world was not being straight with me.

I don't believe Richard had set out to rip me off, but I think he knew he was not giving me the best deal he could.

To compensate he would buy me these incredibly expensive gifts. One time he turned up with this massive Balinese musical instrument, which you played by shaking. It was a huge thing, hand-made out of bamboo, and filled half a wall. Another time, he turned up at my house with this enormous wooden galleon, goodness knows how much it must have cost. It was about eight feet long and the same again high, built by French prisoners of war, during the Napoleonic wars. It was a real, genuine antique and must have been worth a fortune. When things eventually went sour I gave it back to him.

Despite the financial warning signs, I finally had some real money in the bank. It wasn't a fortune, about a hundred thousand pounds, I don't think the big royalties from *Tubular Bells* had come in yet. What with the neighbours complaining, my first thought was to move out of my little golf shack into a proper house.

Initially, I was thinking about having a place built: I'd always had this idea of building my own house, and now I could afford to do so. I thought, 'Hmm, I need an architect.' There was a wonderful architect I had heard about at the time called Keith Critchlow. He was a lecturer at the Architectural Association, and I remember that my very first girlfriend used to talk about how he designed buildings using geodesic domes.

I thought he sounded like an interesting man. I must have somehow got in touch with him and, as it was at the time with anybody I contacted, a couple of weeks later there he was at the door with his family. I thought he was a fascinating character. Then, of course, he was another person I could look up to and respect. I didn't know him like a friend as I was too much in awe of him: he was a professor and he'd written books, he was incredibly intelligent.

In the end I decided not to build, but to buy a house. I started looking around various places and the obvious choice seemed to be the Cotswolds. It was a bit closer to London and there were some lovely stone buildings there, like the Manor, which I loved. I finally found a house in a funny little village called Througham, in Gloucestershire. The house was called Througham Slad; it was a big but not huge Cotswold house, parts of which dated back to the thirteenth century. It had lots of tiny rooms that I wanted to knock together to make three or four big rooms. The other thing was that it was well away from any neighbours. It was right out in the country, in the hills, not really with a view but the closest neighbour was half a mile away. The nearest place was Bisley, not far from Stroud, which was just a village with a pub and a couple of shops.

Througham Slad cost me £82,000. That meant there was enough left over in my bank account for the building work, to knock the tiny rooms into big rooms, and to convert the whole stable block into a studio. Now that *was* exciting – to design and build a studio – last time around I'd been sticking egg boxes on the walls. I didn't want to employ an engineer, but I did want a technical engineer, somebody who could build special devices to do the weird things I might want to do, and who could be there if anything went wrong. In those days a studio took a lot of maintenance, fixing the decks, lining up the tape recorder and so on; there were always jobs to be done.

I had been down to Rockfield Studios near Monmouth for some reason: I heard that a lot of Queen material had been recorded at Rockfield, and Elton John had recorded there. I didn't like the studio much, but I'd met a technical engineer whose name was Paul Lindsay. I called him and asked him, 'How would you like to work for me?' Together we worked out what we were going to need and we hired a local builder, who was actually a friend of Martin Griffiths, to start the work on the house and the studio.

It all seemed to take forever. The building work kept me occupied, but after a while I was getting frustrated because I couldn't work on my music. There were some quite friendly people living in the area, so sometimes I would go and see them. I remember when I had just moved, I was invited to meet a sculptor called Lynn Chadwick: he was famous in the area and he lived in this big old house. I later discovered he was quite a name in the world of sculpture. He had a beautiful house, a big mansion, and its corridors had these huge windows. The whole place was full of these amazing sculptures made out of metal. He had a very strange setup there. He, his wife and a male friend all sat down to lunch together and were completely plastered by about two o'clock in the afternoon.

Another time, the famous author Laurie Lee sent me a letter and invited me over. What a delightful man he was, with a lovely family and friends as well. We had a few beers and a glass of wine and he started to play the violin; I think I had a guitar with me, so we had a jam session. He wasn't a brilliant violinist but he played it nicely and it was all good fun. Right up until he died I always received a Christmas card from him and I sent him postcards. I did try to read *Cider with Rosie* but I didn't quite get through it. I'm not one for those kind of books.

I'd never really felt particularly famous until an incident when I moved to Througham. People knew my name and that I'd moved into the area, but nobody really knew what I looked like because I hadn't done any publicity. I remember once I went into a shop, I wanted to buy a camera. Some salesmen treat you like an idiot: if you don't really know what you are looking for, they roll their eyes, and then try to sell you the most expensive thing. This chap was just trying to get me out the door until he saw the name on the cheque, at which point he became a grovelling sycophant. I really think people are complete idiots when they do that. That was the first time I remember, but it happens all the time now.

12. THE SEMINAR – 1978

At home, I was starting to feel pretty lonely and I wanted to settle down with someone, but I was still unstable. I didn't realise that it would be impossible for me to do that for many years. At the time, however, it seemed like the right thing to do, or at least try to do. I wanted to have a relationship, but I didn't know how to find somebody; we were right out in the country and I didn't want to go to clubs. As it happened, I had a kind of long-distance relationship with Keith Critchlow's daughter, for a while.

I bought three massive dogs for company, a St Bernard, which I called Wellington, and two Irish wolfhounds, one of which was one of Bootleg's offspring. Willy was still around: he was a very sociable person, easy to get on with, chatty and relaxed, but it wasn't really working out. One day I said to him, 'I think you should leave, you should go off and have your own life.' Shortly afterwards he moved to the States and got a job as an assistant to a quite successful fashion photographer, from there I understand he tried to make his own photography career.

When a bit more money came in I was able to change my Mercedes. I bought a Ferrari, which I should never have been let loose with at that age, my early twenties. I would drive at reckless speeds in very bad states, but that was what people did. I still saw Steve Winwood sometimes, Northleach not being far from Througham, and it was about halfway to the Manor. I didn't understand a thing about country life, shooting and all that, so Steve sent me to a place where they had a proper shooting school, shooting clay pigeons, and I took lessons. I bought my own double-barrelled shotgun, quite an elaborate one, a Churchill, I think it was called.

Steve was really into country sports and he always wanted to go shooting. On one occasion, I remember Richard invited me on a shoot. I didn't really know what to expect, it was like a weird ritual. We turned up at this house somewhere miles away; Richard was there and so was Simon Draper. We were told it was going to be cold so we should dress up warm, then we all sat in the back of this truck and people kept having swigs out of their little hip flasks. Eventually we got to a pond and crouched in a kind of hide. Somebody seemed to be in charge, like a game-keeper or something; I sat there in hushed silence for about an hour and a half, freezing and wondering what on earth we were doing there.

Eventually we heard this 'ta-ta-ta-ta-ta' sound and then, quite suddenly, all these old upper-class men, judges or whatever they were, burst out of this hide. It was complete Armageddon, like the First World War had come back to life. They were blasting away, there were ducks falling all around us and dogs rushing around our feet. It was absolute mayhem. I shot off a few rounds, but I didn't really know what the devil was going on. This only went on for about five minutes before it stopped, then they piled all these dead ducks into the truck. We drove back to the house and everybody was very pleased with themselves, still swigging away from their hip flasks.

Someone took some of the ducks back to Througham Slad and I went back with Richard. He said, 'You're supposed to eat them.' I thought, 'Bloody hell, really?' I remember he had the ducks on the kitchen table, plucking them, ripping their feathers out. I was horrified, there were feathers all over the kitchen floor. Richard did something disgusting to one of the ducks with a knife, then we stuck it in the oven and served it up with roast potatoes. It was full of lead shot, though; you couldn't take one bite of it without cracking your teeth.

I couldn't work it out at all. I didn't understand why we couldn't have gone there and watched the ducks come in and land on the water; why did we have to murder a hundred of them and waste all this time trying to cook and eat this poor bird that broke our teeth?

That was the last time I shot anything, I felt so guilty. I kept my guns for a little while but in the end I sold them. I didn't like this hunting and shooting business, so the 'country pursuits' kind of life never really worked for me.

After several months of building work, things started to come together. We'd converted the whole stable block and barn into a lovely studio with a glass window, looking down onto the main room. I even had my own mixing console, built by the same people who used to be the maintenance engineers at the Manor, according to my own specifications. They had started their own company called Rebis, and mine was the first desk that they built. It lasted for years and years. Eventually I had it installed in a live rack and it came on tour with me. It was finally consigned to the scrap heap just a few years ago, so that was a very good investment.

Finally, after taking more than a year to build, the house and studio were finished. I had my own, beautiful studio, and that meant we could finally get some work done.

One day, when we'd just started working in the studio, someone rang up and said, 'I've got this guy here, he's got a lion and he's looking for a home for it, would you like to meet it?' I said, 'Oh, yes, why not, send him over.' So this van arrived with a man and his girlfriend, and out of the back pounced a one-year-old male lion called Clyde. He wasn't completely mature, just starting to grow his mane. The instant Clyde had jumped out he came up to me and grabbed my chest with his teeth, and the man, who had this huge stick, started bashing him off. Clyde eventually let go and he stayed the weekend, with his owner.

Phil Newell, the engineer, was doing some work at Througham Slad at the time. When the lion arrived Phil was busy in the studio, and I remember him coming into the kitchen to make a cup of tea. The lion was there, but Phil hadn't a clue – no one had thought of saying, 'Be careful, because there's a lion around.' I remember poking my head through the kitchen door and Clyde had literally got Phil pinned against the sink. The expression on his face was priceless; he had long ginger hair and a ginger beard, and he was white, like a ghost! I don't think he could even talk. The owner noticed what was happening, and started thwacking Clyde to leave Phil alone. The poor chap nearly had a seizure. It was a bit of revenge for being so anti-me in *Tubular Bells* – unplanned, of course.

Clyde was a very fine animal indeed. Obviously he was a big cat, but his personality was that of a complete brute. He was as tough as you could possibly imagine. He would crawl around the place and look at you and you could see him thinking, 'I'm going to frighten them now,' and then he would roar at you. It seemed he would only respect anyone who beat the absolute hell out of him: if Clyde showed signs of really hurting someone, his owner would come and wallop him with a stick with all his strength. Clyde wouldn't howl, or scream or anything, he would kind of back off. Obviously he could hardly feel it, that was just the only way to control him.

I got on well with Clyde once I got used to beating him up all the time. I didn't like doing it, but then he respected me a bit – if I hadn't done it, I think he would have killed me. I'd never met an animal like him. For food you gave him a whole chicken and he ate the whole thing, just crunched up the bones. We had to follow him around with newspaper because he would spray his scent all over the place, stinking up the walls.

We decided to take Clyde to the pub. It was summer, so everybody was sitting outside, and when we arrived I went to buy some drinks. Suddenly I heard this woman screaming, more than you could possibly imagine. I ran out of the door to see that the lion had plonked his head on the front of her dress, resting on this woman's lap. She screamed her head off and everybody scattered out of the garden, then the lion's owner came and, of course, started whacking the lion saying, 'Bad Clyde, behave!'

Clyde was a complete bully, but I liked him. At home I threw grass at him and played with him like a dog, but he was ten times quicker. He was so quick that I could go a couple of hundred feet away down to the end of the garden; one second I could see him looking at me from the other end of the garden and, in the next second it seemed, he would be right in front of me. At one time I had him inside a courtyard with wire all around it and the dogs started barking at him, so the lion just prowled up to the fence and roared at the dogs. The two Irish wolfhounds, they literally pissed themselves, their tails between their legs. I've never seen animals so scared for their lives. My St Bernard, Wellington, he stood his ground and barked back. I was so impressed with him, he wasn't scared at all.

That night Clyde slept on my bed with me. At about four o'clock in the morning I woke to find this lion on top of me, looking at me in a very amorous way. I gave a massive scream and had to beat him up before he would get off me. Clyde spent the rest of the night in the corner, I wasn't having him on the bed with me any more. The next day the owner said, 'Would you like to have the lion?' I declined the offer but, my God, what an experience that was.

In the end I sent Clyde off to Virgin. I rang Richard up and said, 'I've got a lion here, do you want to meet it?'

Richard said yes and, as I liked to wind Richard up, I gave the lion's owner the address of Virgin Records and told him to take it in there. It probably caused complete havoc in reception, demolished all the offices and had people screaming. I never found out what happened to it in the end. I think Richard turned him down as well, so he probably passed it on to someone else.

That was fun.

Once Clyde had gone, I started to work properly on my new album. At the time, I was listening to a great deal of religious music, which helped me keep calm and sane. I remember my engineer, Paul Lindsay, ridiculing me; he was listening to things like Steely Dan. He just thought I was out of my mind and I suppose he may have been right; I was very disturbed and the music comforted me.

When I started planning things out, my first thought was, 'I have tried *Tubular Bells* with rock instruments in a classical format; I've tried *Hergest Ridge* which was more Celtic; *Ommadawn* was more African.' I wanted to have some magical things in there, so I decided to try using real instruments where I could, real strings and a real flute in the beginning. I'd never orchestrated my own string section, so I thought I'd give it a try. I sat down with a pen and paper and laboriously scribbled out all these crotchets and quavers and all the parts. I hired a string section of about eighteen players and had them in my studio. That was my starting point, just to see where it led.

With that in place I set about working on this really complicated musical sequence. It went sequentially through every key in the musical scale. It was a 'Frère Jacques' kind of round, but the longest anybody had ever written as far as I know. The whole thing was really complicated. If you listen to it carefully, you realise that it is two parts that cross over and take about two minutes to get round. By some fluke I found the right notes to start the second part, twenty-five and three-quarter bars in, all with different time signatures in each bar. Later I got Pierre Moerlen and his brother Benoit to play it, with two interlocking vibraphones. I just loved to watch them go for it, those two were fantastic.

Things came together quite quickly. With this magical mood that I wanted to capture, I decided on the title, *Incantations*, quite early. It just seemed like a good idea. The original plan was to get some real incantations, magic spells and chants, rather than making them up. I'd heard about druids, they still existed and were supposed to be carrying on the traditions of the very ancient peoples of Britain. So I asked somebody at Virgin in the A&R department. He probably wasn't used to a request saying, 'Find me the head druid!' but, lo and behold, suddenly someone turned up at Througham.

He wasn't exactly wearing robes, but he was the kind of person who I imagine would look quite comfortable in such a costume. I said, 'Can you give me some magic spells that I can use in my music?' He was rather reticent about that, and didn't seem to want to. I think he was more interested in converting me to druidism, perhaps using me to get more publicity for the druids; maybe he was trying to decide if I was worthy enough. We talked about it for quite a while, but in the end he drove off. I never actually got anything from him.

Keith Critchlow then introduced me to a couple of strange people. One was a poet called Kathleen Raine, who was a lovely old lady, but I didn't manage to use any of her poems, although I tried to. There was also a very strange shaman, gypsy-type woman, I don't know where she came from. I remember spending an entire afternoon with this old lady, who didn't say a word. I sat there for at least an hour and a half, not even speaking. It was inspiring, in a strange way. I don't get embarrassed sitting in silence with somebody – I love silence.

Somebody at Virgin then put in some research, and managed to send me some bits and pieces about ancient paganism, going back to Gog and Magog, two giants from British folklore. I managed to get a few pieces of incantation, funnily enough they were all about the goddess Diana for some reason. In the end I found some words from Longfellow's *Hiawatha*, which fitted in rather well. But as far as the druids were concerned, that was pretty much a dead end.

Just as I was getting going, everything changed.

I hadn't been paying that much attention to the music scene, or what was popular, as I was totally into my classical music. I used to occasionally look at *Melody Maker* and see how things were doing: for years it seemed that *Tubular Bells* and Pink Floyd's *Dark Side of the Moon* were chasing each other up and down the top end of charts. Meanwhile there were the glitter bands like Slade and Sweet, glam-rock I think it was called. I didn't really recognise, or know much about the other artists.

To me, it felt like rock music didn't know where to go after albums like *Tubular Bells* and *Dark Side of the Moon*. You would have thought that *Tubular Bells* was so successful, every other musician would think, 'I'll do something like that,' but it didn't happen. There weren't any other people coming up with similar albums to continue the lineage, so it ran out of steam. It's always been a mystery to me why no other musicians took the baton and carried it on, did something amazing with it. There have always been good instrumentalists and good songwriters, but to have a composer make something using rock instruments is different. I'm not talking about hiring the Royal Philharmonic and saying, 'Let's all pretend to be classical musicians with classic rock stuff,' but more, 'Let's do something totally unique.'

After a few months I started hearing noises about punk rock. I can understand why the punk movement wanted to destroy the glam rockers, because they were so ridiculous and pathetic; also the people who were trying to make classic rock music, the pompous rock stars with the Royal

Philharmonic – I can understand why that could be annoying. What I couldn't understand was why my kind of music should be attacked as well. From being told by Tony Palmer that *Tubular Bells* was the pinnacle of musical achievement, quite suddenly, I was looking at things like *NME* and *Melody Maker* and finding my name was being blackened. They were slagging me off, calling me a 'rock dinosaur', 'Mike Oldfart' and stuff like that. I was still only in my mid-twenties, for heaven's sake.

I can look back and chuckle about it now, but at the time it was humiliating and distressful. I have come to think of it in terms of the laws of human evolution, that if something stands out as being different to the norm, initially people will follow it, and then they will rebel against it, and try to destroy it. I think this is a natural process, to test its validity. So, if something is good enough to be adopted as generally good, it has got to survive the backlash. I accept that now and I have made peace with the whole issue.

In retrospect I think it has to do with the human instinct to destroy or revolt against anything that is considered to be too clever: everyone hates the school swot or somebody who is too successful. I don't think the media liked me very much; they had got pretty annoyed with me in the past because I wouldn't speak to them. Neither did I come and stand centre stage, be the guru of progressive music I felt they wanted me to be. I wouldn't play the role, go and talk to people, be photographed, go to lunches, do tours, 'look at me', and all that. I just didn't have it in me. As Richard said in his book *Losing My Virginity*, perhaps all I needed was something like therapy – which I eventually found, a few years too late.

Virgin was still having financial difficulties. While *Ommadawn* had been critically acclaimed, in sales terms I think *Tubular Bells* had sold fantastically well and was still selling, *Hergest Ridge* was down to about 75 per cent of that and *Ommadawn* was at about 60 per cent. Even though it was adored by everybody, the people at Virgin were probably thinking, 'Maybe we can't carry this on.' Perhaps that would explain later why they chucked in nearly everything to do with me, and became the punk label.

Everybody's got their own point of view, their own goals, their own objectives in their lives: for me, it was, and is, to make the best music that I can. By some fortune, at the time of *Tubular Bells* the winds blew me towards Richard, who had very different goals as he was a businessman and I was a musician. I had the impression that he liked music but I've since realised that it wasn't like that. He wanted to build a successful company and I happened to be in the right place at the right time to allow the process to begin. As time went on I was looking less and less like sustaining that success so, in Richard's mind, he needed to change direction.

Richard explains in his book that they felt like a laughing stock as a record company, they were known as 'the hippy label', and they had to change their image. I understood later they were debating whether to stop being the progressive label and become the punk label; this was around the time of the infamous Bill Grundy interview with the Sex Pistols where all the four-letter words came out.

I understand why Richard felt it was the right thing to do, probably for his life and his business. The fact that Virgin changed direction towards what seemed to be the antithesis of my kind of music was neither here nor there. It was a commercial decision, which I now understand. That's just the way it was.

In terms of our culture, quite why punk was so successful is another question. Whatever happened, it played into the hands of the media. I do think the media like to feel in control of what is happening in our society. I suppose it could be thought of as a good thing, as they are supposed to be the voice of the people. When these aggressive, spitting, swearing punks came along, I think the 'powers that be' thought they'd found something they could control, some people who would co-operate.

* * *

After I'd got about twenty minutes of music for *Incantations*, the people at Virgin asked if they could come and see what I was doing. They wanted to know what kind of album I was making next, whether it was going to be another *Tubular Bells* probably. One day a delegation arrived at my house. Somebody at Virgin, I think his name was Rob Vickery, had obviously done a deal with Volvo, because everybody turned up in identical Volvos, about eight of them. I remember seeing them all parked up my drive, Volvo after Volvo. Richard was there, Simon was there, Ken Berry was there and a couple of other people. Ken was the accountant, the person who used to sign my pay cheque and give me my luncheon vouchers.

Given everything that was going on, I think this delegation was hoping to be able to influence me one way or the other. Obviously what I'd recorded was a mathematical, classical-sounding piece of music, and it was going to be a double album as well. I remember playing them the first twenty minutes and watching their reactions. They quietly sat around the place listening; at the end, Richard was his usual, cheerful self but everyone else filed out in silence. It was probably just after that, when Richard got together with the others and said, you know, from that moment on Virgin should become the punk label, instead of the progressive rock label. I don't know how it happened exactly, but shortly afterwards Virgin decided they were now in favour of punk rock.

I wasn't marketable, because I'd never played the marketing game. I later learned my albums were being taken off the shelves in the Virgin record shops and punk albums being put in their place. At the time I didn't think they liked me anyway at Virgin, I felt they were probably just glad I wasn't their star performer anymore. I didn't know how I was supposed to feel, I just felt I had been let down. It started getting to me and I became even more paranoid.

The attacks in the music papers became more and more aggressive. I felt I was being vilified and made to feel like it had all been a waste of time. I've since learned it wasn't just me, it was anybody who belonged to that era, that genre of music. Stuck away in Througham Slad, I didn't know what the devil was going on. I was trying to do something new, something that hadn't been done before. What I was doing was interesting and articulate, it was crafted, and meanwhile there were these screaming, crazy, spitting, obscene ... I don't know if you could call them musicians. I was being pushed out to make way for the next big thing.

My work on that album didn't exactly grind to a halt, but I lost all my spark and inspiration. It became a chore again, just like *Hergest Ridge* had been. Meanwhile, I still had this looming tax bill and the lawyer was still saying to me, 'You could get a much better deal.' Eventually, I very politely managed to get another percentage point or two on my royalties. I felt I was getting less than I was worth, but I still wouldn't acknowledge that Richard could treat me badly as he was my captain and I looked up to him.

Finally, the day came. After two or three years, the royalties from *Tubular Bells* started to come in and suddenly I had something like a million pounds. About £860,000 went straight out to the Inland Revenue, which left me with about £140,000. Somehow I found a tax lawyer, not the ones Richard had given me. His name was Paddy Grafton-Green and he was a charming gentleman. He told me I had to get organised and start a company, have employees, pay myself a salary, work on company tax instead of personal tax. I did all that and started keeping the receipts instead of throwing everything away, that kind of thing.

It's because of that period that I have been careful with my money and been organised ever since. I have made much more money since *Incantations* than I ever made from *Tubular Bells*, although that still brings in an income from the back-catalogue sales.

So, I had a bit of money, but it wasn't what people expected, they thought I was a millionaire but I was nothing like that. I had my house and less than a hundred thousand pounds in the bank. I'd bought Througham Slad, built a studio and bought a Ferrari. I didn't spend money on anything else, I didn't go on holidays or travel much. Indeed, I couldn't travel in my state. There was still pressure to move abroad but I just couldn't.

The inspiration for *Incantations* had gone completely. In terms of music, all I heard about was, punk this, Sex Pistols that. Richard and I would still speak but it wasn't the same. I was drinking a lot; I became aggressive, withdrawn, paranoid. Life just seemed to be falling apart, and I was really at rock bottom. By then Keith Critchlow's daughter, Louise, had moved in with me and our relationship became stormy and aggressive, it was awful. Finally she left, so it was just me and my three dogs. I was completely on my own there and I could see that the money would run out before long.

I was looking for something but I just didn't know what it was, and I was terrified about being alone. I had to be blind drunk every night to go to sleep, and my days were empty and full of terror.

My brother Terry came over again, I remember. He tried to help me, we even went for a long drive, down through Europe to Italy. By that time I had some kind of Alfa Romeo. I remember we went to one of the big cathedrals in Milan, and I was desperately hoping I could leave my panic behind me there, the demon that was possessing me. Terry did his best but he didn't really know what to do. You can't understand what it's like if you're not in a completely paranoid, depressed state yourself. The slightest thing could set me off in a breathless panic. I would be sweating, my heart would be racing and I would just want to run somewhere; as if by running really fast, I might be able to escape it, or sweat it off. We drove all around Italy and ended up in Greece; Terry had spent some time in Hydra so we went there for a while.

My father also came to visit me, back at Througham Slad. He had met a new woman called Helga, and they had married. I remember being put out by that, indeed it would take me quite a few years to accept it.

The only person left around was my technical engineer Paul Lindsay, as he lived next door in a cottage. Finally it was Paul's wife Barbara who did it; Paul just mentioned that she had gone on some kind of seminar and said it was wonderful. I asked if she could come and tell me what it was about.

Barbara arranged for the sister of the man who ran the seminar to come and speak to me. Her name was Diana. They wouldn't take anyone who was on any kind of medication or therapy, they were very choosy. I had to fill in a big questionnaire to show I was a person that really wanted to go forward. I didn't need much convincing. I just said, 'All right, I'll do it,' and she booked me in. I remember saying I didn't want to be there under my real name. Everyone was first name only, so I said, 'I'll be Mick.'

I really didn't want to do it on my own, so I spoke to Rosie, my sister's boyfriend, that wayward scallywag. I persuaded him to come with me to keep me company: he was up for anything so he said, 'Oh, OK, I'll come.' As he was going to be there with me, I felt a little bit of security.

The seminar lasted over three days, starting on the Thursday night and ending on the Sunday. As the days passed, I felt a growing sense of foreboding, though I had no idea why: it was as if I knew my whole life was going to be changed, that I would finally be free from the panic attacks. When the moment came, on the Sunday, I was full of trepidation but I just walked up and gave myself over to this guru, Robert D'Aubigny. I didn't know what I was getting into; I simply trusted him, and he somehow made me believe I would get through it.

After it happened I felt nothing but absolute relief and euphoria. The whole process had been like an initiation ceremony: it was like leaping off into the unknown, throwing myself off a really high mountaintop. I have never worried about my courage since then, as that demanded the biggest step I have ever taken. After that, somehow, the huge, blood-crazed demons that had been stalking me for the previous twenty years suddenly disappeared.

I was floating on a cloud.

ON REBIRTH – 2006

I've come to believe that the biggest single cause of my condition was the suppressed memory of simply being born. I think it's been proved that babies do react to light and the trauma of going through the birth canal, out into the cold, bright world. In the foetal stage, you can become aware of the sounds outside, even before you leave the womb. I would hazard a guess that, for many people who suffer panic attacks, it comes back to that same birth-trauma memory. For some, it's too much and they can never recover from it.

At the same time, I grew up in the womb with whatever genetic characteristics had been implanted in me by my parents. I have often wondered whether anything was passed to me, through my mother, from my grandfather's war experiences, which added to the strength of the panic I used to feel. It's possible there may be a residue that somehow gets passed on to the children, perhaps genetically, or maybe spiritually in some way.

Genetics fascinates me. I think I was born as a sort of mutation, without the socialising gene that makes people or animals flock together. I was meant not to fit in. Probably, one way nature advances is to create a number of mutations for every generation, to see if anything is better than the status quo: that is how we progress as a species. At the time, not fitting in was a terrible handicap for me. However, as I look back on it now, I just see that it was meant to be like that, and I'm comfortable.

To compensate, I had my atmosphere antennae. It occurs to me now that some people are born with these windows onto the 'fifth dimension', the spiritual world or whatever it is, but, if they are open just a little too much, their personality is not able to cope with it all. It was like an avalanche of feelings. I think my mother had the same problem: the only way she could block it off was to take her tranquillizers and drink alcohol.

It must have had quite an impact on me, watching my mother go downhill like that. I think when you have certain experiences as a child, it becomes part of your adult programming. I could never accept that things would go permanently right, because I believed things went in cycles of going all right for a while, then going terribly wrong. I found out later on, during the seminar, that I was creating my own cycle of disappointment.

There are physical sensations associated with these feelings – when I got into my teens and started suffering panic attacks, they would terrify me. I thought I must be possessed by some demon, because it suddenly became a very big thing that I was trying to shut off. It was all mixed up with my perceptions, the doors onto the unknown that opened wider still as my family fell apart and I had to survive on my own.

Then, of course, the doors got ripped off completely. They were smashed open with LSD and I've been trying to close them ever since. It's like the doors weren't really supposed to be opened, but were opened artificially, by chemical means. Taking LSD was a terribly powerful thing for me, which led to some great creativity but those absolute horrors as well.

I didn't really regain control of my life until the Exegesis seminar. Robert D'Aubigny, as he called himself (his real name was Robert Fuller), was a kind of guru, a follower of Werner Erhard, the founder of EST (Erhard Seminars Training). Certain people are born leaders, they are charismatic, somehow able to influence or control people. Any great world leader or business mogul has this gift. Robert was, and still is, one of those people; Richard Branson is too, but in a completely different way – he applies his skills to business and also to having fun.

I think charisma is genetic: nature churns out of few of these people every generation. It's a great gift but takes a tremendous amount of responsibility. There are many people who have the ability to make others follow them; the difference is what they choose to make people follow. A really powerful, controlling person could use it for good or evil; I would imagine some of the worst leaders in our history have had that gift. I suppose that kind of mind control exists to a negative degree in some cults, it simply takes a person with that genetic gift.

One of the most important things I learned during the seminar was that you can actually cause events to go wrong in your life. All the little subtle things you say and do, the way you behave, all the decisions you make, they are part of your programming. I used to be completely oblivious to that, I would normally blame bad stuff on someone else. I didn't realise we could subtly manipulate people, and ourselves, by the way we view things.

I realised that a lot of the trouble we get into is self-inflicted, because we are not in control. I'm not saying we should blame ourselves for everything that goes wrong, but that we should take more responsibility in our own lives. Even if you try very hard to do something – say, write a book, make an album or play sports – if you keep failing it may be because you don't allow yourself to do whatever it is properly. You can put obstacles in your way; you'll try your hardest but all the time you'll be unintentionally, subconsciously knocking yourself off the rails.

This can be for several reasons but the main one is to re-create childhood situations that can't be understood at the time. As a child, when you have a stressful experience, its memory can get buried, covered up. It doesn't have to have been a major, life-threatening problem; maybe there was a bully at school or an irritated parent, maybe it was about being sick or humiliated. It resurfaces in your adult life and controls the way you behave. You try to re-create that situation and, in a way, help yourself understand – but in doing so you can prevent yourself from succeeding.

All through my twenties, thirties and even into my forties I could find myself in a situation and I suddenly would feel awful, insecure or angry. It could be some very small, subtle thing: a colour could set it off, or a sound or a smell, or something somebody said. Instantly, in the front of my mind there would be a childhood memory – something that happened at school, in the playground – which would be triggered by these feelings. I would want to get drunk, or get into one of my Ferraris and drive around at ridiculous speeds.

Seeing the way the mind works is just a revelation. It is like seeing viruses deep in a computer program. The mind is a labyrinth of psychological wiring, spaghetti programming, which causes kneejerk, instinctive reactions. It's a mass of electrical impulses telling you, 'I can't do this because my mother did this and my school did that.' Sometimes it can be hilarious to see somebody who hides behind a tough mask, hiding because they are too afraid or insecure to be who they really are.

I am sure there are people who will read this and be cynical; they will think such seminars are a waste of time, but that's just a block. Having said that, it's unlikely that EST would have the same impact now. Back then it was all new, so it was controversial. The philosophy is ancient but it was one of the first times terms like 'ownership', or 'personal responsibility' had been used over here. I think the seminar I did was only about the fourth or fifth one in Britain, and I don't think EST had been going for much longer than two or three years before that. Since then so many people have done these seminars, especially in Los Angeles, that the language has started to appear in the films and soaps. Today, 'EST speak' or similar terminology has become part of our language. We just accept these terms, they've permeated our society.

The terrible possession I experienced, the birth trauma, I still to this day don't really know what it was. What I do know is that, through the seminar, the rebirth experience helped to exorcise it. I was on a high for nearly a decade after that experience. The euphoria lasted several years, but then all the nuts and bolts of my psychology gradually crept back in. I had to deal bit by bit with the mechanics of my problems, all the little details. I went to psychotherapy for two or three years and eventually I learned meditation as well. I have found that helps enormously.

I suppose I've spent all my life learning how to control the doors onto the unknown, to know how to open and close them when I want to. Nowadays the childhood memories are still the first things that come into my head, but I am able to catch them. They're like an alarm bell: what I've learned is that the best way to deal with such feelings is to take ownership of them, saying, 'Here I go again, knocking myself off track, getting jealous, feeling insecure or getting upset when there is no reason to be.' The more and more I do that, the less I am controlled by my own programming.

If there's one piece of advice I could pass on from this story, it's that if you do try to hide from your problems or blame other people, then that's all you're going to do. You can run away from it, anaesthetise the feelings with tranquillizers or alcohol, drugs or whatever, but they are still going to be there. It's much better to start on a journey of self-awareness or education, to find out how not to be scared of them, maybe use them to help you grow, not just as a physical person but as a spiritual being.

In a way, the whole process was for me like completing a circle. While for many years it churned me up inside about my mother and the whole business, it doesn't any more, now I can live with it all. It doesn't make me scared, give me panic attacks, make me unreasonable or mentally unstable like it used to. I am getting pretty good at understanding how the mechanisms work, and I am much more settled than I was. I think I'm pretty much as good as I'll ever be now, in fact. I don't think I'll ever be totally happy and relaxed, but I have come to terms with it and it's all right – that's fine.

13. FLYING HIGH – 1978

After the seminar, my life completely changed: I had to rebuild it from nothing. I needed to find new ways of living, working, having relationships, relating to myself. It wasn't like Part Two of my life, it was like starting a completely different one.

The very next day, I booked myself on a small plane to fly to Minorca, where Richard's parents had a house on the harbour. I'd been invited to visit Richard and his family on holiday, but until the seminar I hadn't felt able to go. I flew from Elstree, in a little Piper two-seater, across the Channel to Paris; from there I flew on to Palma, Majorca. It was magnificent, I felt like a happy child. I found that I didn't mind flying in aeroplanes, though I'd not had the courage to fly in years. I had this thing about coffee as well: on the plane, I was drinking lots of cups of coffee. I was looking down, unafraid; I was even chatting to the people next to me, which was outrageous for me.

In those days, Palma airport was pretty much a chicken shed. I had to wait two hours for the connection flight to Minorca, so I came out of the airport. Just outside were the remains of a windmill. I climbed up onto the base of this old windmill, took my shirt off and sat up there in the sunshine. I felt like I was finally alive, not scared, and not scared of flying any more. At Minorca I met Richard with his family and friends. You know how people get when they go on holiday in a group? After lounging on the beach for a few days, they become a bit lethargic and cabbage-like. Well, I went in there like an absolute whirlwind. Nobody could believe it: I could see them thinking, 'What's happened to him? He's gone mad!' They hardly recognised me, they couldn't understand what had got into me at all. I was friendly, sociable, relaxed, I was making people laugh. I wasn't afraid.

From the moment I arrived back from Minorca, my life began as a completely new person. I wanted to talk to every single journalist that I hadn't wanted to speak to before, so I spent two weeks, doing eight interviews a day. I didn't really know what to say, they asked questions but I didn't have any answers. I'm a bit wiser now. I give answers that I know will satisfy the questions, so they can write a reasonable piece, but at that time I didn't have a clue.

I also was having my photograph taken left, right and centre. I even appeared nude in *Sounds* magazine; I still occasionally see that picture on the Internet. I also got my ears pierced, as it was all the rage; I did have both of them pierced, but one swelled up. I had a diamond stud in there for a while, trying to be hip and cool. For a brief period I got married to Diana, the sister of Robert D'Aubigny. It was an instinctive reaction, and only lasted three months, but it wasn't long after that I settled into a proper relationship. I was a completely different person, liberated from my rabid demons; more than that, it really had felt that it was the devil. I had been possessed and was now exorcised in the true sense of the word.

After a while I had to land somehow, to come back down to Earth. I was still being humiliated by the press; my albums had already been put on the back shelf in the shops, and all the punk albums had been put at the front. Virgin obviously believed they could make more money from selling punk rock than my kind of music. That attitude was probably valid for them, it was just that I didn't see it like that; to make matters worse, the money was now running out.

Ironically it was the possession, the terrible anxiety, that gave my music real voltage and power. My music had been turbocharged, it was nuclear powered because of my paranoia, but now my inspiration had gone. I had to find another reason to make music, a new muse. It was a strange time: I knew I'd reached a crossroads. Luckily I was able to progress out of it and go forward, as I could have easily collapsed and not gone anywhere.

At the time, I just wanted to finish the album. It wasn't a labour of love, and I really didn't feel like doing it, but I couldn't leave it unfinished. I just banged ahead, gritted my teeth and got to work for a month or six weeks to finish it off. It wasn't a tremendous joy. It took a lot of effort, I had to really force myself to make things happen. I got David Bedford's choir (from Queen's College in London) in for a session: I just thought, 'I've got to get this bloody thing done,' so I put a session of that in there.

The photo on the cover was of me, taken maybe two months after the seminar. It was taken on a beach called the Cala Pregonda in Minorca by Carlos Moyse, a friend of Richard's. Carlos was a lovely man who later became a promoter. He was wheelchair-bound and his family had this house on the beach where the photo was taken, the rock in the middle of the bay is like a praying lady.

Once the album was finished, I finally decided to go on tour. Richard was over the moon. At that time I thought I needed a huge band so we had string players, woodwinds, we had a rock band and a folk band, plus a full choir. The musicians I chose were the ones I had worked with on *Incantations*. They had been to my house and I felt, for classical musicians, they were almost on my side. After the seminar I was more able to communicate with people, so I was actually able to explain it to them how I wanted to do it.

We chartered a Viscount, a four-engined propeller plane, and flew around Europe in that. Richard came along as well: with him there, it was like a charabanc holiday. It was like Club Med or something, we were partying up and down the plane. *Incantations* was the main piece of music we played, although we did bits of *Tubular Bells*, *Hergest Ridge* and *Ommadawn* as well.

Richard wanted to record every concert, but without necessarily paying the musicians for every recording. Eventually the musicians, in particular the string players, found out this was going on and we had to dismantle the tape machine and have it on the stage in bits before they would even go on, in case we were secretly recording them. (The resulting album was called *Exposed*, and it was released on DVD in 2005.)

Unfortunately, the tour cost an absolute fortune. Somebody at Virgin tried to warn me, but I said, 'We need this, we need that . . .' It wasn't just me, I didn't realise that if you give everybody a blank cheque then the money starts pouring out like water through a breached dam. Everybody wanted this and that: 'We've all got to have cars, double rooms at the hotel, all food paid for,' and so on. I stupidly didn't realise who was going to end up paying the bill – it was me, of course. Money just started pouring out, and Muggins here got the bill for everything.

Although the tour was a success critically and sold out pretty much everywhere, I wasn't yet a proven live act, so we couldn't play the really big halls, we played two- to three-thousand-seater venues. The income was nowhere near enough to cover the expenditure and at the end, the loss was around half a million pounds from just over a month's touring. I was absolutely horrified. Although I didn't have to pay it back from my personal money, I paid it back through the royalties from *Exposed*, which finally paid off the debt more than ten years later.

It was a major lesson. You can go on tour and have all these people cheering, you all stay in lovely hotels, then you finally get the bill and find out you've been working for the last three or four months and it's actually cost you hundreds of thousands of pounds. It happens again and again; everybody thinks the artist makes a fortune but quite often it is the reverse. It will be the people around the artist making the money, and in the end the artist will be left with a negative bill, a deficit, just from touring.

You've got to learn about being economical, not wasting money unnecessarily and putting money by for important things like tax, not spending it before you have really got it. If the tour is not properly prepared financially, if you get one figure wrong, the whole profit for the two or three months can go out the window, or even turn into a loss. It was quite a lesson for me at the time.

Once *Incantations* was complete, I decided that I had to learn to fly. Before the Exegesis seminar I'd had every phobia you could imagine: claustrophobia, agoraphobia, and, of course, fear of flying. As a result, I had got the feeling in myself that I was somehow a weed, a coward, not as strong as I wanted to be. So, having confronted my demons during the exorcism seminar, one of the first things I wanted to do was to take flying lessons.

After many weeks of training, I actually got my pilot's licence. I used to fly from Staverton flying club near Gloucester. My instructor, John Cole, used to fly a tiny little plane built by Bölkow Messerschmitt just after the war. By God, could he do aerobatics in it. At Staverton air show, they would have the Phantoms and the Harriers flying, and then there would be John in his little Bölkow doing loop-the-loops and barrel rolls down the runway. I looked on him as a sort of grandfather figure: I was his last ever student, but I don't think I could have had any other teacher, nobody else could have given me the confidence. To be honest, I hated every moment of the training. For my qualifying cross-country flight I remember sitting in a Beechcraft plane, on my own, flying over the Severn Bridge. It was absolutely horrible.

For about a year I had my own plane, a Beechcraft Sierra. After I got my licence I tried to persuade Richard to come up with me and, to my surprise, he actually agreed, so one day I took him up. One of the things you do when larking around in the air is to practise stalling: you wind off the power and pull back until the plane starts to lose lift, then the alarms go and it starts to shudder. It's not that difficult to recover, you just stick the nose down and add some power. I'd always wanted to get back at Richard for all his practical jokes, so I thought I'd practise a stall. It was the only time I've ever seen him scared – he was sitting next to me, really sweating. To get Richard panicking was quite an achievement.

For various reasons, I wanted to move house from the Cotswolds, to be closer to London, so I sold my house in Througham and got about £120,000 for it (I saw it for sale recently for £5.5m – maybe I should have kept it!). I found a house in a place called Denham, but due to the tax bills I didn't have much money at all, even with the sale of Througham Slad. So I asked Richard to lend me the money, advancing it against the next album. I think the house cost about £160,000, so I had to borrow about £50,000 of that against future royalties. Once I had the house, I had virtually no money at all, so I obviously needed to have a successful album.

When *Incantations* was released, my genre of music was being vilified in the music press as being worthless rubbish, dinosaur stuff, even though *Tubular Bells* was still in the album charts. My first four albums might have outsold everything I have made since, but at the time it felt that the tide was against me. My kind of music, progressive rock, you might call it, had not only gone out of fashion but was being stamped out, almost becoming illegal. It was all very strange. I didn't understand it but I did feel I had to learn to speak a more popular musical language. I needed to completely change the way I thought about music, to somehow bring it up to date. I had no choice but to bend with the wind and adapt.

The best way to do that, I decided, was to travel. One of the wonderful things Richard had done for me after the seminar had been to invite me out to New York to see Virgin's new offices. It was a tremendous trip. We'd flown on Concorde, which had been just incredible. There's no way I could have done that before the seminar: I could hardly go down to the shops, let alone to New York, flying at twice the speed of sound.

As I was deciding what kind of album to make next, I wondered about going to New York again and hiring a really good studio, and the best studio musicians I could. I thought we could play around with a few ideas and see what happened. That's probably how most artists actually work: get an advance on the album, get the best people in, have a jam and get a few ideas. So off I went, to Electric Ladyland studios in New York.

The end result of my time in New York was *Platinum*. What I learned from that experience was how much I used the studio as a creative tool. From the *Tubular Bells* days and all through *Hergest Ridge* and *Ommadawn*, I had learned exactly how the studio worked. I astonished the engineers in New York with the expertise I had developed on my own. I knew how to use all the equipment, though it was still quite primitive back then. I could use tape loops and so on, I knew how to do things half-speed, and not just in theory. I knew that if you turn the tape recorder to half-speed you have to play things in different ways, then when you turn it up to full speed it sounds the way you want it to.

It was good fun, but hard work as well. I relied a lot on certain musicians to come up with the ideas; the music became a lot more jazz-rock, it was syncopated, it used techniques such as pushing and pulling the beat, making it swing. These were all things that I didn't naturally do, but I learned how to do them and went along with them, because it was considered to be hip and cool at the time.

One of the tracks we recorded in New York was called 'Guilty', which illustrates my point that I not only wrote and played the music, but used the studio as well – it was a production exercise as much as anything else. When I went back to Virgin Records and played it to Simon Draper, he was totally astonished at the change in my music, from *Incantations* to that. I asked Steve Winwood to play a bit of keyboards at the end, and then we put it out as a single.

The next I knew, I was on *Top of the Pops*! In those days, that was quite an achievement, rather than the stupid parody it became at the end.

This time, when I decided to tour, things were very different. Obviously I couldn't take the sixty musicians, or however many we had the time before. I cut it right back, I think I got it down to twelve people. It was still a large band but I thought it was a lot more manageable; it was the first step in working out how to go on tour and come out with a bit of money in my pocket. We started keeping much tighter controls on costs: you really have to be ruthless and nasty with everybody. That's not really a sensitive musician's strength, but you have to make yourself do it, otherwise people are just plain greedy.

We played similar-sized venues to the *Incantations* tour, but this time we came in with a very small profit, a few thousand pounds. Trouble was, on tour it didn't feel like me any more. I wasn't making music that was essentially my kind of music, I was bending myself to fit in with what I thought would be successful at the time. Still, at least it wasn't the terrible financial disaster of the previous tour.

Everywhere we went, I had to go through the rigours of promotion, doing interviews and TV shows. I started to get very irritated by the first question that every journalist would ask: 'Why did you write *Tubular Bells*?' In fact, they would ask 'Why?' about just about everything. In the end, in some interviews, I wrote down the answers to a lot of the questions. When they asked, 'Why did you write *Tubular Bells*?' I would say, 'OK, Number One, where's the card?' I just got fed up with it.

I remember once I was doing promotion and I had a request from Virgin to do an interview with Paula Yates, who was carrying out interviews with celebrities in unusual places. I had my own plane, which I kept at Denham aerodrome, so I suggested we did an interview in the air. When everyone arrived – Paula Yates, the production team and the gang from Virgin – it turned out to be a very foggy day. Because they were there, I felt obliged to get them up in the air, I thought at least we could do a circuit.

Unfortunately I wasn't licensed to fly IFR, which is instrument flight rules, I could only fly VFR, visual flight rules, which means you have to be able to see for at least five miles. We all got in my plane, everybody was looking very confident, ready to have a lovely time; meanwhile, there was me with my hand on the control column, and it was shaking like you wouldn't believe. I thought, 'How am I going to get away with this? I can't back down and say no.' I decided I actually had to take them up. We took off and almost instantly I couldn't see anything, probably just enough to get round and do a circuit.

Of course, when it's foggy, there's no wind whatsoever, and I was used to landing into the wind. We got round and I could just about see the runway. As I turned onto the final approach, because there was no wind, there was no air blowing me back, so my actual ground speed was much higher than it normally would have been. Denham aerodrome has a tiny little runway, so we came in at what I thought was a reasonable height. The plane went 'thump' onto the runway and all the people went 'Oh My God!'

I asked, 'Everybody enjoy that?' then I taxied round and, still shaking, shut the plane down. We then went to the pub, where I downed two pints of lager in about three minutes, then asked Paula Yates if she would like to carry on the interview.

I bumped into Bob Geldof on a *Top of the Pops* a few months after that. He said, 'You . . . you terrified my wife!' I thought he was going to kill me, to beat me up. He was very annoyed.

For the next album, I decided I needed people to work with, as I couldn't work on my own any more, so I asked Simon Draper if he knew anyone. Simon suggested an engineer-producer called David Hentschel, who had produced some of the early Genesis albums. I met with David and got on very well with him. I thought he was very talented, he gave a lot of helpful input and it was nice to work with someone new. I had a few guests on there, like Phil Collins, who came and did some drums. I'm not sure where the title came from, I think it was because on this one track we had somehow created a foghorn noise. It reminded me of a great, big ocean liner: I had the choice of calling it *Titanic* but I thought that didn't bode very well for the success of the album. So I thought we'd call it *QE2* instead.

By this point, my partner Sally and I wanted to start a family. When the time came for my own children to be born, I wanted to make sure they didn't go through the same experience that I had. At that time, in the late 70s and early 80s, there was a movement called 'natural childbirth'. It is fairly common knowledge now, but it was pioneering in those days. When the first baby-boomers where born, back in the 1950s, birth was considered a very serious business. It was almost scientific, with very bright lights, and doctors thought the child had to be slapped on the back or held upside down for some reason. But this new movement decided it was much better to allow a baby to be born, then to leave the umbilical cord connected for a short while. The midwife would put the baby on the mother's tummy, then wait until it took its first breath on its own.

The first time I witnessed that, indeed every time I have witnessed it, I have found it quite stunning to see that first moment of life. I believe it's a very good, natural thing. Animals give birth out in a field, in a safe place, obviously: there is no big rush or panic. I always felt that when my children were born it was a very magical moment, almost a holy moment, much more than anything I had experienced. It was fantastic.

The problem for me was, in the early days, I just wasn't mature enough to be a father. I was still diving deep into my musical world, trying to get closer to God if you like, it was a very spiritual experience for me. I was searching for something that perhaps didn't exist, but I used to be able to find it in my music, momentarily. If I worked on an album for a year, for a few minutes of that year I might be in contact with what I was looking for. Later on, when I learned meditation, I found it a very easy shortcut to get there.

Also, in many ways, the *Tubular Bells* success story was a millstone. I was under immense pressure, constantly expected by those around me, record companies and everybody else, to produce the miracle again. I had spent quite a lot of money on my studio so I could have a professional facility to work in, and I became obsessed with my work. I would spend just about my whole life in there, when I wasn't touring, which was also a struggle. Once I started touring after the Exegesis seminar, I was away a lot and trying to make a tour work, not only musically but financially. All of these things were a huge distraction to me.

It wasn't just fatherhood I had problems with: for some reason, I could never settle down in any of the relationships that I had. I think I was heartbroken that my family split up when I was a child, through the circumstances of the time, my mother's illness and the medical care that was available. That was the state of medical science of the time; if it happened now things would probably be different. I was scared of it happening again, so when things got difficult in my relationships I tended to leave them.

So with regard to my children, obviously I adore them all and I did the best I could for them, given how I was at the time. It probably wasn't what you'd expect from a perfect father, but mind you, it was perhaps better than a lot of fathers. I am sad that I couldn't be a real father for them all the time but I am here, and they are always welcome. They are a part of me and I love them.

I may have scared Richard when I took him up in a plane, but he got his own back. I remember him ringing me up some time in the early 80s. 'I've got just the sport for you,' he said, 'I've just taken my balloon licence. You must come up, it's fantastic!' I wasn't so sure about it. With aeroplanes you're in a technological environment, you've got lots of knobs and dials and you feel a bit safe in there; whereas how I imagined a balloon was, you're in this little basket thing. I didn't want to do it but Richard was determined to persuade me. 'You just go floating across the treetops, and it's silent, you can hear the birds, it's the most beautiful thing!'

I said, 'Have you really passed your licence?'

'Oh, yes, yes,' he replied.

So I agreed to meet him and his buddy at this pub somewhere near Oxford. My girlfriend and a couple of Richard's friends came along as well, and we all bundled into a car. I was a little bit nervous, so I took along a carton of beer. I thought I'd be able to sit there quietly and have a nice relaxing beer, while I was just floating over the treetops, it wouldn't be so bad. They dropped us off right next to Didcot Power Station, which is an enormous industrial complex, with massive chimneys. It soon emerged that Richard and his friend were planning some kind of race, to see who could get the furthest. His friend was a similar character to Richard, with long, frizzy hair, and a great big smile. He got his balloon going first and off he went: I couldn't see where because he quickly disappeared behind the trees.

We gradually inflated Richard's balloon and climbed in; there were a couple of his other friends as well so we were five people in all. It started off really gently. Richard lit the burners and we gradually floated up. For about ten seconds I thought it was rather pleasant. There was a little bit of a breeze blowing, so after a minute we found ourselves gradually sliding up the side of one of the massive cooling towers of the power station. Soon we were literally hanging over the top of it, staring down into the middle. Luckily it wasn't functioning at the time, otherwise I think we would have been incinerated. I started to feel distinctly uneasy at that point; I remember gazing longingly at the treetops, which he'd promised we would be drifting serenely past.

Richard then caught sight of his buddy, who had about ten minutes' start on us. He seemed to be gaining quite a lot of ground and he was doing it by gaining altitude, to get up into the higher airflow. As soon as he saw that, Richard's hand went on the throttle, the burner lever, and it was burn, burn, burn! The levers were almost melting in the heat. We rose up to 500 feet, 1,000 feet, 2,000 feet, 3,000 feet, up and up. I said, 'Richard, do we really have to go so high?' He was just staring at his buddy, who was going even higher.

Five thousand feet is very high in a balloon. I could see the whole of Oxford, so small it was like it was a tiny village. Looking down at my feet, I could actually see through the fibres of the basket. I was starting to get distinctly nervous by then. I know I had trained in aeroplanes but it didn't count for much, it's a totally different environment. I was hanging there, in the middle of nowhere, in a wicker basket. It completely freaked me out. I reached for the beers I had brought, and I think I drank all eight of them in the space of about five minutes.

Of course, we didn't stop there. We went up to 10,000 feet, 12,000 feet, right on the verge of when you run out of oxygen. Richard was still madly pulling on the burner, staring at his friend and saying, 'We've got to get past him, we've got to get past him!' We reached about 13,000 feet, which was when Richard looked down at the gas cylinder and started to shake it. He seemed a little bit concerned. To me it looked like it didn't weigh very much, because it shook rather easily. It made me wonder whether we had got any gas left. Obviously, if we were up that high and it cooled off, we would need a lot of gas to land with, to slow the fall.

By then we were above some kind of industrial estate on the outskirts of Oxford, around Cowley. We started to come down, and Richard was looking very worried indeed. We descended, not exactly like a brick, but so that he would have just enough gas left to cushion the landing. I wasn't sure that was normal, that the balloon should come down quite so fast.

After about five minutes I saw the ground coming up towards us. It felt like a moon landing. There were all these buildings around, and by chance we seemed to be heading for a place in the car park were there weren't any cars. The only noise was the burner going, 'whoosh, whoosh'; Richard was pulling the handle furiously. For one second, I thought perhaps we'd made it, as we came down to the ground with a fairly hefty 'thunk'.

Of course, we didn't stop there, we bounced straight off the car park, and started heading back up into the air again. I saw the roof of this building coming towards us – I learned later it was one of the largest bakeries in Oxford. So we plonked down on top of this bakery, at which point I think one of Richard's friends said something like, 'Isn't there a thing where you let all the air out of the balloon, all at once?' and he said, 'Oh, yes, yes!' He pulled that lever and it all went, 'Pshooooooo!' This time it looked like we had actually made it, but we were still stuck on the roof of the bakery.

Suddenly there were sirens everywhere: there was a whole string of fire engines, ambulances and police, all around us. I couldn't believe the fire brigade, within seconds they had got their huge ladders, and they'd climbed right up to the top of this building – thirty or forty feet high, a great, big factory roof – and within a couple of minutes they'd taken the whole balloon down from there. I can't quite remember what happened next; I was half-drunk by that time. I think one of them might have given me a fireman's lift down the ladder. I remember coming to on the ground and trembling, thinking, 'Was that really my first balloon trip?'

It was certainly my last. I have never experienced what it is like to sail across the treetops with the birds. Of course, then we went back to Richard's house, he's so sociable and gregarious – we had the *Daily Telegraph* there, the TV, the radio, you name it. Richard was happily holding court, absolutely nothing was a problem, that's the kind of character he is. It's exasperating at times, but certainly, life is not boring.

The most horrific flying experience I ever had was when we were on a short Spanish tour (I think it was about seven shows) following the release of *QE2*. Instead of going to airports and flying in scheduled planes, I decided it would be very convenient to hire our own ten-seater, twin-engined plane. It was not only the convenience, but I could get some flying experience: I did a conversion training course to twin-engined planes, so I would be able to fly a little bit as well.

We all arrived somewhere like Luton, and met our captain for our journey. He was a very young chap and I asked him if he had been doing this for long. He told me he had just passed his test, and this was his first trip. It was a commercial pilot's licence so he'd had the training, but obviously not the experience. So, we got in the plane and off we flew down to Spain.

I remember we had just played Barcelona and we were flying to Saint Sebastian, which is across the Pyrenees. It was raining and blustery, the weather didn't look very promising at all. I asked the pilot what the weather forecast was and he told me that, according to the Spanish Met Office, there were isolated thunderstorms. He seemed to be quite confident: with thunderstorms, if they are isolated you can see them and go around them. We didn't have anything fancy like navigational radar or anything, and I wasn't happy about flying in any thunderstorm, but he was the boss and supposed to be qualified.

We took off and climbed up to about 10,000 feet, where we went into cloud. After about half an hour it all started getting a bit bumpy, the clouds darkened and it started to rain. It soon became even bumpier and we had to strap ourselves in; then, the sky blackened and hail started hitting the windscreen with a noise you would not believe. It was making this clattering sound, and you could see the lumps of ice piling against the windscreen. The pilot was gritting his teeth and we discussed turning back, but we thought if we turned back we'd have to go through what we'd already passed; if the storms *were* isolated, we thought we must come out of it before long.

But we didn't. At one point the sky was totally black. We must have been right in the centre of a cumulonimbus. Those are the real thunderstorm clouds: they go up to about 20,000 feet, and we were at about 10,000. We didn't have any oxygen so we couldn't climb over it, because we would have passed out at anything above 13,000 feet. We couldn't go down because the Pyrenees were underneath, and there was no point turning back, so we were literally trapped in this living hell. There was hail hitting the windscreen, and ice was now collecting on the leading edge of the wings. The pilot had some inflatable de-icing system that he was constantly pushing up and down – we didn't have any chemical de-icers then.

At several points, the pilot had the throttle completely closed and the engines idling, but we were watching the rate of climb indicator going up at 4,000 feet a minute: we were being funnelled up inside the cloud at an incredible speed. The poor chap was battling just to keep us in anything like a stable condition while we were going up. Then, some-times, we would come down at 4,000 feet a minute. We'd be going down fast and there were the Pyrenees right beneath us, how close we couldn't be sure. The throttles would be screaming desperately as he tried to get us back up again.

After about 45 minutes, we were all crying. We all thought we were dead, the whole band thought there was no way we could get out of it alive, because it was so extreme.

Suddenly, we popped out of the cloud – shot out like a champagne cork. I can laugh about it now, but nobody was happy at the time. You would have thought we would be crying and hugging but we were not. We were just so shocked, we all sat in silence as the pilot popped us down into Saint Sebastian airport. Everyone there was really surprised to see us. 'How did you get through?' they asked. 'There are no planes flying in the whole of the north of Spain.' They'd cancelled every single flight; we were the only plane to have flown.

I asked the pilot, 'Didn't they tell you?'

He said, 'No, they told me they were actually isolated cumulonimbus, rather than embedded.' That wasn't a mistake, in all fairness, if that's what he was told. We shouldn't have taken off and we were very, very lucky to get through it.

So, if I was looking for inspiration for my next album, I had it. 'Five miles out' is a common saying of pilots when approaching any airfield, even for a rookie, a novice. I went down to my local pub and lined up a few pints of Guinness, a rhyming dictionary and my pilot's books, and with that I wrote down little phrases from my flying experience and made a song out of them.

Working on the song was nearly as bad as the flight. It took about three months nonstop, day after day, working on that one song. Don't ask me why I did it. I went through about six different versions until I was happy with it, until I thought it was strong enough to represent that experience.

A lot of work went into that album. If you look at the cover for *Five Miles Out*, that's what it was like as we came out of the cloud. It was painted by Gerald Coulson, who was a glider-tug pilot as well as a brilliant painter. When my dad had a share in his own glider, Gerald used to pull him up from somewhere in Cambridgeshire.

We decided to do a world tour for *Five Miles Out*. I got a new tour manager, a German chap called Ozzie who used to be personal manager to one of the people in Deep Purple. He knew everybody, and was a larger than life, very sociable character; he made everything a lot of fun.

All around that time, touring was an ordeal. Since the seminar I've always tried to co-operate with the record company and do everything that was expected of me, interviews and promotion, tours and videos. I didn't really enjoy it much but I understood that I had to do it. I would spend six or nine months making an album, then would immediately prepare a tour and do promotion before the tour. Then there would be the tour itself, followed by a couple of weeks' holiday before I went back into the studio again. I gradually started earning some money, which was very welcome. Being able to keep it was the difficult thing.

I did do one good thing. One day I sat down and worked out exactly how much it had cost to bring me up – all my education, my food, the first guitar, the Transit van and everything. I think it worked out at about £28,000, so I got £28,000 in cash, and put it in a little briefcase. Then I got it dropped off at my father's surgery. I think he was quite impressed. I hope my children do the same for me one day!

14. CRISES? WHAT CRISES? – 1981

For my next album, I was looking for inspiration once again. I thought I'd try to do a similar thing to 'Guilty', but with British musicians, so I hired some really good session players. Simon Phillips had a reputation of being a real master on the drums, I got on very well with him as well, so I asked him to help me produce and engineer the album. Simon then recommended a few of his friends, a bass player and a guitarist.

We all got together and jammed in my studio in Denham, and out of that came a whole series of backing tracks. One morning, I scribbled down some chords off the top of my head and said to the others, 'We'll play at this tempo.' I switched on the tape machine and it chugged along for four or five minutes, as we played. It sounded marvellous, some kind of magic must have happened as we were playing together. I can't put my finger on it, but we just loved doing it.

That particular track was sounding really good but at that stage I wasn't sure if it was going to become an instrumental or a song. I didn't know what to do with it, so I invited various people to contribute some ideas. One of them was a very popular punk star at the time, Hazel

O'Connor. When she came along I found she was actually a very nice person. I realised then there was no such thing as a 'real' punk, it was all about the way they dressed and the attitude. She wrote a whole version of a song over the track, with her own lyrics; it didn't quite work, unfortunately.

I worked on that track for about three months solid, just trying to get something to happen. I was pulling my hair out, thinking, 'What can I do with this fantastic backing track?' One day, I just decided I would book a singer for the next day. Maggie Riley used to be a girlfriend of a keyboard roadie in my band. I knew she had a good voice, as she had done some backing vocals on some of the tours. So I thought, 'I'll book her for a session tomorrow and I'll just bloody well have to think of something for her to sing, otherwise the whole day will be wasted.'

That night I sat down with a bottle of wine and my rhyming dictionary and started to automatically write anything that came into my head. It took me the whole night, but I made up a song, which became 'Moonlight Shadow'. As the night wore on there was a moon out, so the moon got in there; then I looked at the shadows from the moon, bits of this, bits of that. I had always loved that film with Tony Curtis about Houdini for some reason, a spiritual story of how he had tried to contact him. A lot of the lyrics happened by accident as one word would rhyme with another, then a gun got in there somewhere and then got a bit *West Side Story*-ish and some people suggested it may have had something to do with John Lennon – I never meant there to be, but as it happened I had been in New York the night he was murdered, perhaps there was something that crept into my subconscious about it. I finished the lyrics at about four o'clock in the morning, thinking that was the best I could do.

Maggie arrived the next afternoon and we started. She doesn't naturally sing the way I wanted it sung; she sang like a soul singer and liked to belt stuff out, 'moonlight shah-doah', but I wanted it all beautifully clean, very restrained, in that pure English folksy style but with a thumping big rhythm section behind it. I hated anybody that sang in an American accent, and still do, which is why I love Robert Wyatt's voice. He is nearly the only singer I have ever heard that sings in his natural talking voice, it's beautiful. I think, though, that perhaps it's easier to sing in an American accent, it's something to do with the way the music is produced in the mouth.

We spent quite a while getting the sound, we would do every word almost syllable by syllable. We'd do 'Moon, moon, moon' about ten times, then 'Sha, sha, sha' until I got that, then 'Dow, dow, dow' until we had 'Moonlight shadow'. I played it again and again, she sang each bit until she got the idea, then she sang it right the way through. There were lots of drop-ins after that; you couldn't cut and paste things like you can now, everything had to be done by hand, so that took a good few hours. By the end Maggie was singing so quietly she was almost whispering, very close to the microphone with a lot of compression, it was like having someone whispering in your ear telling you a secret.

As we were working I got that magical feeling; these days they would call it 'being in the zone'. I was focused on what I was doing, I knew what I wanted it to sound like, and Maggie was able to produce it. At the end I remember sitting there, looking quite flabbergasted that I had managed to produce something like that, as it wasn't what I did naturally. When the record company heard it, they liked it and made a video of it. It was some ridiculous thing, I think we went to Hatfield House or somewhere like that. I hated making videos at the time, but you had to. There was somebody doing weird things with my hair, they made me dress up in funny clothes, and I just had to go along and do it.

We called the album *Crises*. The cover was by Terry Ilott: Lynn Chadwick, the sculptor, was a fan of his paintings, and I'd bought a couple of them as well. We released

'Moonlight Shadow' as a single, and by some miracle it started getting airplay. It started going up the charts, and soon everywhere I went I heard it: coming out of shops, on the radio, people's cars. I was astonished. They thought it was going to be number one in the UK charts: it kept creeping up but had very tough competition from Rod Stewart with 'Do You Think I'm Sexy', Paul Young's 'Wherever I Lay My Hat' and The Police with 'Every Breath You Take'. 'Moonlight Shadow' got to number four but it was the number one bestselling single in the whole of the rest of Europe.

It was amazing: it all meant that suddenly, I was very important again. I remember having a meeting with Richard, and he said I should make lots more albums like that and to not worry too much about instrumental music any more. To me it wasn't that easy. *Tubular Bells* had been hard work, but it was easy because it was my idea; I wasn't squeezing myself into the straitjacket of music that was popular at the time. I wasn't sure I could just do it again.

By that time I was realising that my lifelong ambition of being a pilot was not really going anywhere, it just made me miserable. Just the thought of getting lost used to get me stressed. These days private planes have sat-nav, like cars, but there was nothing like that back then. Chundering along at 140 miles per hour you can't see any signposts, and every town looks much the same as every other.

Instead, I thought I would give helicopters a try. I'd had a flight in a helicopter and it was amazing. With a plane you're stuck – you've always got to do at least 90 miles per hour and you need a runway to land. With a helicopter you can just plop it down anywhere. It was difficult to learn to hover, but it's one of those things, like riding a bike or playing a guitar. Once you have it, you do it automatically, without thinking about it.

I remember when I was on some of my solo training flights, I would get a bit anxious so I would find a nice little field where I could just plonk it down. I would sit there and roll a cigarette, holding the joystick between my knees to stop the rotors flapping about, with the engine running so I could make a quick getaway in case an angry farmer came and chased me off his land. I'd sit there and calm down with a cigarette, then I would wind up the engine and off I'd go again. That was fun, I got much more enjoyment from flying helicopters. I spent a good few years doing that.

I wonder if somehow, all those early flying experiences might have got Richard interested in aeroplanes. One of the next times I saw him, I was on tour in Holland and he invited me to come and see his very first press conference, at the opening of Maastricht airport. I'd got my helicopter licence by then so I hired a helicopter, one I wasn't familiar with – it was a Hughes 500. I remember landing at the airport on a beautiful sunny day and we'd just flown up from Germany, or Belgium or somewhere.

I remember seeing this little tiny speck, miles away in the sunshine. It got bigger and bigger, and a white aeroplane gradually became discernible, with red livery. Seeing this massive jumbo jet touch down and taxi to a halt was quite a far cry from Staverton flying club, with my little Beechcraft that I used to fly. Then the steps were rolled up, the door opened and Richard came out, waving to everybody, very graciously, like a kind of president. Out he came in a captain's uniform, surrounded by this whole bevy of glamorous air hostesses. It was quite something to witness. I couldn't comprehend it. I thought, 'How can anybody afford that, it's obviously going to fall apart in a couple of months and they're going to have to sell it.' Little did I realise it would grow into such a massive business.

Richard did his press conference and all these people were asking him about the airline. I had to leave, because I had to get back for a sound check wherever we were playing. I remember taking off in the Hughes and actually hovering outside, bringing it up to the window and doing a 360-degree turn with the tail rotor, right outside, while he was doing his press conference. All the cameras were going clickety-clack at me. It was one of those special memories, a fun thing to be doing on that lovely, sunny day.

Eventually, the contract I'd originally signed in 1973 ran out with Virgin. The original deal was for ten albums; when I got near the end and had two left, we renegotiated. There was a lot of legal haggling, masses of reams of papers, documents and letters; you wouldn't believe the amount of work that went into working out the agreement, but it all got sorted out eventually. One sunny day in London, Richard turned up to my lawyer's office. He was with his daughter Holly, who was only about six then; I remember she was running around the lawyers and misbehaving and he was telling her off. It was very strange: we agreed everything – an increase in royalties, a very good advance and the return of the management commission, in return for three more albums. Then we all sat down and had a glass of sherry. It was extremely civilised, I had a rather old-fashioned lawyer at the time.

The deal cleared the air and we managed to settle out of court, but it had been difficult for both sides – I didn't speak to Richard for about two years after the settlement. Part of the settlement was a large sum of money, so I agreed to spend a whole year out of the country with my family, as a way to avoid paying tax.

I'd already started work on a score for the film *The Killing Fields*, with David Puttnam, who was a friend of Richard's. Most of the work was done in the house in Denham. It was fantastic: while I was working on the score, they were still filming, so I would get the rushes in from the film set in Thailand. The film was very harrowing as it was so well acted and shot, and it had such a lot of atmosphere you could really feel like you were there – of course, it was a true story. I got very emotionally involved and upset about it: I really got into the whole thing and it would give me nightmares.

From Denham, I went to live in a beautiful chalet in a place called Villars-sur-Ollon, which is in the French-speaking part of Switzerland. Unfortunately, as things turned out, the timing wasn't so good. I already had the tour booked to follow the next album, the tickets were already on sale and, of course, I had to make the album before I could go on the tour. What with the settlement with Richard, I wanted to fit all that into the year that I was spending out of the country. When I got to Switzerland, I finished off *The Killing Fields'* soundtrack, or at least, I made it as good as I could get it; then I started work on my next album.

I'd decided to make an album of songs again, but looking back on it I had pretty much emptied the song-creation cupboard with *Crises*. The songs on what became *Discovery* were hard work, although the environment was just picture-book gorgeous. I never even wanted to ski but I ended up learning, and making a whole piece of music about the ice and the snow. I also made an instrumental about Lake Geneva, a lake almost as big as a sea. With snow coming down on Christmas Day, perhaps my early memories of Christmas made that time in Switzerland all the more enjoyable.

Before long, I started getting phone calls from David Puttnam's office, saying that the score was not finished. They had just started editing seriously, and so I had to carry on working on the music. He wanted it orchestrated as well, so I had to shelve all the work I was doing on *Discovery* and do another couple of months on *The Killing Fields*. David Bedford came out and helped me with the orchestra-tion, then we recorded it in Munich with Eberhard Schoener as the conductor. They were all happy with the result; as a soundtrack it still stands the test of time, I think.

I didn't attend the English premiere of the film. I couldn't even come into the country because of the tax situation, but I would have liked to have been there. It was a bit of a shame, what with all the complications caused by being out of the country while the score was being completed, I think it may have somehow annoyed David Puttnam, and I ended up with a reputation of being difficult to work with. That might explain why I have not worked on any more films. I bumped into George Martin a few years later and he gave me the impression that David Puttnam was rather cross about it all, but it had just been very bad timing.

For me, I had loved working on the film and it had been wonderful to work with all the talented people that were part of it. The editor, Jim Clark, was amazing: to watch him work was incredible. This was before computers were used, and there would be bits of film stuck all over this huge editing room. He was a real master, and won an Academy Award for editing *The Killing Fields*. It was tremendous to work with such people, and it was sad that I never had the chance to do more. If I could work with people like that again, I certainly would.

With the soundtrack finished, I carried on with *Discovery* and when that was complete, I took it on tour. I remember we were playing in an outdoor amphitheatre in Athens. The night before I went out with a couple of the musicians, we went to the local taverna and sat in with some musicians there. My God, every bar they played was a different length. Morris Pert, the drummer, was trying to work it all out: 'That's sixteen beats, then that's five, then that's four, and two bars of . . .' Eventually we got up and started to jam with these Greek musicians. We were having a whale of a time. It was all completely spontaneous: there was no such thing as a beat, you couldn't tap your feet to it. It was like expecting a tree to wave its branches in the wind symmetrically; it just doesn't, it goes where it flows. I think the Greeks found it quite amusing that these foreign musicians were trying to play like them. To them, it must be a completely natural thing.

The *Discovery* tour of 1984 was the biggest tour I have ever done, indeed, at over fifty dates it was the biggest indoor tour of that year in Europe. I played to about

350,000 people, all across the Continent, we spent three or four months on the road. It wasn't long before the act of performing the music became a chore, and it was sometimes difficult and stressful. There is a part of me that loves, and another part that hates performing, I think that's because of all the grief I go through perfecting the performance. Every time in the early days I performed *Tubular Bells* I thought it was a travesty of the original music; it's only recently that I've been able to get a good approximation of that album. (Even that is cheating, really – you use a lot of samples, bits of digital recording. It's all very organised and you can't be as spontaneous.) What I did enjoy was, when the last note had been played, the audience would clap. I loved the reaction and loved the audience, though I didn't like the process much.

Towards the end of that tour something happened to me, a nervous breakdown if you like. My whole world crashed in, and I wasn't sure that I could continue. I had to, of course, because you can't just cancel a tour like that; a doctor came to see me, and gave me some sleeping pills because I wasn't sleeping at all. The panic attacks had returned and it made me realise there was still something there from the early days before the seminar; the exorcism hadn't removed everything. That came as a huge shock to me.

It was like the high from the seminar had lasted a good few years, then all the problems started coming back, not with the same terrible intensity as before, but at the level of 'normal' human psychology. In retrospect, I realised that I still had to deal with all the hang-ups and problems that any person would have to deal with, not only because of my childhood but with the stress and trauma of being thrust into the limelight. When I became famous, suddenly everybody who had ignored me was my best friend, but only because I was successful; then, with the loss of that success, I'd faced the inevitable backlash.

Although I had done the seminar and got rid of the panic attacks, I didn't realise that I still had a lot of bottled-up anger and grief, all of which had still to come out. I had fallen out with my father, I used to blame him for things going wrong and I still couldn't accept that he'd got married again. I can't logically explain why I felt that way, but when I came back to Britain I went into proper, normal psychotherapy, at a practice just off Harley Street. During the therapy, I realised that I had to sit down with my father and talk to him.

One weekend, my dad came over to stay at my house. We went down the local pub and had a few pints together, and I asked him all the things that had been bothering me all my life, including what really did happen with my baby brother. It was the first time I'd been able to sit down and talk to him like another human being, instead of my dad. It was a pivotal moment: ever since then I've been at peace with him. Now I see him not just as Dad, but also Raymond Henry Oldfield, another human being. Together with my mother, he gave me a chance at life, and that was fantastic. I didn't realise for many years the huge influence he had been in my first years of childhood, how important he was to me, what with taking me on his rounds and making model aeroplanes together. Perhaps it was unsurprising that I was so shocked, when everything went so completely wrong.

That realisation came with the psychotherapy, but in the early days I didn't relate to it at all. I was trying to explore, to understand, and I was using my music to do that as well, but it was obviously interfering with my relationships. The whole idea of families confused me; when I got together with somebody, I could never accept they would come with their mum and dad, brother and sister, uncles and aunts. I found it very hard to deal with the whole crowd, because family was such a painful concept for me, like having lost something very important. It was all bottled up inside me. It was incredible, I don't why it happens but children feel somehow responsible, guilty that maybe they made it happen. All these things came out in my psychotherapy. Since then everything has been better, but before I was a mass of bottled-up emotion.

It was shortly after I left therapy that I first learned to meditate. My sister had recommended a teacher who belonged to the Transcendental Meditation group of the Maharishi, the same person who taught the Beatles. I thought, 'Oh my God, I'm going to learn something that's going to scare the hell out of me.' When he came to see me, he first of all explained it all logically, on a white board that he'd brought with him. He explained how the mind works and the subconscious – in a completely scientific way. I think that was a ploy to get my logical mind satisfied and to trust him, so I would be able to do it.

Meditation works on the principle of a mantra, which is a little word you are given that you're never supposed to reveal to anyone. It's your special word, you don't even say it, apart from inside your head. Before he gave me my mantra we conducted a very short ceremony. He showed me pictures of all the gurus going back hundreds of years, and said thanks to each one, paying tribute to these people. Then he gave me my mantra, which I started to repeat quietly to myself.

The brain is an incredible machine. It's like hundreds of TV channels going on all at once, all chattering away. All the insecurities and everything else are a complete, static noise going on constantly. With the mantra it seemed to me that it was all happening on the surface, water bubbling like the surface of a very disturbed ocean in a storm. I could sink down underneath that, and underneath there was a very calm, quiet place. All the stuff was still going on and I was underneath it. It wasn't scary at all; more like, comfortable. Almost instantly my mind went, 'Getting too comfy, quick!' and I jumped up again. I thought, 'Thank God, I'm back into my normal, crazy mind, thinking about this and about that, what's going to happen and so on, babble, babble, babble.' Then, as I repeated the mantra, I sank down again.

It felt to me like I was slowly pushing my head into a different world, in a little bubble. It felt like another reality that was just as real as ours, but it wasn't scary at all. The place that you visit when you're meditating, there's nothing there, it's like pressing the pause on everything. In some ways learning meditation 'earthed' me, it wired in an earth cable so that, when the lightning strikes, I know it's not going to frazzle me like it used to. I've never been able to stay there very long, probably only a matter of seconds, but it is lovely just to have that tiny experience of it. To have total peace and quiet, you'd probably have to live in a monastery.

Around this time I was splitting up from my family and starting a new life with a new person, so it was a very difficult time. I'd loved being in the mountains, so much so that in my new relationship I went to live in a place in France called Megeve, which is near Mont Blanc.

While I was there I started recording an album called *Islands*. I was still in the way of thinking that Richard had instilled in me, that I had to have lots of successful songs. He'd probably forgotten about it years before, but these things tend to stick in my mind. The high spot of *Islands* was the title track: I probably felt lonely, isolated and cut off due to changes in my personal life, but I did manage to put together this beautiful song. I couldn't quite get the vocals right so I ended up asking Bonnie Tyler to come and sing it. As soon as she got in front of the microphone and opened her mouth to sing the first words, it was spine-tingling, exactly the way it was supposed to be.

The last album I made full of songs was *Earth Moving*. I was still trying to come up with another 'Moonlight Shadow', I suppose. I didn't manage it; these things happen when they want to, you can't just produce them at will. After that I got fed up with the whole thing and said, 'Well, it's 1990, my next album is going to be all instrumental, its going to be whatever I feel like doing.'

By this time I was regretting having agreed to do those extra albums, because I was becoming more and more distant from everybody at Virgin in the UK, although I was still getting on very well with the European operation. I decided to set myself no bounds; I wouldn't even have to do something musical if I didn't want to. We recorded some strange noises like footsteps creeping up; I had an old Ferrari at the time and we recorded that, revving up and speeding off down the drive.

I loved working on that album, getting in there at ten in the morning and working the whole day until about seven, just letting my creativity completely run wild. I had all kinds of guest artists: I got Jabula back again, the huge troupe of South African performers. They were magnificent. This was still in the days before they abolished apartheid, and they were all members of the ANC (African National Congress) so they wore their T-shirts. We hired a big studio in London and I thought of some words and had them translated into their language. I'm not sure what it was called but it sounded fabulous. I asked an impersonator to come and do some Margaret Thatcher impressions, and threw in a bit of tap-dancing for good measure.

When the album was finished it was really wild and weird, a complete opposite of the albums before. It certainly didn't have any songs, there wasn't anything on it that could be called a single. I had dinner with Richard and he told me they actually thought very highly of it. I wanted to call it *Amarok* – which I believe means 'tomorrow' in Gaelic – but he said they wanted me to call it 'Tubular Bells II', they thought it was good enough to be called that. However for me, it wasn't 'Tubular Bells II'. I wanted to do a 'Tubular Bells II', but that wasn't it. Also, I thought, I only had one more album to do and then I would be free. I didn't really want to be with Virgin any more, and I knew I would probably have the pick of all the record companies when I finally got free from Virgin. I said 'no' to calling the album 'Tubular Bells II', and as a result they didn't promote it and it didn't sell very well at all.

It's a shame, as it's probably one of the best things I have ever done.

15. BERLIN TO NOW – 1990–2006

By the early 1990s, I realised I needed to go and see a proper therapist again, to extract whatever remained of my psychological baggage. I found the best person I could, who happened to be a therapist from the same practice as Robyn Skinner, with whom John Cleese co-wrote his book, *Families and How to Survive Them*. I went to see the main person there, who recommended that I read that book, along with another couple of books, before I started seeing somebody. That done, I spent a good nine months going there.

It was a very gentle process. It wasn't anything like the seminar, which had been all at once, maximum intensity; it was little by little, each week. I felt like I was carrying around a balloon that was overinflated with grief: the grief about losing my mother, my childhood and my cosy little life had filled it almost to bursting point. At the time I didn't understand what it was exactly, but somehow I needed to let out all that grief. The way I did that was by crying. I must have cried most of the day, every day, for several months. Eventually the balloon began to deflate and became more bearable.

It is hard to believe that at the end of the 1980s and the beginning of the 90s, the whole idea of psychotherapy was very new; the thought of having counselling still had the stigma of mental illness attached to it. I had benefited such a lot from my own therapy that I started a little foundation, called Tonic. I wanted to help other people who found themselves in the same condition that I was. We had a fine lady running it: she would send out pamphlets to different GPs' surgeries and get people to fill in forms, as you couldn't get therapy very easily on the NHS – you would have to wait months and months.

As we started, we found that all kinds of wonderful people were willing to help, doctors and experts in the field. We even had the professor of psychiatry at Guy's Hospital as a trustee. We would hold trustees' meetings in the boardroom of the British Medical Association: it had pictures of all these eminent physiologists on the walls. I loved having all these doctors on the board of trustees. It was funny listening to them talk, it seemed to me that the reason they were psychiatrists was because they had their own psychological problems. They'd say things like, 'I'll have to watch I don't upset my inner child about this' – and this would be someone like a professor of psychiatry. So, don't assume the people you see for a cure, are cured themselves!

I would do a lot of promotion for the foundation on television; I tried to do whatever came up. These days therapy has almost become too much, everybody has counselling for every tiny problem, so it's hard to believe that such a short time in the past, that wasn't the case at all. We ran Tonic for about three years, and after that it just didn't seem to be necessary any more, so we wound it up, but it had been a fantastic experience.

Finally, I came to the last album that I would do for Virgin. I thought, 'What shall I do that I have never done before, on any of my albums?' The only thing I could think of was

to sing, so I thought, 'OK, I can't sing, how do I get to sing?'
I decided to hire a singing teacher, and one day this very
jolly, rotund woman turned up. She folded her arms, got me
in the corner by the piano and we started to do vocal
exercises. She would drill me like a colour sergeant: 'No,
Michael, up and down! Open your mouth! Bring your
tongue down, like this! La ... Aah ...'

I worked really hard at it. I had twenty or thirty singing
lessons, once or twice a week for a good few months. I
thought, 'I *will* bloody learn to sing.' It's all to do with
changing the shape of your mouth to approximate a musical
instrument: that's when I found out why it's easier to sing
in American than in English. With the word 'love', in
English your throat is half closed; in American it's more like
'lurve', and your mouth naturally forms a bigger shape from
the bottom of your throat to the top of your tongue.

I honestly did try to sing, but when I played it back it
didn't sound any good. I just can't physically control my
vocal cords and hit the notes well enough for my ears. I
don't have a great tone either, it's all forced. Nowadays it
would be easier, as you've got these automated tuning
machines, you plug them in and they tune your voice. At the
time we didn't have anything like that, so we had to drop
in every note, almost like 'Moonlight Shadow'. It took ages
and ages.

I did record some songs in the end. One in particular
wasn't too bad, called 'Heaven's Open', which became the
title track. We eventually released it as a single, and some
people played it on the radio. Years later, the Formula One
driver Jacques Villeneuve told me he loved that track. It
probably helped him to drive, it was all about motivation.

I can quite clearly remember New Year's Eve, 1990,
when the contract I signed in the Manor in 1973 finally
came to an end. I hadn't been happy during the last few
years with Virgin, in fact I'd lost contact with them
completely. It was all very weird. We had started off with
such good intentions: I thought, as everybody did in the 60s,

that it was a whole new age of creativity, the end of wars and fighting. Culture was going to progress; we had landed on the moon; everyone thought life was going to become really peaceful, exciting and creative but eventually it petered out. The beginning of the punk period was the end of it, the first nail in the coffin.

On that New Year's Eve, I was in tears. Although it had been my choice to extend the contract, after seventeen years of being tied into a single relationship it felt almost like the end of a prison sentence. Suddenly it was over, and I was free.

Around that time was also the end of my second serious relationship involving children. That split was probably the most terrible time of my life, since my early panic attacks. It was awful, really dreadful, and was made worse by the interference of lawyers. Somehow I managed to get through it, helped by the prospect of being able to start a new creative life. I was finally planning to make *Tubular Bells II*. I thought I would work with a producer again, and my dream was to work with Trevor Horn. As soon as I mentioned that to somebody, there he was at my front door with his big glasses. Trevor lived in Los Angeles, he had a studio in his house there. A few years earlier I had been to LA; you could still do tax years out at that time, so I thought it would be a good opportunity to get an advance and do another tax year out of the country, so I wouldn't lose it all. So we rented a house, up in Beverly Hills and, would you believe, the postcode was 90210. Trevor lived just down the road, in Bel Air.

Working on *Tubular Bells II* was a joy, though it was quite stressful as it had a lot to live up to. I carried on with my therapy while I was working on the album: together, the music and the therapy somehow helped me get through the terrible break-up of my family. It was an inspiring environment and it was wonderful to work with Trevor Horn, although we somehow ended up not working in the same room. He would take bits of music to his house and work on them there, and I would take bits to my place, then we would stick them together later. I'm not quite sure why that was, although I was very pleased with the way it turned out.

I had been lucky enough to find a manager called Clive Banks. Clive used to be the managing director of Island records, and he knew everybody in the business. The fact that this was to be called *Tubular Bells II* was a big trump card, so at that point I had the heads of all the record companies coming to my studio to hear the demos. The amount of interest was unbelievable, even before it was finished: we talked to everybody, from Sony, to Warner, Polygram and MCA. Virgin was also included but I'm pretty sure that it was part of EMI by then. It was strange to meet Ken Berry, the backroom accountant who used to pay me at Virgin: by then he was the head of EMI. I think I asked him, 'Have you got any luncheon vouchers, Ken?'

Eventually I decided to go with Warner, as Clive's wife was the managing director and his best friend, Rob Dickins, was chairman. I loved Rob Dickins, he was helpful, funny and creative. He really wanted to get involved.

After *Tubular Bells II* was released, life was good for a while. The tour was pretty much sold out everywhere, we played big halls, and it was all very successful. We even booked Edinburgh Castle to do a concert. I had a lot of help with that, with a conductor and arranger called Robin Smith. The following Sunday we got the news that *Tubular Bells II* had gone in at number one, which was fantastic. I was live on Radio One playing bits of it. I was back up the top again, for a couple of weeks at least. When it went to number two, I remember I went to see Rob Dickins. 'It's not going to be another *Tubular Bells*,' he said. 'It's going to do well, but it's not going to be another blockbuster.' He was right: it sold fairly well, but it wasn't a runaway success.

For a short time I bought a house in the Hollywood Hills, and it was there that I started working on my next album.

Rob Dickins had the idea of doing a piece of music based around a book by Arthur C. Clarke, called *The Songs of Distant Earth*. I didn't think it was one of his best books, but it had lots of atmosphere and I thought I could make a piece of music about it: travelling through space, landing on a strange world and the events that happen there. The best thing was when I went to Sri Lanka, to meet Arthur C. Clarke himself. He's almost a prophet, so it was quite an honour to go and see him. I became ill in Sri Lanka, though, and I couldn't wait to get back home.

It was wonderful up where we were living, we could make little trips to the desert. Santa Barbara was nice but there was an undercurrent of violence about the whole place, I never really felt safe. Once, when I was driving along Sunset Strip, I actually saw somebody who had just been shot, lying in the street. First of all I thought they were making a movie, because there was somebody with a camera there. Then I noticed the traffic was all bunched up, and I suddenly realised that it wasn't a movie at all. It was then that I made up my mind that I wanted to leave. I would never say it was a mistake to have gone there for a couple of years, but I didn't feel comfortable there.

In 1994 I came back to a house that I had bought a few years before, not far from Denham in Chalfont St Giles: I'd just used it as a base previously. It was around this time that I started getting into computer graphics. There was a quite expensive machine called a Silicon Graphics workstation, which you could use for real-time, 3-D work. I thought music could become interactive: instead of just a CD, I thought it would be great to have some kind of interactive program. You could put it in your PC and tinker with it, play videos and whizz around the place. I had a couple of assistants, and we would do all that as well as working on the music.

Songs of Distant Earth was released in 1994. It was the first CD to have anything interactive on it, I am pretty sure. It didn't do particularly well, unfortunately. I don't know why; they worked very hard to promote it. It's just one of those things you can never explain: I thought it was really good but it just didn't sell that well, it's a mystery.

It was shortly before the album was released that I felt I'd had enough touring, and it had always been my dream to build my own house. I was looking in the *Sunday Times* for land for sale, and a little advert popped up in Ibiza, so we hopped on a plane and found the most perfect piece of land, right by the sea, looking out over Formentera. I remember I got back to London, stopped all work on the interactive CD and used the graphics workstation to design a house. We made a 3-D model and a video flying around it and I thought, 'I will just have to find an architect to say he can build that.'

We did find an architect and started building the house, and about a year later it was pretty much ready to move into. It was only after I arrived that I realised what a party island Ibiza was. I didn't go there because of that; I went because it was such a beautiful place to build a house. During the building work I went mostly in the winter and there was nobody there; most of the places were closed and boarded up, it was like a ghost town. There were only a couple of restaurants open in the town for Spanish people, and for the handful of very weird people left over from the 1960s.

Ibiza is a magical island and that magic can happen in a good way or in a bad way. Gradually I met a few people there. Somebody told me, if you are going to live in Ibiza, there is a spiritual force on the island that tests you, to see if you are worthy to stay. There must be some reason why so many people go there in the summer and get out of their heads. Maybe it's something in the soil, in the drinking water or the wine. There is a magical atmosphere there; it's very beautiful in the winter, although it feels a little cold and lonely, and then in the summer it is just outrageously wild. People do things they would never dream of doing at home.

Funnily enough, the producer-engineer part of me got really excited by techno-dance music, simply because it used technology. I suppose I also liked the trance element, the way it goes on and on, building a kind of atmosphere. *Tubular Bells* works in a similar way, but without the drum-and-bass thumping that's used in the clubs. There was definitely something about it, a spiritual element of some sort. I don't know if it's somehow linked with dervishes swinging round and going into a trance, but to me there is that element to it.

I know people wouldn't expect me to like that, or get interested in it, but I really enjoyed it. I did some experiments myself: I take my hat off, not to the people that make the music, but the people that design the software. It's magnificent: you get a plug-in which you load into your music-creation software and it's amazing, it has all these buttons which do weird and wonderful things. It's actually quite easy to make that kind of music with these programs.

Eventually, I obviously failed the test, because I had to leave Ibiza. I became ill, and not mentally ill – sometimes I felt I was being poisoned by it. I can't explain it. I was just pleased to get out, I felt like I was escaping from a weird place. I needed some kind of stability back again, so the best choice, I thought, was to go back to London. To be honest, I have no desire to go back to Ibiza. I had some of the best times I have ever had there, and definitely some of the worst. I am pretty sure Ibiza has had the same effect on others: there was a ruined house not far from where I lived, which in the 1950s or 60s would have been a palace. I think it belonged to a famous person, an actress; perhaps she fled the island as well.

The house I had built cost twice its original budget, but when I put it on the market nobody was interested. I thought, 'My God, I could be in serious trouble with this. I have spent all this money on it and I can't sell it.' Eventually it was snapped up by another rock musician for little more than half what it cost me to build. I was so happy anyone wanted to buy it, I just said yes. I lost a fortune on that house.

Before I was in Ibiza I'd been working on a Celtic album, which ended up being called *Voyager*. The three albums – *Tubular Bells II*, *Songs of Distant Earth* and *Voyager* – were part of my first deal with Warner. Clive decided to do another deal, but just for two albums. One of them was to be *Tubular Bells III*, Rob Dickins at Warner had asked for that. I'd started work on it in my studio in Ibiza, and after I sold the house I continued working on that album, back in Chalfont St Giles. It was quite enjoyable to work on.

I had the opportunity to do a premiere concert in Horse Guards Parade, right next to Westminster in London, where they have the Trooping of the Colour. It was a great success, although it bucketed down with rain right in the middle of it. One of the generators was shorted out by the torrential rain, so we lost lights; even when we went live on Spanish TV in the dark, nobody seemed to mind.

I decided to do the next album with nothing but guitars. Even the drum sounds were made with guitars, the bass drum would be a finger on a bass guitar, snare drums would be a string sound. Keyboards were played with a MIDI guitar, just a chord here and there. That album was called *Guitars*, unsurprisingly. We decided to do a full tour of that, because I was back into touring by then. We did a hell of a tour all the way around Europe, about 63 shows. It was the first time I'd been to the Eastern bloc countries.

That was in 1999. The opportunity came up to do a concert on the millennium evening in Berlin, in front of God knows how many thousands of people, so of course I agreed to that. They wanted me to write a piece of music for it as well, so I started work on the *Millennium Bell*. When you look back at it now, people say, 'Oh, the millennium, what a waste of time that was,' but before it, everybody was really excited about it. The turning of the millennium was a fantastic thing to live through.

When we played, the immediate vicinity held over 100,000 people but the whole city was full. It was a strange event because of the history of that city. It had already become a beautiful city again, but I really felt like we were starting something new. I hadn't been there since before the wall came down, but to see Berlin completely integrated was just wonderful. It is a fabulous city and will be even lovelier, and I felt I was making a contribution to that, just by doing the concert.

When I stood up at my very first concert, shaking like a jelly, little did I realise that nearly 40 years later, I would be playing at the turn of the millennium in Berlin, with all those people, and feeling quite happy. We had to synchronise the clocks to finish just before midnight, so there were a few spare minutes before we were due to start. I just remembered once seeing Frank Sinatra playing at Caesar's Palace in Las Vegas. In the middle of his set he sat down on this sofa, in a living room he'd had positioned in the middle of the stage. He'd pour himself a Martini or some cocktail and have a cigarette; while the saxophone player did a solo, he would be just sitting there, relaxing. In Berlin it was minus-two degrees, I had about six jumpers on, squeezed under this velvet suit. I walked out on stage on my own, and sat down in front of 100,000 people. I made myself an Old Holborn roll-up, and when I lit it, 100,000 people cheered. I just sat there in front of them, completely happy and relaxed, all on my own.

I've made a bit of progress.

At the start of the new millennium, I was feeling pretty much exhausted. I thought, 'What do I do now?' Rob Dickins had given me a copy of a computer game called Myst, which I'd liked a lot. I needed a change and I'd enjoyed working on the interactive stuff myself, so I thought I would have a go at making a complete 3-D game, using music. I called it music VR, musical virtual reality. I bought a very expensive computer graphics machine: since my first attempt, back in 1994, computers had become about twenty times more powerful and faster. Initially I worked with a couple of graphic artists, but eventually I decided to go back right to the beginning, to work with a computer programmer and design our own graphics rendering engine. It took a couple of years, but it was tremendous fun.

The result was a computer game that I called Tres Lunas. I sent it round to all the games companies but nobody was interested in it; they just wanted the normal computer games, adrenaline-filled driving games or shoot-'em-ups, so I ended up putting it out myself. We had a lovely premiere in Valencia, at what they call the City of Arts and Sciences. There was a planetarium there, and I remember showing all the journalists the game on the big planetarium screen.

In total, we sold about three thousand copies. It didn't pay for itself by any means, it cost many hundreds of thousands of pounds to make. All the same, it's out there, it has a very tiny community, and some people like it. I hope somebody in the future will do something along those lines, and it's nice to have made a little contribution of something that's not corrosive or destructive to human minds, especially children. It was a creative dead end; whether it was ahead of its time or a waste of time I don't know, but I wasn't wasting *my* time – I loved it.

2003 was the thirtieth anniversary of *Tubular Bells*. I thought that it would be a good opportunity to re-record it, technically perfect, as I'd never really liked the way the original was done. I decided to take it very easy: I would spend a lot of time in my conservatory, learning to fly model helicopters. From time to time, I would go into the studio and the engineer would record bits and pieces. He would assemble them and edit them, and I would pop back and check out the result. It was a lovely experience, I enjoyed doing that tremendously.

My local shop at the time was in Amersham, and for years they had the original *Tubular Bells* in the shop window. When the remake came out, they put the new cover up in the window. After about two months, I saw they had put the old one back again because everybody liked the original so much. *Tubular Bells 2003* sold fairly well, but nothing compared to the old version. The original is still the one, I can't explain why; I thought I had done it better. I will probably compare them again one day and prefer the old one!

With that, I was free contractually. By this time, I had split up with my manager, Clive: I just thought the relationship had run its course. By myself, I started looking around for a new deal: some people were interested and others weren't. The original deal for *Tubular Bells* was for 35 years, which means it comes back to me in 2008: as soon as I began to let people know they might be able to get the rights to that, things became a lot easier. Eventually I signed with Universal, and I am very happy there at the moment.

Recently, I decided to move away from the London area again with my wife Fanny and our son Jake. It was quite a big upheaval for me, moving from my house in Chalfont St Giles after so many years. Funnily enough, I am not that far from my old house in the Cotswolds; it's only about half an hour away. When we got here I thought, 'Now I can take life easy,' but that philosophy didn't last long. About ten years ago there was talk about doing a book; I spent time doing interviews with Annie Nightingale, the DJ, but they never came to anything. So I thought perhaps I could get round to it again. Now that is done, I have got my studio together and I've started working on a new piece of music.

Things are changing so much in the music business. In the future everything will probably just be downloadable, the CD will go the way of vinyl. Technology has advanced so incredibly that I have trouble keeping up with it. Luckily I am still at the cutting edge of recording technology: I am a beta-tester for the latest music production software, so I get new versions to test out, which I enjoy.

Also, age is starting to creep up on me. I used to be able to do several tasks at once, but I can't do that so well any more; I get tired when I wouldn't have before; my short-term memory is starting to degrade a little bit, but it's not too bad at the moment. I've had to get used to things like wearing glasses for reading. I have a pair of glasses in every room, because if I only have one pair and take it to the next room, when I go back to where I was, I think, 'Where the bloody hell are my glasses?' So, I have a pair for every room, and I make sure I leave them there.

It really is a new phase in life. If you had told me at nineteen, when I was making *Tubular Bells*, that I would be fifty-three sometime and talking about it all, I would never have believed that possible, but it has come to pass. The whole world has completely changed. I can't believe I am still active, that I still mean something in the music business. Even though things are nothing like they were in 1973, I am very happy with my situation.

What's next? I plan to try to make a piece of more classical music, which is the one thing left that I have never done. After that, I just don't know.

ON ME – NOW

Looking back, what can I take away from all these experiences? Above all, I've gained an understanding of my own place, of the tiny, little place of every human being in the greater realm of this physical and spiritual universe. At the time of the seminar I didn't know about the spiritual side of existence, I just felt the physical, harsh reality. Today, it's the same reality, but now I can experience it without fear, without being possessed by such an evil, but with a feeling of belonging, of rightness.

Tubular Bells was successful beyond my wildest dreams. There have been various people who have called me things like the father of New Age, the godfather of ambient music. All the same, I have tremendous regrets about the period of my life when I was at my most successful. I still carry around a sense of guilt, that I wasn't able to be the spokesperson or figurehead for real, interesting, progressive music. I just wasn't strong enough to do it; I regret not having the confidence in those days. I have met Richard a few times since Virgin Records was sold to EMI and it was a great pleasure to see him again. I am proud of him, and thankful to have been given my first chance back in 1972.

Today, it's a very different world from when I first started out. The utopia we thought was going to exist in the 1960s, all that was going to carry on and get better. By now we should have colonies on the moon, have abolished poverty, have magnificent art and culture; instead we have grossly obscene, voyeuristic television, smothered in degrading advertising that is an insult to human intelligence. Technology has advanced beautifully but culture has suffered, it has almost gone back to barbarism with our yob culture. I don't know what happened, but it's not all doom and gloom; perhaps it has to dip before it gathers momentum again. It might take another twenty or thirty years to get back on track.

Right now we have got this terrible disease of coolness. Everyone has to be 'cool': for me that means wearing sunglasses in dark places, so you can't see anything. It's almost like hiding, rather than being yourself and standing out if you are a bit unusual. The philosophy I try to live my life by these days is to be different and be proud of being different, to speak out. If people like me don't stand up and give their opinion, nothing is going to change. I don't think anybody should be afraid of saying, 'This is rubbish, let's do better.'

Since the seminar I feel I have lost the angst-ridden, creative person I used to be, which is a relief. I used to be able to pick up a guitar and create something amazing; but if I wasn't doing that, I didn't have a life at all. I can still do it, but I am also able to do other things, like if the weather is good I can go for a beautiful walk with the dogs. I don't need to retreat into my space any more, as I have become comfortable in my body and in my life. I can be honest, though; it's been difficult to find the drive to make new music, just to maintain a reasonable career. I've had to recognise that there may never again be that paranoia-fuelled high voltage that used to turbocharge my music.

For a while I felt I'd lost my uniqueness, or at least I hadn't used it for a long time; now I find I'm rediscovering it again. It's not like I'm trying to be the tortured seventeen-year-old, but there was something there, the ability to play, to see deeply into music and understand it. I'm getting that back.

I've had to learn what I am, and it's not a musician, it's something else. To me, a musician gets out his instrument and just plays or entertains. That's not me at all: what I can do is transfer the essence of a feeling or an emotion, express it in music. Musical sounds are pleasurable things, like sunlight or the smell of warm bread. I'm an interpreter, a sonic mood translator if you like. I can take the beautiful feelings you get in life and the horrible ones as well, and I can turn them into aural sounds, give form to them in music. Plus I love the physicality of the studio, the feel of the strings when I play the guitar, the mechanical nature of it all. I may not understand the link between physical and spiritual, but it still excites and inspires me.

From now on, my music is not going to be cool, it's not going to be hip or sexy. It's going to be hand-played and mathematical; it's going to be as complicated as I feel it needs to be. I'm not going to care if anybody likes it or buys it, which is exactly the way I felt when I was nineteen. In the back of my mind, I do hope that there will be a renaissance for progressive music at some point, which will involve people delving into that world where every instrument is alive and can speak, has a character of its own. If I can somehow persuade people how to play again properly, to stop concentrating on how good they look on TV and really start to do interesting things again with music, then I'll try to do that.

I could certainly do without the angst, however. I'd rather have the peace.

ACKNOWLEDGEMENTS

I would like to thank Jon Collins for helping me to edit and compile this book. Thanks also to Ed Faulkner, KT Forster and all at Virgin Books for their support.

INDEX